HORSE DRAWN SLEIGHS

HORSE DRAWN SLEIGHS

Compiled by Susan Green
Librarian
Carriage Museum of America

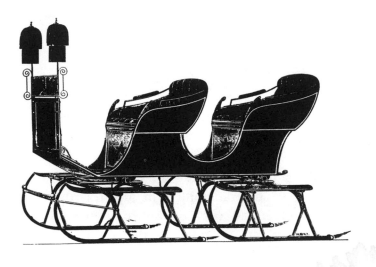

The Astragal Press
Mendham, New Jersey

Published by
The Astragal Press
P.O. Box 239
Mendham, NJ 07945-0239

The material in this book was derived from the reference collection of the Carriage Museum of America, P.O. Box 417, Bird-in- Hand, PA, 17505.
Tel: 717-656-7019.

Book design by Martyl J. Pollak
Manufactured in the United States of America

Library of Congress Catalogue Card Number: 95-79983
ISBN 1-879335-68-9

TABLE OF CONTENTS

Introduction   i

Albany or Swell-body Sleighs   1

Portland and other Cutters   21

Speeding Cutters   68

Four-passenger Sleighs   84

Box-body Sleighs   121

Traps and Sporting Sleighs   133

Canadian Sleighs   144

Rumble-seat Sleighs   150

Cabriolet or Victoria Sleighs   161

Vis-a-Vis Sleighs   175

Closed-body Sleighs   187

The Construction of Sleighs

    Ironing   194

    Body design   214

    Painting   230

    Trimming   256

Index of Sleighmakers   267

INTRODUCTION

In some cultures the use of a sleigh or sledge for either travel or transporting of goods precedes the use of wheeled vehicles. Although sleighing is looked upon by many modern admirers as romantic, in earlier times travel during the winter was a serious business in which people and horses could lose their lives if proper precautions were not taken. Horses needed winter shoeing to prevent the balling up of snow in their shoes and to avoid slipping on the ice. Occupants of sleighs needed to dress in the warmest clothing; there was much use of furs for coats, lap robes, and carpets. My aunt recalls that my great grandfather would heat bricks and place them in the vehicle for the trip from the farm to town in the winter. Any mail order catalog could supply more elaborate foot warmers, into which a piece of burning charcoal would be placed.

If one did not have to travel out of necessity, winter could be a fine time for socializing, and sleighing became a great winter sport. Members of the Tandem Club in Quebec were fond of parading their sleighs tandem style; New Englanders, having time off from farming, made trips to neighbors and organized gay winter carnivals; New Yorkers made a great spectacle with their sleigh turnouts in Central Park.

There are as many different types of sleighs as there are different types of carriages and wagons; in some instances, in order to maximize the utility of a carriage, runners were provided that could be slipped onto the axle spindles once the wheels were removed. The idea of adapting a carriage to a sleigh was more common in Russia and Europe, where winters were longer.

The most popular two-passenger sleighs in America were the Portland cutter and the Albany cutter, or Swell-body sleigh. The Portland cutter was the most popular sleigh style in North America, being the cheaper and easier sleigh to build. Peter Kimball of Hamlin's Gore, Maine, is generally given credit for building the prototype of a Portland cutter in 1817.[1] He had his shop on the west side of "The Whale's Back," a ridge extending from Hamlin's Gore to Portland. The following rhyme was quoted by Dr. Jefferson Gallison at a Woodstock reunion in 1890:

Peter Kimball built the cart wheels
By the Whale's Back on the Gore,
Made strong sleighs once painted yellow
And they last forever more.[2]

The Portland cutter, or Kimball cutter, had a body style of angular lines, deep in the seat and with a fairly straight back. The curves of the forepart and the runners were gentle. Kimball's sleigh evolved into a lighter one, with lighter paneled front, back and sides, as opposed to the heavy planking and timber braces used in the original sleigh.

This lighter sleigh was made popular by Peter Kimball's sons, James and Charles, who, independently of each other, set up shops in Portland, Maine. James had set up a shop in 1852 with a partner, Edward Clement. In the same year Charles opened a sales room in Portland, and by 1854 his entire shop was moved to Portland from Norway, Maine. Charles became the most famous carriage builder of Peter's six sons. About 1876 he sold his business in Portland and formed a partnership with the Brewster Company to produce the Kimball-Brewster sleigh. The partnership lasted about a year; Charles eventually established a large carriage company in Chicago, C.P. Kimball & Co.

The Portland cutter style sleigh was extensively manufactured throughout North America by many different carriage and sleigh companies.

The Portland cutter was the leading sleigh both in numbers built and in the variety of styles. Two variations found ca.1900 were the speeding cutter and the comfort cutter. The speeding cutter, modeled after the modern Portland, had the front constructed in such a way that the horse could be hitched very

PORTLAND SLEIGH, 1817.

i

close to the sleigh. But even at full speed, the animal's heels could not come in contact with the runners, beams, or knees. Speeding cutters sat high and were light and stylish.

The Comfort cutter, also ca.1900, was a modification of the Portland cutter of that era, whose design went back to the original Peter Kimball sleigh. The original sleigh was more comfortable, with longer body style and lower runners. The Comfort cutter tended to be lower to the ground and roomier.

The Albany cutter, also called a Swell-body cutter, gets its name from its place of origin, Albany, New York. James Goold of Albany is known to have made a sleigh in 1816 with a curved frame, but it wasn't until the late 1830's that the body styling of what is now called the Albany cutter started to take

ALBANY SLEIGH, 1816.

form.[3] In a letter dated February 1880, Abraham Efner took credit for making the first swell body cutters with rounded backs in Albany, 1835-1836. He was then working for Robinson & Vanderbelt; the following year he was to build 18 of these sleighs, priced at $23 each. George R. Groot, also working for Robinson & Vanderbelt around 1832, was the first to build the exaggerated goose neck for sleigh fronts. A wealthy customer, who was noted for the odd-looking turnouts he ordered, brought a four-seated phaëton to Robinson & Vanderbelt to have the body placed on runners. The forward ends were required to run up and form "goose-necks," scrolled at the end and curved for about 10" to 12" back. George Groot had the job of making the goose neck; this was also the first sleigh to have wings or sleigh fronts.[4]

In later years, this style of sleigh became somewhat of a trademark with the James Goold carriage shop of Albany; it became popular with sleigh owners who wanted something more stylish than the Portland cutter. Oftentimes this sleigh was also decoratively and ornately painted, and plush upholstery with a long cut pile (many times printed with a floral pattern) was generally used.

The editor of *The Hub* had this to say about the Albany sleigh in 1902:

"The modern Albany or full swell body cutter which was evolved from the old Albany, was a sleigh built on artistic lines, but it was improved until it lost the comfort-element which characterized it at the time of introduction. It was set too high and the great bend of the runners imparted a trembling motion which contributed largely to impair its popularity. The making of the body of the Albany cutter was a piece of work that called for the utmost skill, and there were very few workmen who could build a perfect body. Every piece in the frame work was bent and so full was the side sweep both on the horizontal and perpendicular lines, that it was necessary to use 1/3 inch basswood panels, and these were often spliced on the center strainer, as it was impossible to work in the double sweep without the panel buckling."

From November 19th to 24th, 1877, the Brewster Company of New York City held a grand sleigh opening and exhibited a line of sleighs unlike any that had been shown before. One hundred models were displayed, 18 different patterns, embracing the well-known Kimball-Brewster cutters, Albanies, Four-passenger sleighs of many styles, and 15 varieties of fancy sleighs, including the Russian, Russo-Canadian, Cariole, Tandem Whitechapel, Cabriolet, and Victoria sleighs both square and round, with and without rumbles. One was a true Russian sleigh, four were made by James Goold & Co., and all the rest were made by Brewster & Co.[5] A year before the company decided to produce something unlike the styles so long in use, it made a study of the sleighs used in other countries, particularly those of Canada and Russia; the best of these foreign sleighs were Americanized. This caused other builders to start out in new directions; the result was a variety of patterns unequaled in style and finish [6]

This book is divided into eleven different categories, each being arranged chronologically. Sleigh styles and colors varied frequently through the years. In 1894 the C-back Portland, ogee-back Portland, full-back Portland, Albany cutter, Goold's Albany sleigh, Goold's Albany Swell-body cutter, Utica jumper, New York cutter, Vis-a-Vis sleigh, Gentlemen's driving sleigh, and Four-passenger square box sleigh of eight years earlier were reported to be out of fashion; the more popular sleighs of 1894 were the Phaeton, Cabriolet (with or without rumble), Victoria, German, Russian, Danish, Canadian, and curricle.[7] In 1883 F.B. Gardner reported that no ornamental work was to be allowed on the finest models, excepting it be a simple monogram or coat-of-arms.[8]

The information presented in the book is as it was originally reported in the monthly trade journals for the horse-drawn vehicle manufacturer's trade. It is hoped that the reader will gain a sense of the vast complexity of the horse-drawn vehicle industry. Many books try to interpret information and in so doing lose some of the original intent; the reader is left with the writer's opinions on design concepts and developments. I have tried to avoid this by presenting selections of the original material.

As one can see in these old trade journals, the horse-drawn vehicle industry changed from year to year, even from month to month. The fashion plates and descriptions of the sleighs in this book are taken from the two leading American trade journals. The first was published in September 1865 as *The Coach-Makers International Journal* in Philadelphia; in April 1873 it changed its name to *The Carriage Monthly*. The second was first published in New York in June 1858 as *The New York Coach Maker's Magazine;* then changed its name to *The Hub and New York Coach-Maker's Magazine* in March 1871, and in January 1884 became *The Hub*.

Sleigh building was first concentrated in New England, later it was centered in New York State, and by the 1900s was largely found in Michigan and Wisconsin.

Only a few manufacturers specialized in making sleighs. This was a seasonal trade, generally carried on in the winter by companies that made carriages and wagons during the rest of the year. These companies usually started planning around July or August[9] for the winter season, a very risky business for most manufacturers because an abundant snowfall was essential to hold prices and to dispose of stock.

In June 1891, *The Hub* published the results of a study made of the number of sleighs built in the United States. The federal census listed 4572 carriage-building companies in 1890. *The Hub's* survey included only those manufacturers who made over 125 sleighs a year and, as the list on the next page indicates, not all the large manufacturers returned the questionnaire. It was estimated that the number of sleighs shown was two-thirds of those actually manufactured.

FOOTNOTES

1. "Sleighs and Sleigh Riding," *The Hub*, January 1894, p.808.

2. Letter of Ruby C. Emery, Bryant Pond, Maine, March 7, 1980.

3. "Sleighs and Sleigh Riding," *The Hub*, January 1984, pp.807-808.

4. George R. Groot, "Forty-Seven Years Ago The Origin of Albany Cutters in Question." *The Hub*, February 1880, p.497.

5. "Grand Sleigh Opening in New York City," *The Hub*, December 1877, p.415.

6. "Sleighs and Sleigh Riding," *The Hub*, January 1894, p.808.

7. "Sleigh Styles of 1894," *The Carriage Monthly*, April 1894, p.2.

8. F.B. Gardner, "How Are Sleighs Painted This Season," *The Hub*, March 1883, p.744.

9. "Sleigh Styles for 1894," *The Carriage Monthly*, April 1894, p.2.

Susan Green
Librarian
Carriage Museum of America

	Year when established.	1885–86	1886–87	1887–88	1888–89	1889–90	1890–91
S. R. Bailey & Co., Amesbury, Mass	1856	1,500	2,500	2,500	900	500	200
S. E. Bailey & Co., Lancaster, Pa.	....	400	700	600	....	....	....
Bay City Buggy Works, Bay City, Mich.	....	....	....	500	....	....	....
E. C. Bassett, Sterling, Ill.	....	400	300	900	500	250	250
Bean & Anderson Mfg. Co., McGrawville, N. Y.	....	....	....	42	8	None.	None.
Belknap Wagon & Sleigh Co., Grand Rapids, Mich.	....	146	267	487	862	637	716
Berry Spring Sleigh Co., Concord, N. H.	1889	....	....	....	200	None.	None.
Jas. H. Birch, Burlington, N. J.	....	3,000	2,500	1,500	800	600	None.
Birdsall, Waite & Perry Mfg. Co., Whitney's Point, N. Y.	....	....	....	18,000	9,200	6,000	2,000
Brewster & Co., of Broome-st., New-York City	....	100	100	100	....	....	....
W. N. Brockway, Homer, N. Y.	....	640	955	1,456	2,500	500	None.
Buffalo Carriage Co., Buffalo, N. Y.	....	....	....	200	300	400	None.
Burg Wagon Co., Burlington, Iowa	1851	432	500	1,000	200	None.	None.
John A. Chockelt, South Bend, Ind.	....	....	....	....	....	....	500
City Carriage Works, Fort Wayne, Ind.	....	150	200	500	200	None.	None.
Clark & Co., Lansing, Mich.	....	....	....	....	....	....	500
A. A. Cooper, Dubuque, Iowa	1850	593	897	1,360	682	767	680
Cortland Mfg. Co., Cortland, N. Y.	1885	....	....	....	....	....	250
Jacob J. Deal, Jonesville, Mich.	....	....	....	....	400	None.	None.
Fisher Mfg. Co., Limited, Homer, N. Y.	....	....	....	1,150	1,500	200	100
Forbes Sleigh Co., Westboro, Mass.	....	1,300	1,500	1,500	1,000	900	750
Ferd. F. French & Co., Boston, Mass.	....	50	70	90	30	20	24
J. & F. French, Keene, N. H.	....	150	150	150	150	150	100
Jas. Goold Co., Albany, N. Y.	1813	100	100	100	75	50	40
Groton Carriage Co., Groton, N. Y.	....	1,000	1,500	2,000	3,500	2,000	500
W. T. Helms, Reiglesville, Pa.	....	52	18	27	....	....	....
Hitchcock Mfg. Co., Cortland, N. Y.	....	12,257	15,000	18,887	....	....	....
Henry Hooker & Co., New-Haven, Conn.	....	....	25	50	160	50	1
Hurlburt Mfg. Co., Racine Junction, Wis.	....	400	600	500	None.	None.	None.
Kalamazoo Wagon Co., Kalamazoo, Mich.	....	2,800	2,500	2,500	None.	None.	2,000
C. P. Kimball & Co., Chicago, Ill.	....	100	100	100	....	None.	None.
Kingman, Sturtevant & Larabee, Binghamton, N. Y.	....	3,000	6,000	6,000	6,600	5,500	3,000
La Crosse Wallis Carriage Co., La Crosse, Wis.	....	100	150	250	100	150	35
J. A. Lancester & Co., Merrimac, Mass.	....	100	112	150	....	....	None.
La Porte Carriage Co., La Porte, Ind.	....	....	....	....	800	1,000	None.
Long & Silsby, Albany, N. Y.	....	25	25	25	25	25	25
Lowell Cutter Co., Lowell, Mich.	1889	....	....	....	....	10,000	15,000
Loud Bros., Merrimac, Mass.	....	100	125	140	....	....	....
Martin, Pennell & Co., Portland, Me.	....	50	50	50	....	....	....
J. B. McCrillis & Son, Manchester, N. H.	....	75	50	50	40	25	6
International Carriage Co.	....	70	63	58	None.	None.	1,260
Michigan Buggy Co., Kalamazoo, Mich.	....	2,000	2,500	3,000	5,000	4,000	3,000
Michigan Cutter Co., Lowell, Mich.	....	....	....	3,000	3,000	25,000	None.
Minnesota Carriage & Sleigh Co., St. Paul Park, Minn.	1887	....	....	1,200	600	600	None.
H. A. Muckle Mfg. Co., St. Paul Park, Minn.	1887	....	300	600	1,000	3,000	4,000
Northwestern Mfg. Co., Fort Atkinson, Wis.	....	1,900	2,150	2,600	2,000	2,300	3,000
G. W. Osgood, Amesbury, Mass.	....	210	250	250	....	....	....
Pratt & Chase, Coldwater, Mich.	1882	....	4,838	6,250	4,948	1,350	506
Reed & Forman, Poughkeepsie, N. Y.	....	25	20	None.	None.	None.	None.
Rogers Mfg. Co., Mason, Mich.	....	....	....	....	500	310	153
Rumsey Mfg. Co., Milwaukee Junction, Detroit, Mich.	1887	....	....	250	650	None.	None.
Peter Sames, Rockford, Ill.	....	....	....	....	....	....	500
Orville H. Short, Syracuse, N. Y.	....	813	None.	600	600	600	None.
W. H. & F. Sibley, Westboro, Mass.	....	500	500	500	....	....	....
St. Anthony Hill Sleigh & Carriage W'ks, St. Paul, Minn.	....	306	345	425	157	None.	None
Staver & Abbott Mfg. Co., Chicago, Ill.	....	2,000	2,000	3,000	1,500	500	None.
A. Streich & Bro., Oshkosh, Wis.	1860	10,000	10,000	10,000	12,500	15,000	30,000
Sullivan Bros., Rochester, N. Y.	....	800	1,000	1,000	....	....	....
B. F. & H. L. Sweet, Fond du Lac, Wis.	....	1,000	1,225	1,300	1,300	1,500	1,600
C. V. Taylor & Co., Pontiac, Mich.	....	....	....	....	....	None.	None.
Tiffin Agricultural Works, Tiffin, O.	....	1,000	1,500	1,000	500	500	1,000
Zenas Thompson & Bro., Portland, Me.	....	71	92	77	70	102	30
I. S. Tower & Bro., Chicago, Ill.	....	200	225	300	None.	None.	None.
Troy Carriage Works, Troy, N. Y.	....	75	85	105	10	6	2
H. E. Tyler, Morrisville, N. Y.	1871	....	440	440	600	300	350
Union Carriage & Gear Co., Watertown, N. Y.	1888	....	....	....	800	650	550
Geo. J. Warden & Co., Cleveland, O.	....	30	None.	None.	None.	None.	None.
Saml. J. White, Wilmington, Del.	....	None.	None.	None.	1,000	1,200	None.
C. R. & J. C. Wilson Carriage Co., Detroit, Mich.	....	....	....	....	1,000	250	100
L. & M. Woodhull, Dayton, O.	....	300	None.	None.	None.	None.	None.
O. P. Wright & Co., Nyack, N. Y.	....	....	....	16,000	18,000	18,000	14,000
Totals		53,310	64,426	118,919	84,267	104,892	86,728

ALBANY or
SWELL BODY TYPE
SLEIGHS

CUTTER SLEIGH.—½ IN. SCALE.

Engraved expressly for the New York Coach-Maker's Magazine.—Explained on page 132.

New York Coachmaker's Magazine
December 1859

BINGHAMTON, N. Y., Nov. 1, 1859.

MR. STRATTON : *Dear Sir*—Inclosed you will find a draft of a cutter after the Albany style. It is drawn one-half inch to the foot. This style of a cutter makes a fine sleigh when neatly finished, and sells from $60 to $100, according to the costs of finishing. In this design a carved eagle-head is shown, with patent leather arm-pieces, neatly stitched or stamped ; the former looks the neatest. The wings are covered sometimes with patent leather, very often with russet leather unfinished ; when covered with unfinished leather the front side of the wings should be painted of the same color as the running part, a light orange (some paint the running part vermilion), and the back part of the wings the same as the body, either lake or a blue color. Some paint the arm-piece a Chinese white, which gives the job, when done, a light appearance, finishing it with a gold stripe, three sixteenths of an inch wide, with a hair stripe added to each side. I think that plain striping looks the neatest. The back is finished with a sweep-back, to which a moulding is applied, giving it the appearance of the back of a coach.

We make the runners track from three feet to three feet two inches wide. The body-raves for a swelled side should be placed two feet six inches apart on the beams, measured from the outside. Splice the top-rave to the arm-piece, and afterwards lap and fasten the ends to the body rave, and let it project four or five inches from it, so as to give it a side-swell.

Trim the arm-pieces and back with red plush, using seaming lace ; and from the patent-leather arm-pieces to the necks use three-eighths angle moulding. This makes a nice finish. If you think this cutter looks well enough to publish, please introduce it to the craft.

Yours in haste,
S. W. SPALDING.

ALBANY SWELLED-SIDE CUTTER.

PLATE NO. 10.—This style of sleigh, for symmetry and beauty of outline, is unsurpassed. Track : 39 inches, 30 inches on front seat.

PAINTING : lower panels ultramarine blue, striped with gold, and edged with Canary color. The upper back quarter painted imitation of cane work, or Scotch plaid. Running part painted a bright straw color, striped black and fine line of blue.

TRIMMING : reps or fancy figured Brussels.

ALBANY SWELLED SIDE CUTTER.

Coachmaker's International Journal
December 1868

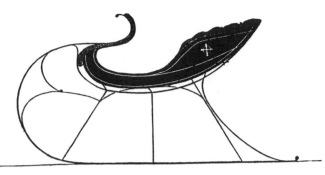

KENNEDY SLEIGH.

Plate No. 48.—Half-inch Scale.—

Coachmaker's International Journal
September 1869

KENNEDY SLEIGH.

PLATE No. 48.—This is a good style of Albany cutter, very light and graceful, and when properly constructed will be serviceable as well as attractive.

DIMENSIONS.—Width of bottom side, outside: 2 feet. Fenders: frame, 9 inches outside of bottom side. Track: 3 feet 3 inches. For further description, see Plate No. 43 in the August number.

TRIMMING.—Purple plush.

PAINTING.—Body: Munich lake, bordered with Milori green, edged with gold. Runners: black, elaborately scrolled and striped with gold and colors. The scrolls may be transferred. These can be obtained of Chas. Palm & Co., of Cincinnati. The body panels may also be scrolled and connected with stripes.

NAUTILUS CUTTER.

PLATE No. 45.—The beauty of a cutter depends almost entirely on the style of the body. When it is inclosed by lines which give a jaunty appearance, and the entire finish is of a cheerful order, nothing but the "beautiful snow" is required to have them sell rapidly. The Albany and Portland styles, although so different in their construction, each have their admirers, and will doubtless long continue to be built. The sleighs built at Keene, N. H., resemble the Albany pattern, and are generally very gaudily painted. The Nautilus has the bottom side bent to the same sweep as the Albany cutter. Sides and backs to be taken from thick poplar or white wood to produce a heavy swell. The panels may be fluted, or painted in imitation of flutes. The latter method is probably the most desirable. Track: 39 inches. For shoes, use steel. The front knee should be framed about 3 inches in front of the bearing of runner on the ground.

PAINTING.—Body: white, striping in imitation of fluting, gold. Running-part: drab, mixed of white, umber, yellow and lake, striped with brown and gold.

TRIMMING.—Crimson plush, with orange plush welting.

NAUTILUS CUTTER.

Plate No. 45.—Half-inch Scale.—

Coachmaker's International Journal
August 1870

No. 56. ALBANY CUTTER. SCALE, ONE-HALF INCH.

THE ALBANY CUTTER illustrated is very similar to Mr. James Goold's standard pattern. This style requires a finely swelled body; and, on the skill with which this is worked out, its beauty of effect depends very largely. Outside of New-York City the Albany pattern is yearly becoming more popular, particularly in the West, and we have seen specimens in certain Western cities which were fully equal to the best Eastern work.

We add the principal dimensions commonly employed in an Albany cutter of standard pattern:

Width of body over all, 37 inches. Turn-under, 7 inches. Side-swell, 7 inches each side. Runners, ⅞ x ¾ inch. Beams, 1⅜ x ¾ inch. Knees: at beams, 1⅜ x ¾ inch; at runners, ¾ inch square. Shoes, ¾ x ⅜ inch. Track, 3 feet 4 inches.

Painting, blue, red and gold striping. Trimming, blue plush.

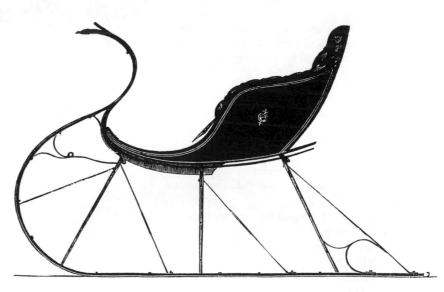

WAGNER'S SWELL-BODY CUTTER. (65)

EXHIBITED BY G. W. WAGNER, OF PHILADELPHIA.

THIS pattern shows several original features, and its effect is unquestionably good. The somewhat increased cost of the body, caused by swelling the sides, is amply repaid by the fine appearance of the body when painted.

The seat-frame is 35 inches wide. Track, 39 inches.
Painting.—Body, light vine color, with black border.

Albany or swell body type sleighs

Swell-Body Cutter.

PLATE NO. 48.

In this plate is represented a late style turned out by The Beach Carriage Manufacturing Co., Ypsilanti, Mich., a drawing of which was kindly furnished the agent of the MONTHLY, Mr. Wm. H. Sparks, while traveling through the Western states.

Dimensions.—Same as No. 46.

Painting.—Running part: Naples yellow, striped with fine line of super-ultramarine blue. Body: light scarlet lake. Moldings: Quaker green, ornamented with gold.

Trimming.—Crimson plush.

Carriage Monthly
September 1877

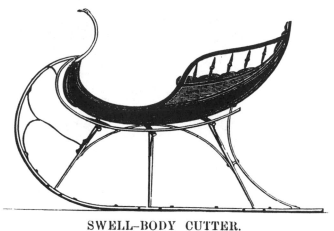

SWELL–BODY CUTTER.

PLATE No. 48.—HALF-INCH SCALE.—

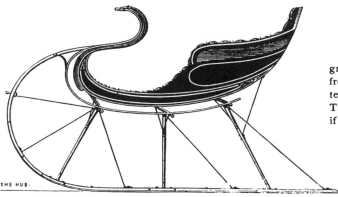

No. 107. PONY SLEIGH.—SCALE, ONE-HALF INCH.—BUILT BY ISHAM, BRUNDAGE & CO., OF PLATTSBURGH, N. Y.—

"THE PONY SLEIGH (Plate 107) has these dimensions: track on ground, 56 in.; height to top raves, 15 in.; dash, 42 in. high; length from front to back beams, 56 in. A Canadian screen is used as protection from drift snow. Painting: carmine and black; plating, gold. Trimming: cloth or plush to match painting; a top may be added if desired; weight of sleigh with top, 165 lbs."

The Hub
August 1878

ALBANY CUTTER.

(See Plate No. 46.)

THE principal novelty of this design consists in the pointed shape of the body, which should be made still more apparent by painting the triangular space at the front of the body in a bright color, such as English red, with either gold striping or an ornament. This will set off the darker part of the body, which narrows to the width of a molding at the extreme front.

Dimensions.—Width of body on seat, 34 in.; on bottom, outside, 26 in. Runners, $\frac{7}{8}$ x $\frac{3}{4}$ in. Beams, $\frac{3}{4}$ x $1\frac{3}{4}$ in. Knees, $\frac{3}{4}$ in. Track, 3 ft. 6 in., out to out.

Painting.—Body panels and seat-rail, dark chocolate brown; three-cornered panel under toe-rail, light carmine. Moldings black, striped with fine lines of light blue. Panels striped with $\frac{3}{16}$-inch stripe of gold, edged with fine lines of vermilion and white, and on carmine panel with blue and white. Runners, dark blue, striped with fine lines of pure white.

The Hub
August 1879

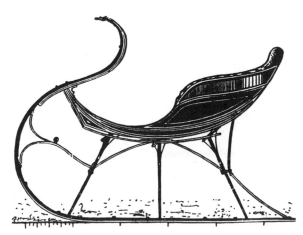

No. 46. ALBANY CUTTER.—SCALE, ONE-HALF INCH.

Working Draft of Swell-Body Cutter.

Numerous letters from Canada and elsewhere have reached the office of the MONTHLY, requesting the publication of a working draft for a swell-body cutter. We intended to comply with these requests in our last issue, but were unable to do so, on account of lack of space; therefore, taking advantage of the first opportunity, we produce drawings illustrative of the construction of a cutter. The drawings show, in a clear manner, the different views, which will readily be understood.

Fig 1 is the side view, showing working draft and cant. *A, A, A,* is the bottom sill; *B, B, B,* the fender; *C, C, C,* the rave; *D, D,* the seat arm; *E,* pillar; *F, F, F, F,* strainers; *H,* seat; *I, II, III,* knees; *K, K,* runner; *L,* turn-under; *N,* cross-bar, shown to better advantage in *Fig 2*; *O,* back; *P,* dash; *V,* bottom of dash.

In *Fig. 2* are shown corresponding parts, as viewed from the front; while in *Fig. 3* the same are given as viewed from the back.

Fig. 4 is a draft of the knees and beams; *I, II, III* representing, respectively, back, front and center knees.

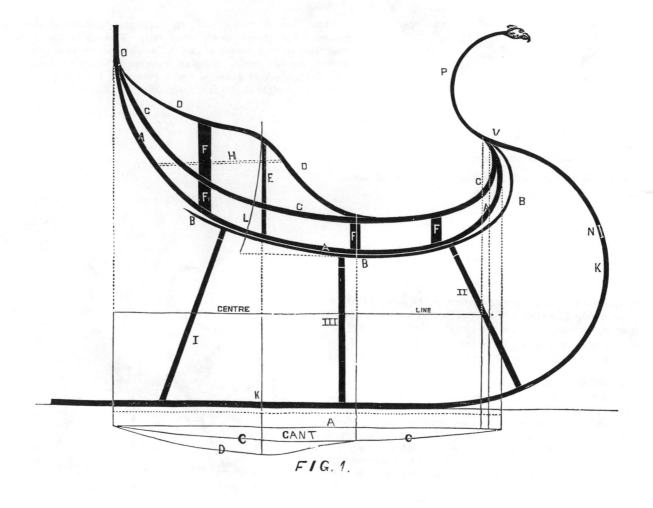

FIG. 1.

Carriage Monthly
December 1877
(second page of two)

FIG. 2.

FIG. 3.

FIG. 4.

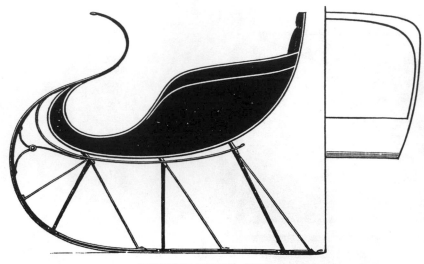

DETROIT SWELL CUTTER.
PLATE NO. 45.—HALF-INCH SCALE.

Detroit Swell Cutter.

PLATE NO 45.

A sketch and description of this cutter was furnished us by Mr. John Kemp, of Detroit, Mich., who, in his letter to us, says:

"My chief aim in this design is to simplify its construction, and do away with much of the hard labor in the common swell cutter. The stuff bent for ordinary swell cutters can be used in this. The raves should be one inch thick, the side panel grooved into them. They should be set 26 to 27 inches from out to out on the beams. The turn-under of main pillar at the front of seat is 5 inches on each side, making the body 36 or 37 inches wide at this point. The rave may be swelled a little sideways, that is, from the back to the front, say $\frac{1}{4}$ or $\frac{3}{8}$ inch. It will make the panel slide in easier. The back should be two inches narrower at the bottom than at the main pillar, the front drawn in some to suit the runners. The side panel can be put in in one piece, 19 inches wide, or it may be jointed under the molding, the top edge finished with hard wood. The easiest way to make the back is to mitre it into the back raves, put the panel on in one piece, 28 by 37 inches, the moldings as per design. Groove the neck panel into raves, and finish with wings placed on in the ordinary way. No change in the runners. Portland runners may be used with short raves, or swell raves with short runners."

Albany or swell body type sleighs

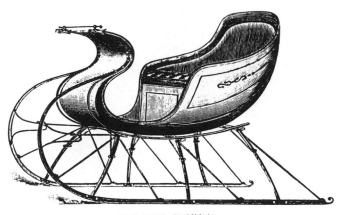

ALBANY CUTTER.

PLATE NO. 29.—VOL. 24.—HALF-INCH SCALE.

Bottom frame 23 inches wide; width of body at center, 38 inches; body 19½ inches from floor. Runners: width of track, 37 inches. Thickness and depth of runners, ¾ by ⅞ inch; shoes ¾ by ¼-inch round edge steel.

No change has been made in the construction of Albany cutters similar to our illustration for the past fifty years with the exception of the curved knees. The body consists of a light frame and bent panels.

Painting.—Body: deep carmine, lower part black. Runners: deep carmine, striped black. Body striped and ornamented in black and gold.

Trimming.—Red plush. The back, sides and seat are trimmed perfectly plain, with the exception of the roll across the top and sides to relieve the plain appearance. Carpet plain, without figures.

Mountings.—Gold. ———

Carriage Monthly
July 1888

No. 47.—SHALLOW-SIDE ALBANY CUTTER.

The Albany or Swell-side Cutter, notwithstanding its age, is always a favorite pattern, and it gives abundant opportunity for changes in the form of the body and the manner of molding. Our present design shows a very light and graceful body, the bottom line of which is well drawn up under the seat, giving a shallow and airy appearance. The seat-sides have one upright slat, with a round collar or medallion in the center.

The back has three slats, the one in the center only having a collar. The manner of ironing the gearing is that usual in the West.

Dimensions.—Width of body, outside, at bottom, 29 in.; at front of arm-rail, 35 in. Dash, 32 in. Runners, ⅞ x ¾ in. Knees, ¾ in. Fenders, ⅝ in. square.

No. 48.—SCROLL-SIDE ALBANY CUTTER.

This pattern has a fuller and heavier body, such as is made in some parts of this State. The moldings forms an ogee in the back, and a scroll in front; the latter finish is original and may be produced by a broad gold stripe. The gearing is ironed in the usual Albany style.

Dimensions.—Width of body outside, at bottom, 31 in.; at front of arm-rail, 36¾ in. Dash, 32½ in. Runners, ⅞ x ¾ in. Knees, ¾ in. Fenders, ⅝ in. square. Track, 40 in.

The Hub
July 1881

Albany or swell body type sleighs

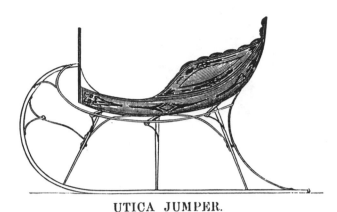

UTICA JUMPER.

Carriage Monthly
September 1877

This neat, jaunty style of cutter has long been in use in the central portion of New York State, differing from the Albany cutter only in the finish of the dash, which is framed of pieces. ⅜ by 2¼ inches, curving over the top and down the sides, made with two panels, upper and lower.

Dimensions.—Width of body outside on bottom : 29 inches. At back arm rail and lower corner of dash, the same. At front end of arm : 35 inches. Dash : 32 inches. Runners : ⅞ by ¾ inches. Beams : ⅜ by 1¾ inches. Knees : ¾ inches, tapering on inside to correspond with the beam at top and runner at the bottom. Fender : ⅝ inches square. Track : 39 inches.

Painting.—Running part : English vermilion, striped with black. Body panels : Tuscan red. Moldings, body : lake, ornamented profusely with gold.

Trimming.—Green plush.

No. 64. SHAW'S FOUR-PASSENGER ALBANY SLEIGH, WITH CALECHE TOP.

EXHIBITED BY P. H. SHAW, OF ALBANY, N. Y.

A LIGHT and graceful looking sleigh, although the proximity of the seats prevents the possibility of making a good-shaped top.

The principal dimensions are :

Width of front seat, 36¾ inches ; width of hind seat, 38 inches. Track, 39 inches. The runners at the forward extremity are contracted to 18½ inches.

Painting.—Blue, striping in gold, carmine, yellow, and white. *Trimming.*—Crimson plush.

The Hub
September 1876

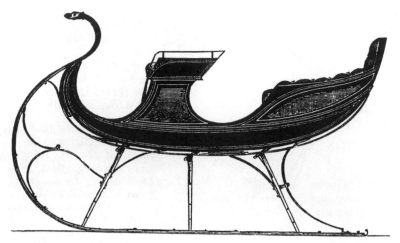

No. 72. SWELL-BODY FOUR-PASSENGER SLEIGH.—As built by Mr. A. Acker, of Sing-Sing, N. Y., and others.—Scale, one-half inch to the foot.

THIS design, although the lines of the Albany pattern are generally observed, shows some minor variations, particularly in the moldings and the striping of the hind quarter of the body. It illustrates a style built at present in several cities of this state, notably by Mr. A. Acker, of Sing-Sing.

Another feature of this design is the shortness and compactness of the running-part, which, measured between the extremities of the runners, is nearly one foot shorter than generally made.

The principal dimensions are as follow: Width of front seat on frame, clear, 36 in. Width of hind seat, clear, on front of frame, 38 in. Width of body at back, 26 in. Runners, $1\frac{5}{8}$ x 1 in. Knees on top, $\frac{7}{8}$ x $1\frac{1}{2}$ in. Benches, $1\frac{5}{8}$ x $1\frac{7}{8}$ in. Shoes, $\frac{1}{4}$ x 1 in. Track, 3 ft. 4 in.

Painting.—Let us make this a rather showy job. The swell-side panel, back panel, inside panel, and seat of this job may be painted with a darkened vermilion ground, glazed with carmine; the rear arm-pieces and blocks or risers of the front seat, a medium blue glazed with ultramarine; moldings, black. Stripe the body panels, arm-rests, risers, etc., with a broad stripe of gold, say $\frac{3}{8}$ inch wide, edged on one edge with vermilion, and on the other with white, and with distance fine lines of white or very pale cream-color; make the running-part and the front of dash (the latter being always painted the same color as the gear) in light blue glazed with ultramarine, thus forming a very rich sky-blue; and stripe with a double heavy "round" line of white. There should be no other ornamentation except a monogram or crest.

Trimming.—Crimson plush, with laces to match.

Mountings.—Silver.

The Hub
September 1877

No. 89. FOUR-PASSENGER, HALF-TOP SLEIGH.

BUILT BY A. ACKER, OF SING-SING, N. Y.—SCALE, ONE-HALF INCH.

THIS illustration, photographed from one of the jobs in the repository of Abram Acker, Sing-Sing, N. Y., has the following dimensions: Length, 5 ft. 4 in., from back of neck to back of sleigh. Knees, spread on runner, 4 ft. 8 in. Beams, spread at top, 2 ft. 9 in. Width of body on top of beams, 2 ft. 5 in. Width of back seat, 3 ft. 5 in. Track, 3 ft. 2 in.

Painting.—Body panels, dark green; seat riser and armpiece, French green; moldings, black, striped with gold and fine lines of white; runners, dark Indian red, striped with fine lines of straw or gold color, or with gold-bronze.

Trimming.—Dark green cloth. Mountings, gold. See further facts in regard to the styles of painting and trimming sleighs this season, under the article "Shifting-seat Sleigh," on opposite page. These suggestions were made by Mr. F. B. Gardner.

The Hub
October 1878

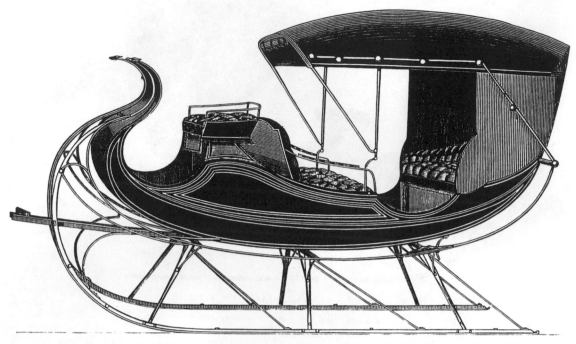

No. 120. SIX-PASSENGER ALBANY SLEIGH.—BUILT BY A. E. & J. H. CHRISTIE, OF NYACK, N. Y.

SCALE, ONE-HALF INCH.

THIS drawing represents one of the fall styles built by A. E. & J. H. Christie, the well-known sleigh-makers of Nyack, N. Y. No marked novelties are introduced in its outline or finish, but both are characterized by taste and elegance. This is known by the makers as their "Full Top Six-seat Pattern." Its principal dimensions are as follow :

DIMENSIONS.—Knees spread on runner, 6 ft. 3 in. Width of beams at top, 4 ft. 5 in. Width of body on beams, 2 ft. 7 in. Width of seats inside, 3 ft. 6 in. Length from neck to back, 8 ft. Height of panel, 4½ in. Runners, 1½ by 1 in. Beams, 1 by 2 in. Track, 3 ft. 4 in.

PAINTING.—In dark, rich colors, varied to suit the taste of customers.

TRIMMING.—Maroon plush. Top lined with reps to match plush.

The Hub
December 1878 (drawing)
and January 1879 (written description)

14

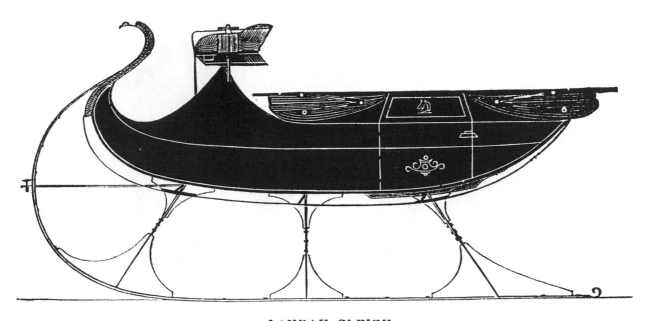

LANDAU SLEIGH.
Plate No. 44.—Half-inch Scale.

LANDAU SLEIGH.

PLATE No. 44.—As has been our custom heretofore, we introduce, thus early in the season, designs for sleighs, giving ample time for sleigh builders to prepare for the incoming season. This pattern will, when completed, furnish a winter vehicle of massive proportions, possessing a degree of stateliness heretofore unequaled. This being the first Landau sleigh published in America, and as the cost of the body will be about equal to that of a Landau carriage body, we do not expect that it will be built outside of the great sleigh-making centres; but wherever the sleighing season will warrant the building of such fine work, this design will certainly be of value. The boot is brought up very sharp, with rounded neck, being the latest coach style. Lamps are introduced of the column pattern. For hinging, the bows should be made of a straight pattern, so as to draw the front bows on both the front and back divisions of the top when the top is laid down.

DIMENSIONS.—Width of body over all: 50 inches. The turn-under must be governed by the dropping of glass frame. There is a drop rocker under centre of the door. The seats should be constructed to admit of being elevated when the top is down, which was explained in the description of the Elm City Landau.

PAINTING.—Body: crest panel and lower division of body, English purple lake. The middle division, which is connected with the boot, black; mouldings, striped gold. Running-part: carmine, painted on a dark ground work, striped black and gold. We have selected colors which will agree with the character of the vehicle, (deeming it in bad taste to introduce a display of scroll work and flashy colors,) thus placing this sleigh, in its whole make up, on a par with a fine carriage.

TRIMMING.—Turkish morocco. There might be an objection to this goods on account of its being colder than others that could be selected, yet in the summer season it would not be liable to damage from moths, and is more durable.

Coachmaker's International Journal
August 1870

No. 68. SIX-PASSENGER EXTENSION-TOP SLEIGH.—DESIGNED BY MR. A. MULLER, OF NEW-YORK.

SCALE, ONE-HALF INCH TO THE FOOT.

THIS fine design represents a style of Six-passenger Sleigh which cannot be excelled, we think, for the beauty and grace of its lines.

The finish of the front part of the body, and the connection of the middle seat therewith is always one of the most difficult parts to manage in designing these bodies, and in this instance it is made with much taste, giving to the whole an easy and well finished appearance, preferable to the several small panels which we see on some patterns, and which are of necessity objectionable to the painter. The inside of the body can be closed all around by curtains, including a storm-curtain dividing the driver's and middle seats. The dimensions are:

Width of body over all, 50 in. Width at back, 34 in. Width of body under front seat 33 inch. Runners, $1\frac{1}{2}$ x $1\frac{1}{2}$ in. Knees on top, $1\frac{1}{4}$ x $1\frac{5}{8}$ in. Beams, $1\frac{1}{4}$ x $1\frac{7}{8}$ in. Fenders, $\frac{7}{8}$ in.

Painting.—Body, swell side panels, back and seat, dark purple lake. Arm-piece and front seat-riser, dark green. Stripe with $\frac{5}{8}$ gold stripe, edged on the lake with light green, and on the green parts with vermilion. Distant fine lines of pale cream color on all parts. Running-part, light English vermilion ground, striped with gold or its imitation in paint.

Trimming.—For interior, crimson plush, driver's-seat, black leather.

Mountings.—Silver.

The Hub
September 1877

SHIFTING-SEAT SLEIGH.

We are indebted to Mr. Abram Acker, of Sing-Sing, N. Y., for this design of sleigh, as also for two others which are illustrated in this issue of *The Hub*. The following dimensions have been furnished us:

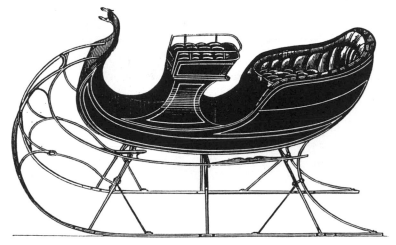

No. 88. SHIFTING-SEAT SLEIGH.—Built by A. Acker, of Sing-Sing, N. Y.

SCALE, ONE-HALF INCH.

Knees, spread on runner, 4 ft. 5 in. from outside to side. Track, 3 ft. 2 in. Height of knee, 20 in. from floor to bottom of sleigh. Width of beams at top, 2 ft. 4½ in. Height of panel, 3½ in. Width of back seat, 3 ft. 2 in. Length, from back of neck to back of sleigh, 4 ft. 8 in.

Painting.—Body panels, lake; the moldings and arm-pieces, black; runners, black, striped with fine lines of gold-leaf over all parts.

Trimming.—Crimson plush made up very elaborately. Mountings, silver.

It may be added here that it was formerly the custom of sleigh-builders to employ a variety of fancy colors, stripes, ornaments, etc., but of late years plainness and simplicity have been preferred by city customers. A sleigh of this description, if built for the New-York market, might be painted with dark lake or green panels; black moldings; the runners, vermilion or light green, and striped with plain colors in as neat and simple a manner as possible.

In trimming, greater display is allowable, and it is now the custom to employ a variety of rolls, biscuits, puffs, squabs, etc., according to the taste or ability of the trimmer. It would seem now to be a general idea that the more elaborate the trimming is, the better; while, as before remarked, the painting should be subdued, and this will serve to heighten the effect of the trimming.

The Hub
October 1878

NO. 123. SMALL PONY SLEIGH.—BUILT BY A. E. & J. H. CHRISTIE, OF NYACK, N. Y.

SCALE, ONE-HALF INCH.

THIS engraving has been reproduced with care from a large photograph of a Pony Sleigh just completed by A. E. & J. H. Christie, of Nyack, N. Y., and represents one of the most tasteful and pleasing patterns that has come to our attention this season. It is furnished with both pole and shafts. We are told by the builders that this pattern is becoming very popular, having the appearance of a full-size Pony Sleigh, while weighing no more than an ordinary shifting-seat pattern. The front seat turns on hinges, from top of risers, to facilitate access to the rear seats.

DIMENSIONS.—Its principal dimensions are these: Knees spread on runner, 4 ft. 6½ in. Width of beams at top, 2 ft. 8 in. Width of body on beams, 2 ft. 2 in. Track, 3 ft. 2 in. Width of seat, 3 ft. 3 in. Length from neck to back, 4 ft. 10 in. Height of panel, 3¾ in. Runners, 1⅛ x ⅞ in. Beams, 1¼ x ⅞ in.

PAINTING.—Body panels, dark green; arm-pieces and moldings, black. Gold-leaf lines are added on body, with fine line of lighter shade of green. The running-parts are painted light green, and striped neatly to suit the taste.

TRIMMING.—Dark green plush. Mountings, silver.

The Hub
December 1878

Albany or swell body type sleighs

No. 58. SIX-PASSENGER ALBANY SLEIGH, WITH EXTENSION-TOP.

SCALE, ONE-HALF INCH.

THE class of sleigh illustrated herewith is the so-called Albany pattern, which has taken a firm hold in all the Eastern States. Large as the surface of its body is, it is nevertheless difficult to make material changes in its lines. As a slight variation, we have altered the shape under the front seat, resting the seat upon a kind of riser, 3 in. deep and 8 in. wide ; this riser should be painted in a prominent color, such as carmine or yellow. The front crest-panel, represented in tint on our cut, is inclosed at its top by swept lines of a new shape ; the back-quarter has an ogee finish with scroll-ends.

Dimensions.—Width of body over all, 50 in.; at back, 34 in. Width of body under front seat, 33 in. Runners, 1¼ x 1¼ in. Knees on top, 1¼ x 1⅞ in. Beams, 1¼ x 1⅞ in. Fenders, ⅞ in.

Painting.—Principal body panels, under the "wing-panel" and "arm-piece," vermilion glazed. "Wing-panel" and "arm-piece," Paris green. Outside of the panels, chocolate brown, and the moldings black. This will give a lively effect, but one, we think, that will not be inharmonious. Stripe the body panels with a quarter-inch gold stripe, edged with white and orange. Stripe the black moldings with a single fine line of gold. Running-part, chocolate brown, striped profusely with vermilion glazed.

Trimming.—Crimson plush. Driver's-seat, black enameled leather. Lining of top, dark green cloth. Mountings, silver.

The Hub
September 1879

19

Constructing Swell Body Cutters.

Detroit, Mich., Nov., 1882.

Mr. Editor :—Noticing in the Monthly, a question asked by a correspondent from Lyons as to the best method of making swell cutter bodies, I will try to explain the way it is done here, although it may not be the best.

After the stuff is bent to the required shape, the raves are fastened to a trustle the necessary distance apart, say 20 inches, extending from the extreme back to the extreme front; they are then routed on the outer edge to receive the side panel, and also on the inner edge on the back part to receive the back panel.

It is best to take the back top rail, round back corner, back quarter and part of the front rail out of one piece, this requiring stuff 4 feet 8 inches long, 11 inches wide and ⅝ inch thick, bent diagonally so as to make the highest part of the back and extend around the back corner, and from the back quarter above the side panel to the front of seat, from there being tapered down to a plain rail for the purpose of splicing on the front rail which extends to the front of the raves. The front splice is about half way between the seat and front, and the back splice is in the middle of the back. The bottom edge of this piece is routed out to receive the top edge of side panel.

The routing out is done by a machine cutter, either by hand or steam power, it requiring two men to run it by hand. This machine is a journal, 1 inch thick, fitted to boxes in a frame so as to apply pulleys or a crank to increase the speed or power or both; to this ground is fastened a small circular saw, 1¾ inches in diameter or ⅜ inch around the journal, cutting the groove for the panel ⅜ inch deep. This piece is spliced in the middle of the back, lapping 4 or 5 inches, the back panel being put in before fastening the splice. Before paneling any more have your frame all glued up and the splices made and cleaned off.

The side panels are in two pieces, meeting about the center and fastened with a batten, the front panel being driven toward the front and the back panel toward the back, being bent sufficiently to allow them to double into the groove.

The front panel or dash was formerly made in two or three pieces, but now that they saw them out around the log it can be made in one piece; this is placed on the outside of the rave, and the runners outside of that.

To do this work advantageously two men should work together, doing half a dozen jobs at a time. They should have a working draft, showing the lower line of the body when on the benches, the top line of the benches on which the body rests, the runner line on the ground, and also the leaning in of the back and front benches. This will show the lengths and bevels of the legs and benches, without which the workman cannot make his body and runners come together properly.

Yours, truly,

JOHN KEMP.

Carriage Monthly
December 1882

Bass-Wood Panels.

Bass-wood panels are only used for sleighs and work of similar kind. It is admirably adapted for Albany sleighs on account of the great side swell and turn-under, as there is no wood that bends easier than this kind. For carriage bodies yellow poplar is preferred, it not being as much affected by atmospheric changes as bass-wood; for instance, a straight, wide panel of bass-wood is liable to buckle, which will greatly show uneven surfaces. A bad practice in the body-shop is to nail the panels, sink the heads below the surface, and apply hot water to it. The hot water soaks the glue, rendering it unfit for holding anything, will rust the nails in a short time, and these nail holes will always show through the varnished surface.

Carriage Monthly
May 1885

PORTLAND
and
OTHER CUTTERS

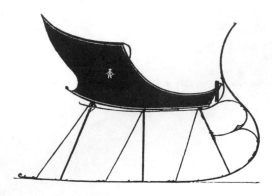

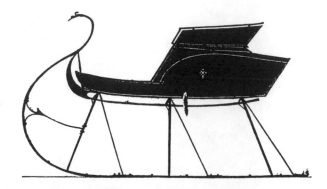

NEW HARTFORD JUMPER.—½ IN. SCALE.
Engraved expressly for the New York Coach-maker's Magazine.

COAL-BOX SLEIGH.—½ IN. SCALE.
Engraved expressly for the New York Coach-maker's Magazine.

NEW HARTFORD JUMPER, AND COAL-BOX SLEIGHS.
Illustrated on Plate XIX.

Both of these designs have been furnished us by our attentive and ingenious friend, E. Hallenbeck, Esq., of New Hartford, New York. The first—the jumper—in the drawing may have in the judgment of some, an unfavorable appearance, yet we have the assurance of the designer, that it makes a beautiful thing for the purpose intended. We have been supplied with the following details in regard to it: Bottom of the box, 3 x 2 ft. 3 in.; top, 2 ft. 7½ in. across, in front of the seat. The back corners should start at the bottom, perfectly square, and (by inserting large corner blocks) the top may be rounded to the desired fancy. The rest for the arms at the top edge on the side, are formed by a half-inch strip projecting five-eighths of an inch beyond the body, and running out at the back corner. For a very rakish looking job, the top of the dash may be thrown forward three inches, preserving the same crook above the top of the body in front. This—Mr. H. says—is decidedly the finest cutter in use, and will well pay the expense of getting up, because of its ready sale. The price of such a 'jumper' is $125.

The second design is a coal-box sleigh, which can be made and sold for $100. The box at the bottom is 3 ft. 9 in., by 2 ft. 3 in., to which of course the proper flare should be given. The center beam is 4 ft. 8 in. long. The upper panel is routered into the center of the runners, and the lower one rabbeted into the back side. By putting to it a 2½-inch sunken-bottom, the sleigh will look much lighter. The beams should be made to run through this sunken-bottom, the front one being rounded up for a foot-rail.

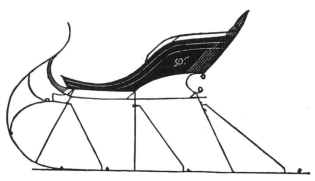

MERRIMAC CUTTER.

Plate No. 51.—Half-inch Scale.

MERRIMAC CUTTER.

PLATE NO. 51.—An improved style of Portland cutter. The draft shows a round corner, and the back panel is swelled. The sides are taken from $\frac{1}{2}$-inch poplar, and have $2\frac{1}{2}$ inches flare. The front of body rests on the two front beams, while the back part is swept up and supported by scrolled iron braces, producing a very light appearance. The hind beam is rounded or chamfered, except where the foot of scroll iron rests. This plate cannot fail to find admirers, as it introduces a pattern of cutter entirely outside the old beaten path.

DIMENSIONS.—Width on seat, 31 inches. The running part should be taken from good hickory, and made very light. Size of runners: $\frac{3}{4}$ inch square; beam: $\frac{3}{4}$ by 1 inch. In ironing, use straight stays, placing them where they will support or resist the greatest strain. Steel shoes. Track: 39 inches.

PAINTING.—Cutters admit of an almost infinite variety of styles in painting, and they will bear an amount of display which would be out of place on carriage work. We would prefer this body painted with lake or Bismarck, relieved with two or three different colors in striping, and the running part carmine, with cuir (kweer) fair leather-colored coarse lines, and fine lines of black and gold. At Portland, Me., Amesbury and Westboro, Mass., white, drabs of various tints, delicate greens and browns are employed, and the striping selected to contrast.

TRIMMING.—Red plush, with green plush welting and edge finish. Trimmings portable.

THIS original design for a cutter, by Mr. Adolphus Muller, will, no doubt, be approved by those of our readers who are interested in sleigh-making. Our cut presents a plain yet pleasing outline of the body, which is greatly increased by the ornamentation to be painted thereon.

This style of body, the Portland pattern, is the favorite in most sections, both with makers and customers. It is usually given square corners, but the corners on our cut are rounded. Square or edged seats have of late been made by many city builders on all classes of work; but are on the decline already, except in the case of stick or slat seats. Country makers, with large custom, and of undoubted ability for manufacturing and selling, have told us repeatedly that their customers object to sharp corners, as they are looked upon in the country as denoting cheap work. Our own experience has disclosed this fact, and we are far from blaming makers so situated for not following this or any other taste that may rule in the cities.

To make the body look best, the swell and bevel of the sides should not be less than from 3½ to 4 inches. The ornamental stripe is intended to run over the back of the body.

The usual dimensions are as follows:

Width of seat, 2 feet 8 inches.
Runners, ¾ inch square.
Beam, ¾ x 1 inch.
Track, 3 feet 2 inches.
The "goose-necks" are contracted to 1 foot 6 inches on the top, and the shoes are made of cast-steel.

Straight stays are preferred at present, they being considered not only more stylish than the old curved stays, but also more durable.

For painting, we recommend for the body, dark blue; for the broad lines of the ornamental stripe, gold; and for its fine lines, straw color, or New-York red. Running-part, red, striped black.

Trimming in plush is always taking for sleighs.

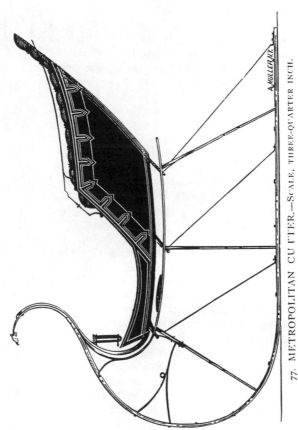

77. METROPOLITAN CUTTER.—SCALE, THREE-QUARTER INCH.

DESIGNED BY ADOLPHUS MULLER.

The Hub
September 1872

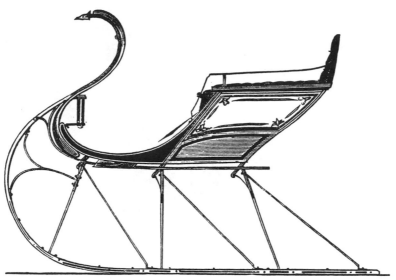

No. 64. CONCAVE CUTTER. SCALE, THREE-QUARTER INCH.

64. CONCAVE CUTTER.

This neat design for a two-passenger sleigh presents some decidedly novel points in the finish of the sides. Concave-convex bodies are at present a leading style for English quarters, and it seems to us that for sleigh-bodies, which require considerable turn-under, the same finish is very appropriate. Nor does this finish cause so much extra work as it would appear at the first glance, for if the side-pieces are taken of sufficient thickness, the concaving can be worked out. The Stanhope-pillar is glued on, and then shaped to its proper form.

The following dimensions apply both to this and the " Plain Portland Cutter :"

        Track, 3 feet 4 inches.
        Width of seat-frame, 31 inches.
        Turn-under of sides, 3 inches.
        Fenders to project 8 inches from body.
        Runners, ⅞ inch square.
        Beams, ¾ x 1 inch.
        Steel shoes.

In conclusion, we will make a few general remarks on the subject of painting and trimming sleighs.

We have, in former years, frequently cautioned our readers against gaudy ornamentation, and in the spirit of the taste of to-day, such work is not considered first class. We do not object so much to striping or belts, even when profuse ; but these stripes should be rather heavy, quiet, and on a dark ground. For instance, if we take a dark blue body, and the same color for the running part, we may stripe with one ⅛-inch line of light blue (white and ultramarine), and, at no less than half an inch from this line, add a gold stripe, ¼ inch wide. Fine lines or hair lines have no effect at a distance, and the object of striping should be to give an effect, not for the stable, but for the road. For this reason, carriage-makers of the best taste in Paris and London very seldom stripe with fine lines, and in the case of light work, which can bear no heavy striping on the body, city makers in this country often avoid striping altogether. Ornaments on a sleigh should be as few and small as possible.

For trimming, we recommend dark colors exclusively, with binding in yellow, red, or similar prominent colors, and tufting with buttons of the same shade. Cloth cushions and leather backs are fashionable.

The Hub
September 1874

No. 63. RUSSELL'S PORTLAND-CUTTER.—Exhibited by Jos. Russell, Portland, Me.

RUSSELL'S PORTLAND-CUTTER. (63)

EXHIBITED BY JOSEPH RUSSELL, OF PORTLAND, ME.

This is a handsome cutter, plain and tasteful in both design and finish. The body has a pleasing shape, which is the more praiseworthy because the simplicity of its lines gives little room for the display of form. The front-finish of the body is the latest used for this pattern of cutter.

The principal dimensions are as follow :

Width of seat, 33½ inches ; width at bottom, 30 inches ; width of body over all, 34¾ inches. Track, 36 inches out to out.

Painting.—Body, vine color, with black border and a fine line of gold. Running-part black, with gold striping ; trimming in pink plush.

The Hub
September 1876

No. 87. PORTLAND CUTTER.—BUILT BY A. ACKER, OF
SING-SING, N. Y.—SCALE, ONE-HALF INCH.

PORTLAND CUTTER.

THIS neat design of cutter was kindly furnished us by Mr. Abram Acker, the well-known sleigh-builder of Sing-Sing, N. Y., who also gives the following dimensions : Width of track, 3 ft. 2 in. Height of knees, 20 in. from floor to bottom of sleigh. The spread of knees on runner, 4 ft. Spread of beams on top, 2 ft. 5 in. Width of body at bottom, 2 ft. 3 in. Flare of sides, 3½ in. to the foot. Width of seat, 2 ft. 9 in. Length over all, from front to end of runner, 5 ft. 10 in.

Painting.—Body, dark ultramarine blue. Runners, dark carmine. Stripe on all parts with medium fine line of gold, using gold-leaf on body, and a good bronze on runners. For city trade, this style of sleigh is painted plain.

The Hub
October 1878

GRANGER CUTTER.

(See Plate No. 48.)

THIS is a style manufactured for the trade by a large Western firm, who are numbered among our subscribers. We have changed a few points on it, the principal of which is the short bracket front, first introduced by Messrs. Brewster & Co. (of Broome-street) on the Kimball-Brewster Cutters ; and we have also altered the lines of the moldings and striping, so as to give space and opportunity for fancy painting. This cutter is the most suitable for cheap work, of the four published in the present number.

Dimensions.—Width of body on top, over all, 34 in.; at bottom, outside of rockers, 28 in. Runners, ⅞ x ¼ in. Beams, ¾ x 1¼ in. Knees, ¾ in.; to taper on the inside to fit beam and runner. Track, 3 ft. 6 in.

Painting.—Body black, striped with gold; and, where desired, ornamental corners may be added (see page 213 for designs of fancy striping). Runners, dark brown, with fine lines of bright yellow.

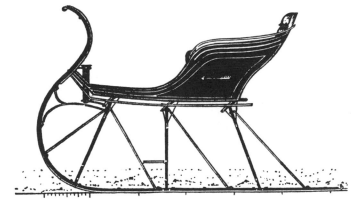

NO. 48. GRANGER CUTTER.—SCALE, ONE-HALF INCH.

The Hub
August 1879

HOW TO MAKE A JUMPER.

A LIGHT sleigh, of primitive country make, is in some sections known as a Jumper. It may be made of hard-wood poles cut and bent into shape, a few bolts, and a light body or box.

The accompanying engraving, made from a sketch of a recently constructed Jumper, will serve as a guide to any one who wishes to provide himself with a light sleigh at a trifling cost. Two hickory poles, for the runners, are dressed down, the smaller ends bent to the proper curve, and fastened until they will retain the bent shape. The posts are mortised into these runners and the bench pieces, which latter are firmly fastened together with bolts. The braces and their positions are shown in the engraving. A floor is laid upon the bench pieces, and extends beyond the sides of the box or body. The box may be plain, or ornamented in various ways. The one shown has the sides and back flaring. The shafts are fastened to the curved ends of the runners with eye-bolts.

The Hub
July 1882

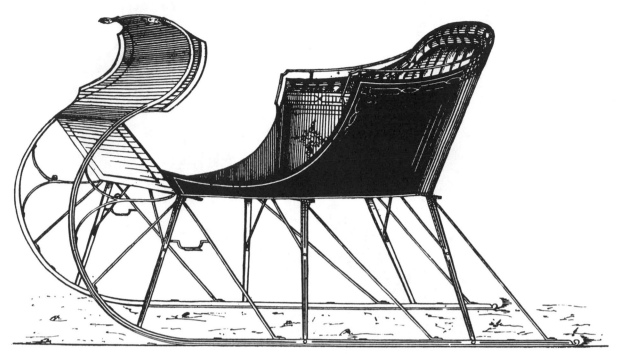

No. 58. MARSHALL'S ROUND-BACK PORTLAND CUTTER.—SCALE, THREE-QUARTER INCH TO THE FOOT.

MARSHALL'S ROUND-BACK PORTLAND CUTTER.

(See Plate No. 58.)

IN this plate we show a standard pattern of Portland Cutter, as built last season in considerable numbers by Messrs. A. P. Marshall & Co., of Lancaster, N. H. Our engraving has been reproduced from a pen and ink sketch kindly furnished us by the senior of the firm, whose skill as a draftsman is quite unusual and highly creditable in a carriage-builder upon whose shoulders rests the weight of a large business.

Mr. Marshall has kindly furnished the following list of dimensions, and description of its finish, to accompany the drawing.

Dimensions.—Height of dash, 47 in. Width of runners, 39 in. Length of body, 35 in.; width of body at bottom, 28 in.; width of body at handles, 35 in. Height of back, 27 in. Height of sides, 19 in. Height of seat, 14½ in. Length of posts, front, 20 ½ in.; length of posts, middle, 20 in.; length of posts, rear, 21 in. Shoes, ⅞ in., common style; or Kimball patent, 1¼ in.

Painting.—Plain black, with Indian red stripe, glazed with carmine; or, if preferred, black body, with Indian red running-part glazed with carmine; body striped with fine-lines, dark green. The irons are black on gear, with very fine gold stripes on irons. Posts and runners fine double black stripe.

Trimming.—Material, dark green broadcloth. Buttons, a light shade of green (covered). Trimmings stitched with light green silk. Green carpet to match, with light green figure.

The Hub
August 1882

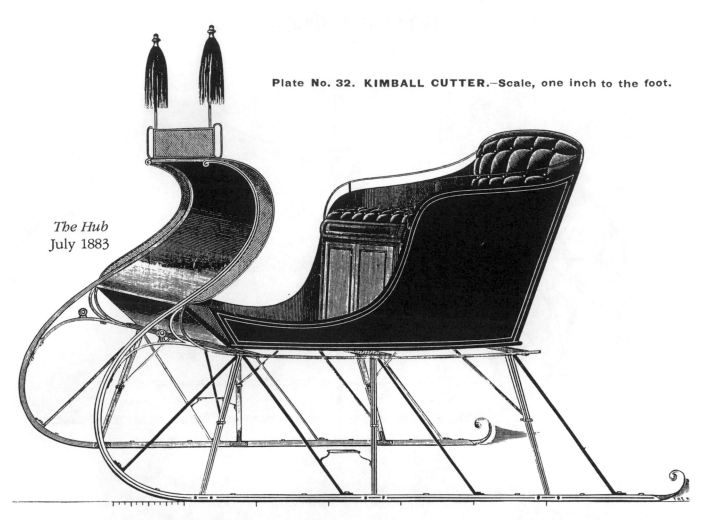

The Hub
July 1883

THE Kimball Cutter, although plain in outline, is always attractive and popular. The general outlines of Plate No. 37, in this number, closely resemble those of the above pattern, but on this Kimball pattern the back is straight, and there are no moldings on the sides and back. Plumes and wire fenders have also been added to this design, and will be found to greatly increase the attractiveness of the sleigh, and therefore improve its salable quality. The wood work on the running-part is made extremely light, and well braced by iron stays. The stays are made out of the very best iron, and reduced to the smallest practicable size.

Dimensions.—Width of body on top, 35½ in.; ditto on the bottom, 29 in.; giving a flare of 3¼ in. on each side. The uprights and cross-pieces for the benches are light, and made of the best hickory or white ash. The horizontal pieces of the benches are also made of hickory or white ash, 1 x 1¾ in. The uprights are 1¾ in. thick, by 1 in. wide at the top, and ¾ in. at the runners. Runners, ¾ in. square. Shoes for the runners, ¾ x ⁵⁄₁₆ in. Side-stays, ⁷⁄₁₆ in. round iron. Cross-braces, ⅜ in. round iron; the latter to be clipped to the uprights. The stays receiving the jack-clips for the shafts are ⁹⁄₁₆ in. round iron. Track, 39½ in., from out to out. It will be noticed that the dimensions of the above body closely resemble those described in detail for Plate No. 37 in this number, (page 220) and the dimensions of the different iron parts adapted to Plate No. 37 will also answer equally well for this model.

Finish.—Painting: For the body color we would recommend dark blue, with a half-inch black stripe around the outer edge of the body, and a fine line of canary yellow ⅜ in. from the black stripe. The running-part can be painted either canary yellow or bright carmine. In the former case, the running-part may be striped black; and in the latter case, gold striping may be put on the running-part, and on the body a fine gold line in place of the canary yellow. Trimming, blue plush for back, cushion and fall. A roll may be applied around the outer edge of the back, and the rest laid off in squares. A raiser, ⅞ in. wide and 1 in. from the outside edge, goes on the fall, and is made out of the same material as the other parts. Carpet, blue, with small figures to match the color of the running-part. Plumes, blue. Mountings, brass. The wings or fenders are made of ⁵⁄₁₆ x ⅝ oval iron, filled in with wire-work, and the whole being brass-plated.

The Hub
July 1883

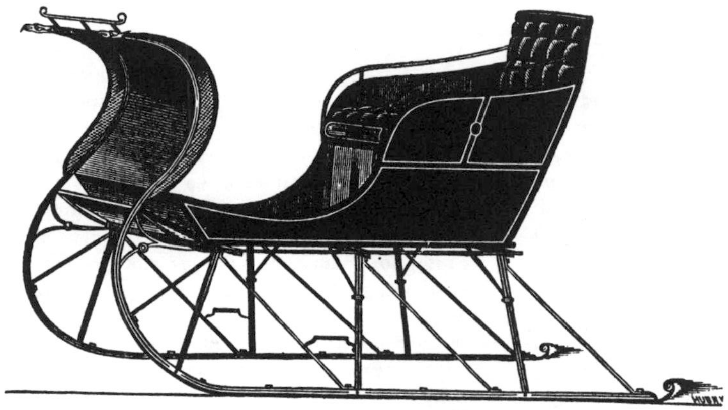

No. 37. PORTLAND CUTTER, WITH MOLDED PANELS.—Scale, one-half Inch.

PORTLAND CUTTER, WITH MOLDED PANELS.

(See Plate No. 37, on this page.)

THE Portland Cutter, in various patterns and under numerous titles, is built in increasing numbers every season, and has become the standard two-passenger sleigh throughout the United States and Canada.

The new design represented in the accompanying fashion plate, is light in appearance, and the construction is simple, reducing the cost considerably. For the panels of the body, half-inch whitewood will be sufficient, which can be lightened to $\frac{3}{8}$ in. on the top edge. A molding goes all around the body. The bottom molding is formed by the bottomsides, which are made of hickory. The upper section of the side-panel at the seat, as will be seen by the drawing, is relieved by horizontal and vertical moldings, the latter to have a medallion. All these moldings may, however, be dispensed with, where plainness or inexpensiveness is specially desired. The moldings are to be rounded on the outside $\frac{1}{16}$ in.

The uprights of the inside frame-pieces on the body, extend in most cases about $\frac{3}{4}$ in. below the bottom edge of the body-panel, forming a tenon, which is framed into the bottomsides. This tenon could be dispensed with by having the plates, which secure the body to the bottomsides, screwed against the uprights, forming an angle at the bottom end. Screw the plates on the body so that the bottom end will come within $\frac{1}{32}$ in. from the bottom edge of the panels. This will give sufficient draw to hold the body firm to the bottomsides. Six plates are used, made long enough to have three holes drilled in them, the center one to receive a thread for a screw-bolt, and those at the ends for a $\frac{3}{4}$ in. No. 12 screw. Two of these plates are used for the center uprights, two on the front corner blocks, and two for the corner-pillars, all to be let in even with the top of the bottomsides. The angular plates have to be let into the pillars flush with the wood. The body is then fastened to the bottomsides by means of screw bolts. A light dowel will be necessary on each side of the body, fastened into the bottom edge of the side panels to keep the body from sliding while putting it together after it is painted. The bottomsides and bottom nearly always remain on the running-part while being painted, and we have often noticed that the bottomsides, at the mortises for the reception of the tenons before-mentioned, frequently shrink at this time; and the mortises in some cases show wear, caused very likely by the moving of the body, the same not being screwed up properly. This may be avoided by following the before-mentioned method of applying angular plates to the uprights, etc.

Dimensions.—Width of body on top, $35\frac{1}{2}$ in.; on the bottom, $28\frac{1}{4}$ in. The uprights and cross-pieces for the benches are light, and should be made out of the best hickory. The cross-pieces are $1 \times \frac{3}{4}$ in. The uprights are $\frac{3}{4}$ in. thick, by 1 in. wide at the top, and $\frac{3}{4}$ in. at the runners. Runners, $\frac{3}{4}$ in. square. Shoes for the runners, $\frac{3}{4} \times \frac{1}{4}$ in. Side-stays, $\frac{3}{8}$ in. round iron. Cross-braces, $\frac{5}{16}$ in. round iron; the latter to be clipped to the uprights. The stays receiving the jack-clips for the shafts are $\frac{1}{2}$ in. round iron. Track, 39 in., from out to out.

Finish.—The panels may be painted either black or dark blue, and the moldings edged with a fine line. Running-part, canary yellow, striped black. Trimming, blue plush for the back and cushion, to be laid off in squares. Carpet, to match the color of the plush. Mountings, brass.

A. K.

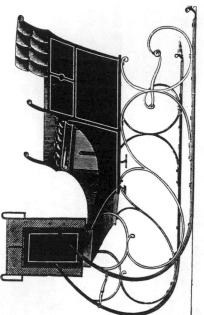

PLATE NO 46: *BERLIN JUMPER.*

(Scale, one-half inch to the foot.)

How or where this sleigh derived the name of "Berlin Jumper," we do not know ; and whether the style of this neat-looking vehicle had its origin in Berlin, the capital city of Germany, or whether it is an American invention, we have not been able to ascertain. The first specimens came under our observation in this city, and they were all constructed either in New-York City or its suburbs, the firm of A. E. & J. H. Christie, of Nyack, N. Y., who are noted for the excellence of their work, not only in outline, but also in general finish, being one of the more prominent builders of this style.

The corner, middle pillars and bottomsides of this sleigh are made of ash. The corner-pillars are framed into the bottomsides, and the moldings on the pillars and bottomsides are worked on, and have a groove for the reception of the panels. Pieces are framed into the corner-pillars on the sides and back at the height of the center molding, and also a vertical piece near the corner-pillar, which is mortised into the bottomsides and lapped to the horizontal piece. The panels consist of two sections, being jointed in the center of the frame-pieces. The joint is then covered by the moldings. (See drawing.) The bar framed across on the back can be utilized for the fastening of the seat-boards. The dash is made of wood, and should not be made too light ; and, preferably, not from whitewood, as sycamore or cherry will give better satisfaction. A wire fender is attached to the sides, to keep the snow from being thrown into the sleigh when in motion.

A study of our fashion-plate in connection with the foregoing particulars, will show that this sleigh is not only quite a novelty, but very comfortable ; and we will now offer a suggestion how, in our opinion, its body might be improved. If the lower section of the panel should

be set in from the outside 1¼ in. on the sides, the upper section would then form a more distinct portion of the body, similar in appearance to the seat of the T-cart or Extension-top Phaeton. It is obvious that this method would greatly improve the appearance of the body, and no extra labor would be incurred by this change.

To continue our description, the upright, before-mentioned, instead of being framed with the same flare as the outside of the pillars will have to be framed in such a manner as to set in 1¼ in. on top. Allowance must be made in the thickness of the back corner-pillar, which would be at the middle 2 in. thick, while 1¹⁄₁₆ in. at the bottom will be sufficient. The lower section of the panel is made of one piece in length, and is grooved into the back corner-pillar. The middle pillar is glued to the outside of the lower panel. The moldings are rounded off ¹⁄₁₆ in. on the outside.

Dimensions.—Width of body on top of the back corner-pillars, 38 in.; ditto at the bottom of the body, 29 in. The runners are ⅞ × ⅞ in. The shoes for the runners are ⅞ × ⅝ in., steel. The stays are ¼ × ⅝ in., oval. Track, 38 in., from out to out.

Finish.—Painting : body and runners, dark green ; moldings black, with carmine fine lines. Runners, striped with black on top, and gold on the face. Dash, striped with a broad panel stripe of carmine, and minor fine lines of gold. Trimming, green cloth for the back, cushion and fall. It is necessary to make the back very full on top, and thinned down towards the seat, as the back corner-pillars have considerable flare from the seat upwards. A plain green carpet will best suit this job. Mountings, silver.

The Hub
August 1883

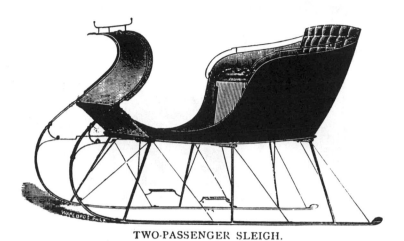

TWO-PASSENGER SLEIGH.

PLATE No. 50.—FIVE-EIGHTH-INCH SCALE.

Two-Passenger Sleigh.

PLATE NO. 50.

This design and Plate No. 51 below represent purely American styles, manufactured by Messrs. R. M. Bingham & Co., Rome, N. Y. The change for the coming season over those of last year is in the back corners and bottom line of body having more curve.

Painting.—Body: ultramarine blue, striped broad lines of black. Runners: deep red, striped two fine lines of black.

Trimming.—Red plush. Back, block pattern, red plush buttons. Cushion, block style, leather welts. Rug, plain, bound with fringe.

Mountings.—Gold.

Carriage Monthly
September 1883

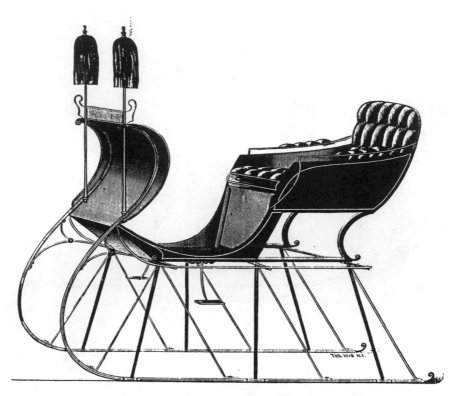

Plate No. 26. NEW-YORK CUTTER WITH OGEE BACK.—Scale, three-quarter inch.

NEW-YORK CUTTER, WITH OGEE BACK.

(See Fashion Plate No. 26.)

THE Cutter occupies a position among sleighs similar to that of the buggy among wheeled vehicles, one of its chief requisites being combined lightness and strength, and, to attain these two conditions, good material and workmanship are both necessary.

The two principal styles of Cutters are the Portland and Albany, the first-named having straight sides, and the latter swelled sides. The back of the Portland Cutter may be flared, but is straight in the majority of cases. We noticed, last winter, a noteworthy departure from this style in a cutter built by Mr. R. M. Stivers, of this city, wherein the back of the body was slightly inclined to the ogee pattern, being straight at the bottom crosswise, but gradually curving out toward the top edge, until it there formed a full round corner. Both wood and ironwork were extremely light and graceful, and the painting was remarkably attractive, the color of the body being a rich blue, and the runners carmine, striped with gold.

The Hub
July 1884

Plate No. 26. SHELL-BODY CUTTER.—Scale, five-eighths inch.

The outlines of the body of this Shell Cutter, together with its runners and stays, are characterized by graceful and easy sweeps. To build such a body in a proper manner requires skill and experience on the part of the body-maker. The sides are made of heavy whitewood of about 3 in. thickness, which is lightened out to ⅞ in. The back has round corners, and the flutes on the sides and back are carved on. The seat is of good depth, allowing comfortable seat-room, and the trimming of the back is heavy, and made very soft. Some sleighs of this class have runners made straight in front, as on the Curricle Sleigh shown in this number. The dash panel does not extend to the front of the scroll, but wire-work is inserted instead, and plated in either brass or silver.

Dimensions.—Width of body at the rear end, 33 in.; ditto inside of the seat at the cushion in front, 39 in.; and ditto at front bracket, 32 in. Turn-under, 6 in. Runners, 1 × ⅞ in. Shoes, ⅞ × ⅜ in., cast-steel. Track, 38 in., from out to out.

Finish.—The painting of such sleighs can be widely varied. We would suggest for the body a medium shade of blue or green, striped with carmine or gold, or both; and the runners, carmine, or a lighter shade of the body color, striped somewhat elaborately. Trimming, cloth, in color to harmonize with the painting. Large figures are preferable for the back and cushion tops, and the square pattern is suggested in our drawing. Mountings, brass.

The Hub
July 1885

BERLIN CUTTER.

Plate No. 29.

Width across front bracket, 34 inches; across the bottom, 33 inches; across the top, 38 inches. These measurements apply to straight sides only; if the sides are made concave, the cross widths are as follows: Across the front bracket, 33 inches; across the bottom, 33 inches; across the body at molding, 10½ inches from bottom, 36 inches; across the top, 40 inches. When the seat is made separate from the body, the cross widths are as follows: Bottom of body, 32 inches; top of body, 35 inches; bottom of seat, 37 inches, and top of seat 40 inches; the amount of turn-under for body 1½ inches for each side, the same for seat. Track, 40 inches. Size of runners, ¾ inch square. Size of steel, ¾ inch, round edge, by ⅛ inch.

This style is not entirely new, having been made for the past two seasons, but we have remodeled and changed the outlines to give it better proportions and finish. These bodies have been made with straight sides, but it gives them a heavy appearance; it is best to let the seats stand over the body proper 1½ inches on each side, or, in other words, the top of the body 3 inches narrower than the seats; back and front of the body moldings can be made level with the seat, or can be set in, either method being good. The sides can also be made concave, with the same sweep as the back corner. The seat and body are molded with ⅝ by $\frac{3}{16}$-inch moldings, the front bracket panel being also molded, as is also the front dasher as illustrated, but this latter can be striped as desired. The wire screen fenders are straight, from 6 to 8 inches wide. The stays are two perfect circles on each side, combined with a horizontal bar, and stiffened sideways with a cross-bar; the back end of the cross-bar also has a bend and a well-finished cross-bar.

Painting.—Body: black; medallions, light carmine, moldings striped a fine line of light carmine. Runners: light carmine, striped one $\frac{3}{16}$ inch line of black.

Trimming.—Green cloth. The back has a fullness requisite for comfort, and is of the block and pipe design; green tufts are used throughout. The cushion has plaited top and blocks, 1⅞-inch facings. Rug, green, with a green lace binding. Plumes, red and green.

Mountings.—Silver.

———

Carriage Monthly
July 1885

PORTLAND CUTTER, THREE-QUARTER SIZE.

PLATE NO. 43.—HALF-INCH SCALE.

Portland Cutter, Three-Quarter Size.

PLATE NO. 43.

There is no difference in the dimensions and size for the side elevation of this sleigh than usual, the three-quarter size designating the width of the body. The cross-width of an ordinary Portland sleigh, carrying two passengers, is from 36 to 38 inches wide from out to out, although sometimes they are ordered 40 inches wide. The medium three-quarter size width is generally 30 inches from out to out; width across the back, top, 27 inches; at bottom across the back, 24 inches; across the front the same width, 24 inches. Length between shoulders for front and back cross-bars, or between raves, 20¾ inches. The raves, or bottom sides as they are called, are not more than ½ inch thick when finished, and from 1⅜ to 1¾ inches wide; for three-quarter size bodies 1⅜ inches is the regular width. These raves are generally bent pieces, the front bracket being bent up at the required angle, which makes it very strong, and gives lightness to the raves. The sides and back panels are screwed against the frame, and to make good work these side panels should be bent on a form in the required shape before they are screwed on the sides. For further information as regards details and construction, see working draft of Portland cutter, *Figs. 1, 2* and *3*, supplement accompanying the September number, 1884.

Painting.—Body: dark blue. Runners: dark blue, striped two fine lines of white, ¼ inch apart; striped also two fine lines of white around the edges of body.

Trimming.—Light blue plush. The back is made perfectly plain, and finished with welts of light plush. Cushion, plain top, with drab buttons or tufts; drab cloth welts, and 1½-inch front facing. The fall has plain 1-inch raisers and edges turned over. The rug may be blue or black, blue or red, to match the painting.

Mountings.—Gold.

———

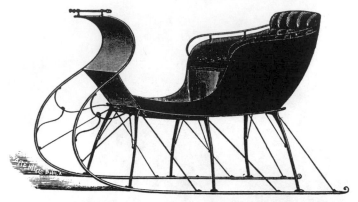

GENTLEMEN'S DRIVING SLEIGH.

PLATE NO. 27.—HALF-INCH SCALE.

Width across front at bottom, 24½ inches. Across the back, 24½ inches. Width of frame, 25 inches; standing over the body ¼ inch each side, forming molding. Width and thickness of side pieces, 1½ by ⅝-inch bent stuff. Across front top of body, 26 inches. Width across body, from out to out, at the height of seat, 37 inches. Across back, on top of side panel, 37 inches. Widest part of body, 38 inches; 1 inch swell in back panel. Runners: width of track from out to out, front, 37⅝ inches; and back, 37 inches. Width across the runners at foot-board, 30½ inches. Across top front of runners, 28¾ inches. Thickness of runners, ¾ by ⅞ inch deep. Shoes ¾ by $\frac{5}{16}$-inch steel. Stays, $\frac{9}{32}$-inch steel.

Mr. S. R. Bailey, of Amesbury, Mass., makes a specialty of this style of sleighs, which possesses artistic beauty in style, workmanship and finish. The construction of the body possesses interesting features for body and sleigh builders in general; for instance the backs and sides are made separately; that is, forms are made for the backs, the end pieces are placed in the form, the panel bent to shape, and glued to the frame-work over the form; as the back has swell from both sides the same as the side panels, the consequence is that by glueing these panels in this way assures not only good glueing, but also a perfect shape, it being impossible for the panel to sink in, as is nearly always the case when panels have swell from both sides. Also all backs are alike, as are also the sides, and can be substituted for each other, as they are bent and glued over the same shaped forms. The same system is carried through with all the other pieces of the sleighs; they are all alike in shape and finish; all runners have the same graceful sweep, and one piece can be substituted for the other, which is not only a great advantage to the builder when the factory is run on that system, but also to the customer; in case of accidental breakage, the broken parts can be repaired in a very short time.

Painting.—Body: cherry red; sunk bottom, black, striped a fine line of black around its edges. Runners: cherry red, striped two ⅛-inch lines of black, ⅜ inch apart.

Trimming.—Crimson plush. The seat is trimmed with a diamond pipe-and-block back, which is plaited; it has buttons covered with plush; the back is made heavy across the top and is finished with leather welts. The cushion is made in blocks, which are plaited. The front facing is 1¾ inches high, with an inch plain raiser; the welts in cushion are plush. The fall is made with a plain 1-inch raiser and is sewed to the cushion.

Mountings.—Silver.

———

Carriage Monthly
July 1886

OLD COMFORT SLEIGH.

PLATE NO. 27.—VOL. 24.—HALF-INCH SCALE.

———

Old Comfort Sleigh.

PLATE NO. 27.

With this plate we give a last years style changed somewhat in the application of the moldings. The appearance is heavy, but some builders and customers desire this to give it the characteristics of the Old Comfort sleigh. The body is molded with ½-inch wide half round moldings. The upper moldings pass around the body on the back, which has also three sectional moldings to correspond with the side panels. The upper edge molding is ½ inch thick, rounded off from the top edge, and finished with a rosette. The runners are finished different from usual, ending with a light scroll at the front. The knees and stays are a combination of iron stays and the well-known Baily knees, which have been so extensively used for the past two seasons.

Width across the body front at bottom, 30 inches; at bottom back, same width, 30 inches; across the top back, 38½ inches; at center, where the body is widest, 41 inches. Width of dash on top of the body, 35½ inches, having one width from top to bottom. Runners: width of track from out to out, 40 inches; across back of runners, ⅜ inch less. Thickness and depth of runners, ¾ by ⅞ inch. Shoes, ¾ by ⁵⁄₁₆-inch round edge steel. Knees manufactured by S. R. Bailey, of Amesbury, Mass.

Painting.—Body: wine color. Runners: orange yellow, striped two ₁³⁄₈-inch black lines. Moldings on body striped a fine line of yellow, also the dasher front. Inside of dasher painted the same as the body, and striped yellow.

Trimming.—Cloth, wine color. The back is a portable back, and is trimmed in the block-and-pipe design, made up very heavy and full in appearance. The sides are plain and painted only. The cushion is made a block top, 1¾-inch front facing, ⅞-inch plain raisers and patent-leather welts. The fall is sewed to the cushion, and has ⅞-inch plain raisers. The rug is wine color, with small yellow figures.

Mountings.—Gold. ———

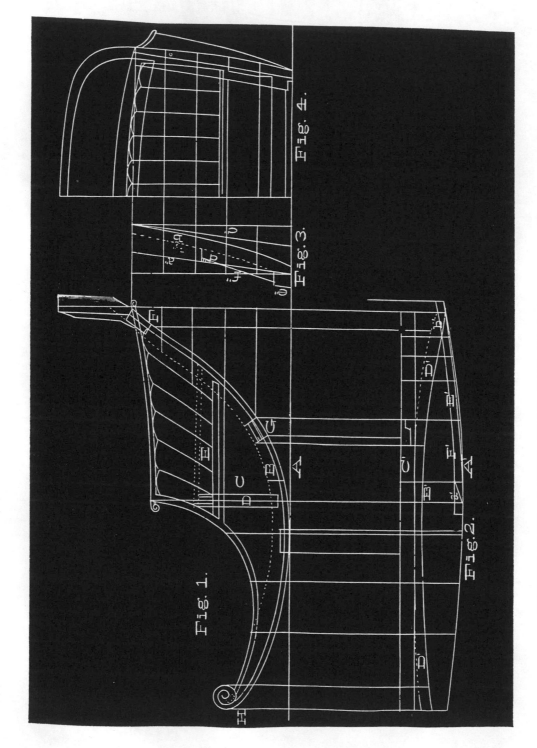

Fig. 1.

Fig. 2.

Fig. 3.

Fig. 4.

WORKING DRAFT OF LIGHT CUTTER WITH SHELL SEAT.—SCALE, ONE INCH TO THE FOOT.

Fig. 1 shows the side elevation; Fig. 2, the cant; Fig. 3, the standing-pillar; and Fig. 4, the half back view.

The principal measurements have already been stated in the description of the Fashion Plate, by referring to which it will be found that the width of the body in the center is $43\frac{1}{2}$ in.; ditto back, $38\frac{1}{2}$ in.; ditto front, $35\frac{1}{2}$ in., and turn-under, 5 in.

If the bottomsill B is made of bent wood, a plate can be dispensed with; but, if sawed out, the use of a light plate will be advisable. The bottomsill B extends the full length of the body. The part marked C is the side, made of thick whitewood; D, an upright for framing the body; E, a horizontal piece framed into the upright D and the bottomsill rail; F, the top cross-rail; G, the bottom cross-bar; and H, the front bar.

On the cant, Fig. 2, the line A' represents the outside swell on top; B', the swell on the bottom when pricked off; and C, the outside bottomsill line. Dotted line D' shows the location of the bottomsill when in its proper position. The line D' is produced by the inclination of line a'', Fig. 3.

To produce a more satisfactory result in the case of the outside swell of the bottomsill B, we have to employ the cheat line, which is represented by line E', Fig. 2. The line F' is the inside of the sides on top.

On Fig. 3, line a'' shows the inclination for the bottomsill B; b'' the turn-under; and the space between the lines a'' and c'' indicates the thickness of the whitewood for the sides. By inclining the bottomsill, the thickness of the whitewood may be reduced considerably. The dressing of the bottomsill, when thus inclined, necessitates somewhat more labor than when it is placed in a vertical position; but this objection, if it is such, is fully counterbalanced by the lesser thickness of timber required for the sides. When the bottomsills have been dressed and the cross-bars framed into them, the bottomsills, before gluing, are then lightened to nearly the proper thickness.

The upright D is framed by the dotted line d', Fig. 3, and the horizontal piece E is lapped to D and B. The piece D has more flare than the inside line of the side, as will be seen by the difference between the lines a'' and d''; and a space will have to be cut out from the sides when fitting the same to the bottomsill. To ascertain the proper position of the upright D, hold a straight-edge on the inside of the bottomsill B (see Fig. 3), and measure the distance at the top end of piece D, from the straight-edge to the line f', which represents the inside piece of D. Pieces D and E are glued to the bottomsill before the sides are fastened permanently.

The scrolls at the front and rear ends on top of the sides are made of hard wood, and are spliced to the sides as indicated by the lines a' and b', Fig. 2. These scrolls are fitted and glued to the sides before they are fastened to the bottomsills. The sides, after they are glued and dry, are cleaned off before putting the body together.

The parts forming the shell are so worked as to come $\frac{1}{4}$ or $\frac{5}{16}$ in. below the surface of the molding. It is not necessary to take the $\frac{1}{4}$ or $\frac{5}{16}$ in. off the whole length of the ribs or shell pieces, as $\frac{1}{8}$ in. in the center will be all that is required; and this will give more roundness to the sides.

After the sides have been finished, the bars are then put into their places temporarily, and the back panel is marked off and fitted. When this has been done, both sides and the panel are put together simultaneously. The ribs are then worked on the rear panel, and the center molding is glued on. We will add here that the rear panel is placed in a groove.

The front cross-bar H, Fig. 1, is the full size of the scroll, and can be made of whitewood mortised into the bottomside, as shown in the draft. The upper back has considerable swell. If bending and steaming facilities are at hand in the shop, 1 in. whitewood will answer for the back; but if such is not the case, then $2\frac{1}{2}$ in. whitewood will be necessary. The necessity of using $2\frac{1}{2}$ in. whitewood throughout the whole length can be avoided by using $1\frac{1}{4}$ in. for the center, and then gluing on blocks on the inside of the $1\frac{1}{4}$ in. piece.

The back is put into proper shape as far as possible before fitting it to the top cross-rail. The molding is glued and nailed on, or, if preferred, it can be worked on. In the latter case, the full depth of the molding is not worked out of the center, but it will be sufficient to take out $\frac{1}{8}$ in. in the center, and the remainder can then be finished gradually toward the edges to $\frac{1}{4}$ or $\frac{5}{16}$ in., as the taste of the builder may dictate. To secure the upper back in its proper position, three wooden strainers are introduced on the inside.

A. K.

The Hub
July 886
Diagram on previous page.

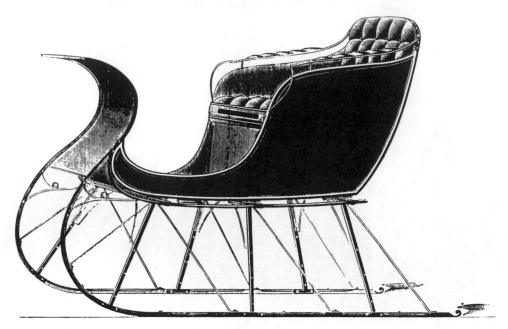

PLATE NO. 42. ROCKY MOUNTAIN CUTTER.—SCALE, THREE-QUARTER INCH TO THE FOOT.

As an introduction to the following article entitled "Design for the Running-part of a Medium-size Cutter," we present on this page our Fashion Plate of the so-called "Rocky Mountain Cutter."

As will be seen, it resembles the Portland Cutter in most respects, but the sides of the body are higher, the back is curved, and the formation of the front is somewhat different. The bottom line at the front is also so arranged as to form a continuous curve with the runners. A knob is fastened to each side of the dash to keep the reins in place.

The general construction and dimensions of this body, other than we have above indicated, are the same as for a regular Portland Cutter, which have so often been presented heretofore that they do not need to be repeated here; and the ironwork is fully described in the article immediately following.

Finish.—Painting of body, black; and runners, carmine, striped with two fine lines and a round line of black. Trimming, green cloth, made up in squares for the back and cushions, while the facings of the cushions are left plain. The fall has one raiser. Mountings, silver.

EDITOR OF THE HUB—DEAR SIR: I feel compelled to go somewhat into sleigh-building in order to retain my wagon custom. The roads in this section of the country are rough and hilly, and the best Eastern cutters fail to hold up, and I have had but little experience in sleigh ironing, and wish to ask that *The Hub* lend me a hand in this line of work. Yours truly, J. T., OF OREGON.

* * *

ANSWER.—In Northern New-York, Vermont, New Hampshire and the border towns of Canada, sleighs are built expressly for use on rough and hilly roads, and the accompanying sketches and description, obtained from a builder in that section, will, we hope, prove useful not only to our correspondent but to many others.

Fig. 1 gives an outline of the under part, both wood and iron-work, A being the top plate or strip; B, the runner; C, the dasher; D, the front stake; E, the center stake; F, the hind stake; G, G, G, branches or stays from the stake plates to the beam; H, H, H, the back stays; K, the front or bucking stay; L, the drag-iron; M, the bracket plate; and X, X, X, X, X, the points for fastening on the stays, etc.

Fig. 2 shows an outline of the stay of the front stake, at the point of

The Hub
August 1886

(continued on next page)

its connection with the runner, with two fastenings back of the stake and three in front. The part marked *b* is the lower end of the stake plate; *c*, the upper end of the same; *e*, the offset; *f*, the branch; *g*, the point where it fastens to the beam; and *d*, the point where the upper section of the plate turns off and fastens to the beam.

Make *a* the width of the runner, and ¼ in. thick at the T, tapered to each end. Make *b* and *c* the width of the stake, and swell from the T to

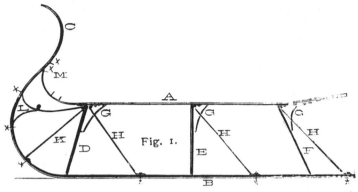

Fig. 1.

½ in. at the upper end. Taper *d* to $\frac{3}{16}$ in., and make it 3 in. long, and fasten with a ¼ in. bolt. Make the offset *e* ¾ in. long and oval; *f*, also oval; and *g*, flat; and fasten with one $\frac{5}{16}$ in. bolt and one ¼ in. bolt, three inches apart. Make the plate and stay of the center stake the same, with the single difference that two rivets are to be placed on each side of the T. On the back stake let the hind end of the T go clear back to the end of the runner. We advise making these stays oval in order to offer less resistance in passing over deep snow and unbroken roads.

Fig. 3 shows an outline of the stays which extend from the beam to the runner. Make *h* $\frac{7}{16}$ in. thick, and taper to $\frac{5}{16}$ in.; and fasten it with one ¼ in. bolt, and one $\frac{3}{16}$ in. bolt. Make *k* of $\frac{7}{16}$ in. round iron for the two central stays, and of ½ in. iron for the back stay and the bucking stay *k*. Make *l* flat, $\frac{7}{16}$ in. thick, and fasten with a $\frac{5}{16}$ in. bolt. Make *m* ¼ in. thick, and fasten to the top plate with a ¼ in. bolt. We advise, where the bolts pass through the beam, that the heads be made thin and flat, to avoid interference with the bottom of the body and the oil-cloth or the carpet.

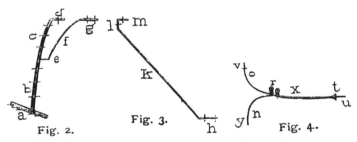

Fig. 2.   Fig. 3.   Fig. 4.

Fig. 4 shows an outline of the drag-iron, *r* being the shackle for the shaft-eye, which make ⅜ in. thick (for the ears), and about 1⅜ in. clear; and use a $\frac{7}{16}$ in. bolt. Make *x* $\frac{9}{16}$ in. round, and taper to $\frac{7}{16}$ in. Make the collar *t* to suit the eye on top of the stay K, Fig. 1. Make *u* ⅜ in. Make *n* and *o*, at the shackle, $\frac{7}{16}$ in., and taper to ⅜ in. at *v* and *y*; and fasten to the back of the runner with ¼ in. bolts. Make the bracket-plate M, Fig. 1, of ¾ × $\frac{5}{16}$ in. half-oval iron, and fasten with four rivets.

For shoes, use 1⅛ × ½ in. Bessemer steel, and let this extend to the place where the stay *k* rests on the runner. Make a long splice with the shoe and dasher-plate, long enough to take the two bolts of the stay K. Make the dasher-plate half-oval, and let it go clear to the top. The $\frac{7}{16}$ in. T-rivets will be strong enough for all the riveting; and ¼ in. bolts will suffice for the shoes if a sufficient number is used.

A cutter built after the above design will carry two or three full-size persons over the roughest roads with complete safety, and will last a lifetime with ordinary care and timely repairs.   NYSSUS.

The Hub
August 1886

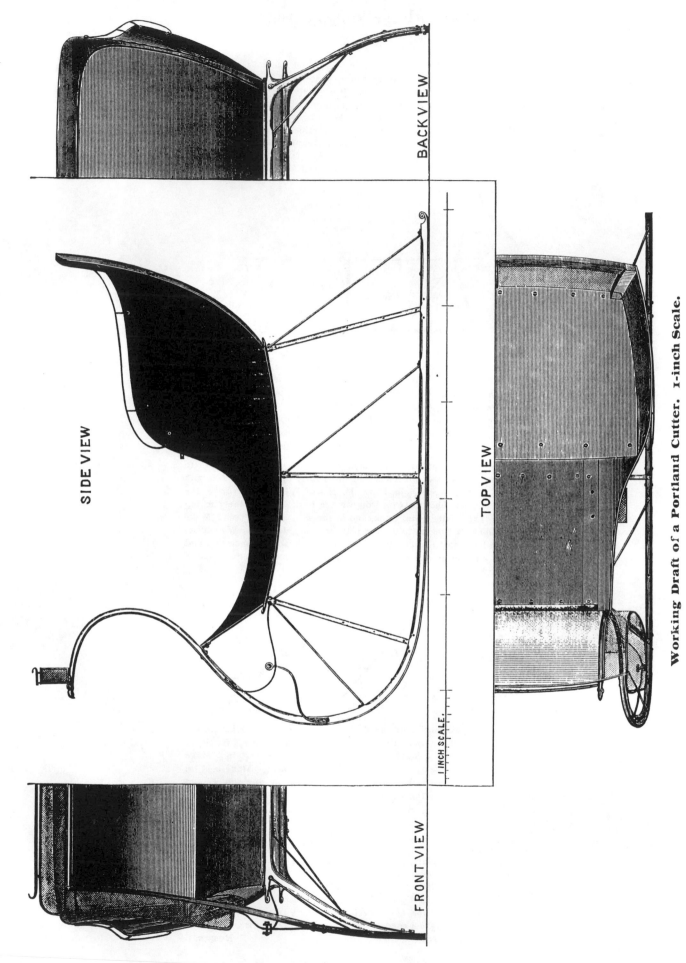

BACK VIEW

SIDE VIEW

TOP VIEW

1 INCH SCALE.

FRONT VIEW

Working Draft of a Portland Cutter. 1-inch Scale.

44

Portland and other Cutters

Working Draft of a Portland Cutter.

SIDE, FRONT AND BACK ELEVATIONS, AND ALSO HORIZONTAL TOP VIEW OF BODY AND RUNNERS.—ONE-INCH SCALE.

This cutter is designed and constructed according to the rules practiced by the well-known sleigh-builder, Mr. S. R. Bailey, of Amesbury, Mass., who is considered one of the best builders of Portland cutters carrying one or two persons. The body of this design is, of course, light, with graceful outlines. The position and shape of runners will be noted as scientifically correct, having the required raise in front for easy running; they are short, and the fullness apparent on the majority of the work of other builders is avoided. The principal object is the shortness and easy running of the runners, which not only gives a better appearance to the sleigh, but is also the only correct method to be practiced in sleigh building.

The bottom frame is only $\frac{5}{8}$ inch thick and $1\frac{1}{2}$ inches wide, and bent to shape. It will be noticed that the front part of bottom frame is slightly more curved than the back, notwithstanding which it has the appearance of a circle sweep; if it really was a circle sweep it would look as though it had less curve front. The upper main sweep of the body from back to front is of latest style, harmonizing well with the bottom and back sweeps. The back sweep is full and must also have swell as shown; the back panel straight across the body, considering the outlines, would not look well.

The side and back panels are only $\frac{5}{16}$ inch thick, and should be bent over forms before they are glued on, to avoid the strain. We have always noticed that side panels strained on before bending always have a bad sweep between the seat-rail and back corner pillars. This is also true with the back panel; if bent over a form it makes superior work, and where many sleighs are made of the same pattern it pays both the employer and workman to have forms made. The back corner pillars are of bent stuff, very light, $\frac{3}{4}$ inch thick by $1\frac{1}{4}$ inches wide when finished. The seat-rail is $1\frac{1}{4}$ inches wide by $\frac{5}{16}$ inch thick; seat-rail pillars $\frac{5}{8}$ inch thick by $\frac{3}{4}$ inch at seat-rail, tapered toward the top and bottom ends. The width of body at bottom frame is 26 inches from out to out, and frame $26\frac{3}{8}$ inches, forming a $\frac{3}{16}$-inch molding on each side, which is rounded. The body and frame is generally made straight at bottom, but a slight swell of about $\frac{3}{16}$ inch on each side is commendable, and improves the appearance of the side surfaces. The width across back panel on top is $35\frac{1}{2}$ inches, and across bottom $25\frac{1}{2}$ inches, a difference of 10 inches, or 5 inches turn-under each side for back corner pillars. The width across the panels at its widest part is $38\frac{1}{2}$ inches from out to out, and at bottom of panels $25\frac{1}{2}$ inches, giving the amount of turn-under at that part $6\frac{1}{2}$ inches each side. The front of body on top edge of foot-board in regard to the widths must be made to suit the cross width of the runners. The shape of the runners viewed from the front is of great importance; they should be well bent, and if they are not in conformity with the widths of the runners, they will detract from its good appearance, which can be well seen on the front view. Suppose the runners were out of shape, and also its cross-widths did not correspond with the widths as given; it would throw the runners in a bad position, and the general appearance would be very undesirable.

The knees are of different shape from styles heretofore given, being convex-concave and bent to shape; they are either mortised or lapped in the bench bars, and are dressed $\frac{5}{8}$ inch thick, but are well rounded and finished to give them a very light appearance. The bench bars have the same thickness, and are well lightened and finished, with a light scroll on each end. The runners are $\frac{3}{4}$ inch thick by $\frac{7}{8}$ inch deep, lightened toward the front; at the dash they are $\frac{5}{8}$ inch square. The front dash panel is $\frac{1}{4}$ inch thick, and is rabbeted into the runners, the joint covered with the shoe which runs up to the extreme front end, well rounded and finished; at the front end it is but $\frac{1}{8}$ inch thick. All the stays are $\frac{9}{32}$-inch round steel, shoes $\frac{3}{4}$ by $\frac{5}{16}$-inch steel, bolted to the shaft iron, the balance being screwed. Track back 39 inches, and front $39\frac{3}{8}$ inches.

Carriage Monthly
August 1887
(continued from previous page)

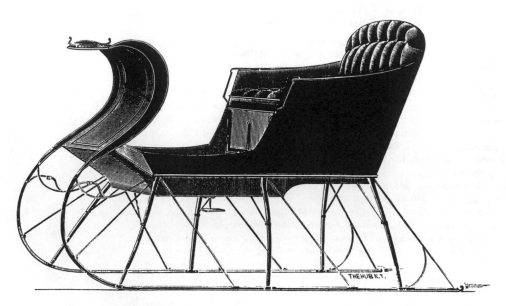

'Plate No. 27. PORTLAND SPEEDING CUTTER.—Scale, three-quarters inch.

FROM the numerous patterns of Portland cutters now popular, we have chosen the accompanying design of a light speeding cutter, which differs but little from the regular Portland cutter in appearance, yet shows many variations in the manner in which it is constructed.

There are no beams in the running-part, the body framework forming a substitute for the beams. The sills are made of $\frac{7}{8}$ × $1\frac{1}{8}$-in. ash. The knees are framed into the sills. There is an end-sill both front and back, forming the beams and taking the stays. There is a drop bottom, 3 in., of the shape shown in the design. This drop is formed on the inside of the knees. The stay on the center knee is made in one continuous piece, secured by two belts in the center. These drops allow ample leg-room and easy sitting.

The body is made with two corner-posts in the back, two in the center, and two corner-blocks at the front end. There is a bar framed into the back, 10 in. from the top of the sill, for the back of the seat to rest on ; and a bar is framed into the center posts, 11 in. from the sill, for the front of the seat to rest on. The framework of this should be got down very light.

The sides are mitered on at each corner, and $\frac{5}{16}$-in. whitewood is used for the panels, with a slight swell to the sides and back.

Dimensions.—Width of body on top, 35 in.; ditto at back, 33 in.; and ditto at bottom, 27 in. The runners are $\frac{3}{4}$ × $\frac{5}{8}$ in. Knees, $\frac{1}{2}$ × $\frac{5}{8}$ in. Shoes, $\frac{5}{8}$ × $\frac{1}{2}$ in., steel. Track, 40 in.

Finish.—Painting of body, deep lake, edged with a fine line of carmine ; and running-part, carmine, striped with two fine lines of gold. Trimming, garnet cloth, made up in blocks. Carpet, to match cloth, with red figures. Mountings, silver.

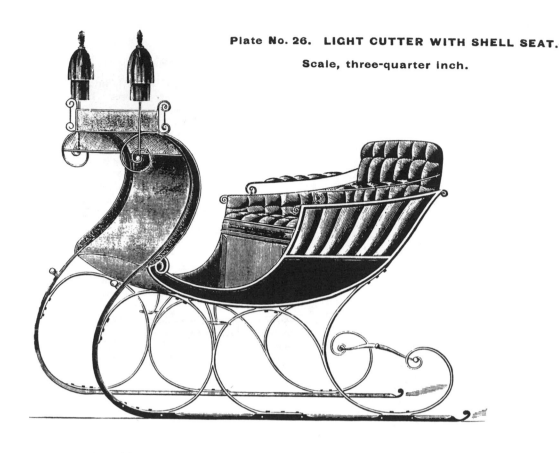

Plate No. 26. LIGHT CUTTER WITH SHELL SEAT.

Scale, three-quarter inch.

THIS is a light cutter of new and graceful outlines, and its beauty can be greatly enhanced by painting it tastefully, while much also depends on the proper selection of the trimmings.

The sides of the body are made of thick whitewood, 3½ in. stuff being recommended for this purpose, and the turn-under and the side-swell can then be worked on. The framework of the body consists of the bottom-sills, the back top-rail and three cross-bars. Each bottom-sill consists of two pieces, if made of sawed wood, or of one piece if made of bent timber. To obtain the necessary turn-under and side-swell, the bottomsills are inclined about 2½ in. on each side. After the framework has been fitted together, the thick whitewood pieces are then glued to the bottomsills, and, when dry, finished off. The moldings and the shell-work are carved on the solid whitewood, and the ribs forming the shell are worked down from ⅜ to ¼ in. below the outer surface of the moldings.

The rear panel is made of ½ in. whitewood, placed in a groove. The bars and rear panel, after the latter has been fitted, are glued together at once. The rear panel is made of one piece, and extends to the point where the rear stay leaves the body.

The molding indicating the depth of the seat on the sides is carried across the back and nailed on. The ribs on the upper section of the back, like those on the sides, are worked on. The carving of these ribs necessitates making the panel ½ in. This panel, after the body has been finished, should be canvased thoroughly.

The upper portion of the back is made of I in. whitewood, and is fitted to the back rail, where it is glued and further secured by dowels and wooden strainers on the inside. The scrolls at the top ends of the runners are made of iron, and riveted to the wooden runners.

Dimensions.—Width of body on top in the center, 43½ in.; ditto at rear, 38½ in.; and ditto in front, 35½ in. Turn-under, 4½ in. Runners, ⅞ × I in. Shoes, ⅞ × 1⁶⁄₁₆ in., cast-steel. Track, 38 in., from out to out.

Finish.—Painting of lower part of body and moldings, black; and the upper or ribbed part of the body blue, striped with gold. Runners, carmine, striped with black and gold. Trimming, blue plush. Square figures of medium size are used for the upholstery. The back should be made full and soft, to give all possible comfort, and the same rule should be followed with the cushion. The fall is made plain, with but one raiser, but it might be finished with plaits if preferred. Carpet, plain blue. Mountings, gold. The plumes should match the color of the painting.

The Hub
July 1886

ROAD CUTTER.

(See Fashion Plate No. 10.)

THE accompanying design of sleigh is intended for two passengers, and is well adapted for speeding purposes. It is light and compact in appearance and substantially constructed. The seat is covered with cane, and the portion below the seat is left open. The ogee sweep at the rear is made of one bent piece, and extends to the top of back with a scroll worked on the upper edge. The sills are of one straight piece with leaf scrolls carved at the ends. The scroll on the upper end of the runner where it intersects with the body, should be bent, rounded off, and lightened out to the scroll. The scroll irons in the running-part are quite plain, yet in harmony with the lines of the body, curved lines being generally introduced in this design. The steps are riveted to the oval, and the step-shank is bolted to the sill. Wire screens are introduced at the top and sides of the dash.

Dimensions of Woodwork.—Width of body on top, at arm-rail, outside, 37 in.; and at bottom, outside, 26 in. Width of seat at bottom, 30 in. Extreme length of body, 4 ft. 8 in. Size of runners, 1 × 1⅛ in. Size of shoes, 1 × ⅜ in. Scroll-irons in running-part, ½ × ¾ in. oval iron.

Painting.—Moldings, dark blue, striped with fine line of carmine. Portion below seat, inside of moldings, white. Running-part, carmine, with one broad line of blue.

Trimming.—Blue cloth. Mountings, silver.

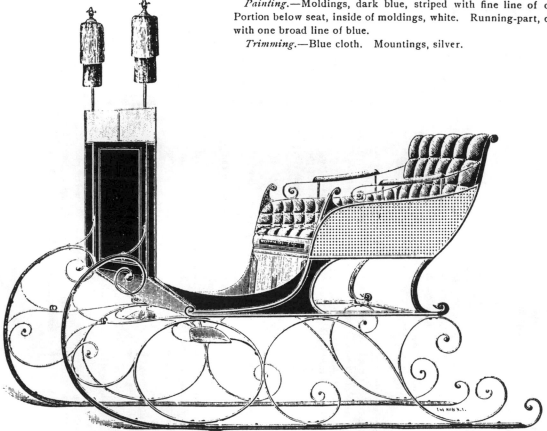

PLATE No. 10. ROAD CUTTER. SCALE, THREE-QUARTERS INCH.

The Hub
May 1890

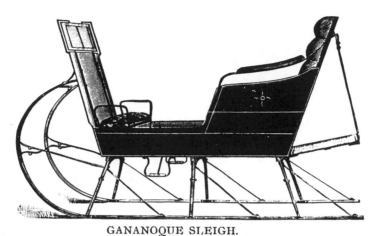

GANANOQUE SLEIGH.

PLATE NO. 32.—VOL. 24.—HALF-INCH SCALE.—*Explanation on page 89.*

Width of body at bottom 30 inches ; width across the back at the height of the side panel, 38 inches. Width of dash 34 inches. Height of body from the floor 16 inches. Runners : width of track 37 inches front, and 36⅝ inches back. Thickness and depth of runners, ⅞ by 1 inch. Shoes, 1 by ⅜-inch round-edge steel. Stays, ⅜-inch iron.

This is a business sleigh of peculiar construction ; the back seat is made to carry two persons, while the front one is a child's seat only. At the back the board, which is hinged at the bottom of the body and held up with two straps, one on each side, is a plain suitable arrangement for carrying packages or anything in that line. The bottom of the body is straight, as are all the other outlines. The dash is made of a panel, and is also straight. The back panel and sides of body are relieved with ⅜-inch wide moldings, finished by taking the corners off slightly with sand-paper. The upper dash has a light frame, finished on the inside with wire screen, and ¼-inch diameter side handles. The front seat is hinged to the front of body, and the side rail has knuckles, which turn over on the cushion, and when not in use are turned over towards the dash and strapped to it. The runners are constructed as usual. This style is manufactured by the Gananoque Carriage Co., Gananoque, Ont., Canada.

Painting.—Body: black. Runners: black, striped with two fine lines of carmine ; moldings on body striped a fine line of the same color.

Trimming.—Green cloth.

Carriage Monthly
July 1888

THIS design of physicians' sleigh represents one of the latest styles in this line of work, including several changes in the body and ironwork. The ironwork is not as elaborate as has been the custom for some seasons past, but it is of graceful design and in harmony with the body.

The runners are fastened under the bottom of the body by means of bolts passing through the stays and the sill of the body. The stays are also bolted through the runners. The stays are ¾ in. at center, and ⅝ in. at the runners and body, and are fastened with ⁵⁄₁₆-in. bolts. The runners are ¾ × ⅞ in., with a ⅜-in. steel shoe, and are tapered up to the dash, which is connected at the ends with a turned bar.

This sleigh can be used with either pole or shafts. At the dash and connecting with the step is a wing, 7 in. wide, covered with leather, and tapered toward the end of the runner. The running-part is finished with scrolls at the ends.

The body is made similar to that of a physicians' phaeton, but it does not require to be as heavy as a phaeton body. The sill is one piece, sawed out, 2¼ × 1½ in. The end sills are lighter. Under the seat are two uprights framed to the sill. A piece, ⅞ × 1½ in., is framed across, to which the seat is fastened. A corner-post is framed in the back, similar to that in a square-box buggy, to which the panels are glued. A ⅜-in. panel is used for the sides and back.

The seat is made with solid sides, and is set on top of the seat frame. The seat-frame forms the moldings at the sides and back. The other moldings are worked on. A corner-pillar is set in the corner, to which the back and sides are glued. A high back is used, the same as on a physicians' phaeton. Under the front of the seat is a piece of white-wood, glued on the outside of the body, and finished up as shown in design. The top has four bows, with an oval light.

Dimensions.—Width of body on top, 44 in.; and on bottom, 28 in. Track on bottom, outside, 36 in.

Painting.—Body, black, and running-part, dark blue.

Trimming.—Green cloth is used throughout, made up in blocks. The fall is made up in two large diamonds, and is bound with leather. Head-lining, green. Carpet, green. A wooden dash is used. Mountings, silver.

COLORED PLATE No. XCIX.   PHYSICIANS' CUTTER WITH SCROLL RUNNING-PART.

SCALE. THREE-QUARTERS INCH TO THE FOOT.

Portland and other Cutters

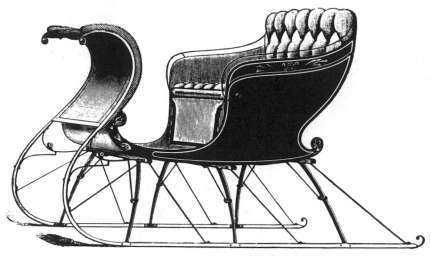

NEW YORK CUTTER.

PLATE NO. 27.—VOL. 28.—FIVE-EIGHTHS-INCH SCALE.—*Explanation on page 98.*

PLATE NO. 27.
NEW YORK
CUTTER.

The construction of this cutter is as usual, excepting that the panels rest against the side surfaces of the frame, instead of on the top of the frame, as generally made. The bottom sides can be bent as usual. It is a great advantage for the front part of body, makes it much stronger and lighter, and avoids the cross grain. To construct these bodies to the best advantage, bend the panels to shape over a form. Four panels can be bent over a form at once. Leave them on the forms till needed, and take care that they are well dried after steaming. The side pieces of the frame are 1 inch thick by 2½ inches wide, the end pieces the same size, and the bottom boards are rabbeted in from the top. The back corner pillars must be dressed to suit the inclination of the side panels, framed to the bottom with a small tenon, and drawn tight to the shoulders with one screw for each pillar. All moldings are glued and bradded on. The carving on belt and front bracket is sawed out to shape, six or eight pieces together, glued against the panel, and finished after it is glued on. The back panel has carving, same as the sides, excepting the design is larger.

The runners are constructed as usual; size, ⅞ inch square; knees, ¾ inch thick for heavy, ⅝ inch thick for medium, and ½ inch for light. The stays are straight, and are ½ inch thick.

Painting.—Body, deep green; belt, yellow; moldings, black; carving on belt, deep blue, high lighted with light blue and yellow; carving on front bracket, light blue, high lighted with yellow; runners, deep green, striped with two pale green lines and one blue line in center.

Finish.—Fenders and rails silver.

Carriage Monthly
July 1892

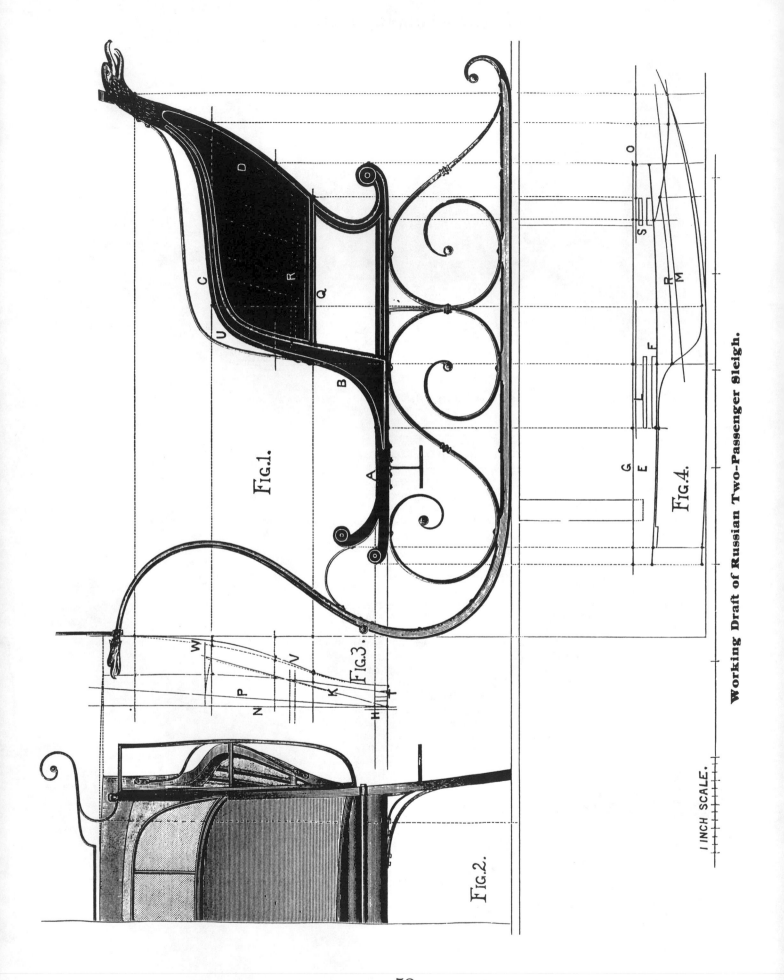

Fig.1.

Fig.2.

Fig.3.

Fig.4.

Working Draft of Russian Two-Passenger Sleigh.

1 INCH SCALE.

Working-Draft of Russian Two-Passenger Sleigh.

ONE-INCH SCALE.

This style of sleigh appeared in our fashion plates last year, but we have remodeled the main outlines somewhat, and changed the body to appear lighter by showing daylight under the seat, also changed the shape of moldings. With these changes the sleigh is greatly improved, and to facilitate the construction of the same, we have drawn this working-draft to one-inch scale.

The body, as will be seen, is of particular construction, and differs entirely from those working-drafts we have given heretofore, and some remarks in regard to its construction will be useful to body-makers. Suppose the body would be constructed without daylight, that is, one panel over the entire surface for inexpensive work, the entire side could be made out of single pine, and a 24-inch wide plank would be necessary. This is not done to our knowledge, because all such sleighs are sold at good prices, and sleigh-builders can afford to panel those bodies, but we mention this in case such bodies are wanted. For cheaper work, a great deal of labor could be saved.

In this case the body is framed and paneled; A, the bottom side; B, the pillar, bottom side; A, Fig. 1, is shown on E, Fig. 4, and line F, indicates that the bottom sides have some side swell, but can be made straight if desired. Those we examined were straight, but a trifle side sweep has a better appearance, and will give less twist to the body. The bottom sides are dressed square, see line H, Fig. 3, and also line G, Fig. 4. Pillar P, Fig. 1, is inclined after line K, Fig. 3, and square horizontally, see line L, Fig. 4. Arm rail line C, Fig. 1, is dressed square horizontally, but is contracted longitudinally; see contracted line M, Fig. 4. Back pillar D, Fig. 1, can be dressed square, see line N, Fig. 3, and line O, Fig. 4, but too much timber is required, and generally this pillar is inclined as shown on line P, Fig. 3, and some thickness of timber can be saved. The cross bars of course are dressed square, the width of the bars as drawn, and are to be level with the bottom sides, top and bottom. Piece R, Fig. 1, is $1\frac{1}{2}$ inches thick and about 2 inches wide, must have side sweep as shown on line R, Fig. 4, and should be level on the inside pillars B and D, Fig. 1. This piece R is dressed square, and seat is above as shown by dotted line R, and does not rest on Q.

The framing of the pillars B and D, Fig. 4; on those pillars there is a tenon and a lap for pillar B, Fig. 1; the tenon and lap is shown on T, Fig. 3, and mortises are shown on L and S, Fig. 4. This manner of framing is the best method that can be adopted; it has less surface of joints, and combines the rockers with the pillars so perfectly that when well fitted, those small joints will hardly show through the varnish. Line K, Fig. 3, can be squared at the bottom up to the thickness of the bottom sides, and then the tenon and lap can be gauged from the inside surface of pillars, same as the bottom sides; the only difference is, allowance must be made for the space the pillars stand toward the outside. To understand this correctly, see inside surface of rocker H and tenon of pillar T, Fig. 3. Now joint U, Fig. 1, which combines the arm-rail with the pillar, wants explanation, because pillar B is inclined and arm-rail C is contracted, and cannot be gauged from the inside. Body-makers who understand working-drafts, prick the tenon off from both of the inside surfaces of B and C, Fig. 1, but that takes experience, and we will explain another method, which is not as correct, but will do in the majority of cases, as follows:

Prick off the pillars B, Fig. 1, after turn-under line V and K, Fig. 3, and plain that sweep on the pillars very accurately; do the same with arm-rail C, Fig. 1, use for pricking off the arm-rail for front part, line V, Fig. 3, and for back part of arm-rail, dotted line M, Fig. 4. It must be understood there is wind in the back corner pillar; if the turn-under line V, Fig. 3, is taken for front and back part, there will be twist in the arm rail, and the object is, as much the back corner pillars are proportioned, the arm-rail must be proportioned also; for this reason, we have dotted line W, Fig. 3, to prick the back corner pillar by, and consequently the arm-rails on back end must be pricked off from the same line.

This is the simplest method to proportion back corner pillars, and a little experience in body drafting will teach the mechanic how much is to be taken off; as in this case, it would not hurt if the back corner pillars would be flattened a trifle, because it is too round as drawn.

GENERAL DIMENSIONS.

Body: width across bottom at center, 34 inches; across front on scroll, 33 inches; across back on scroll, $32\frac{3}{8}$ inches; all widths are taken at the bottom line. Width across back on top, $36\frac{1}{2}$ inches; width across back on bottom molding, that is, under the side quarter molding, 35 inches. Across the center where the body is widest, 45 inches; amount of turn-under, 6 inches each side. Moldings $\frac{3}{4}$ inch wide and $\frac{5}{8}$ inch thick; back and side panels grooved into the frame work.

Runners: width of track, 39 inches front, and $38\frac{1}{2}$ inches at the back. Width across runners on front scroll, 32 inches. Thickness and depth of runners, $1\frac{1}{2}$ by $1\frac{5}{8}$ inches. Shoes, $1\frac{1}{2}$ by $1\frac{5}{16}$ inch, round edge steel. Size of stays, $\frac{3}{4}$ by $\frac{1}{2}$ inch iron.

Carriage Monthly
August 1889
(diagram on previous page)

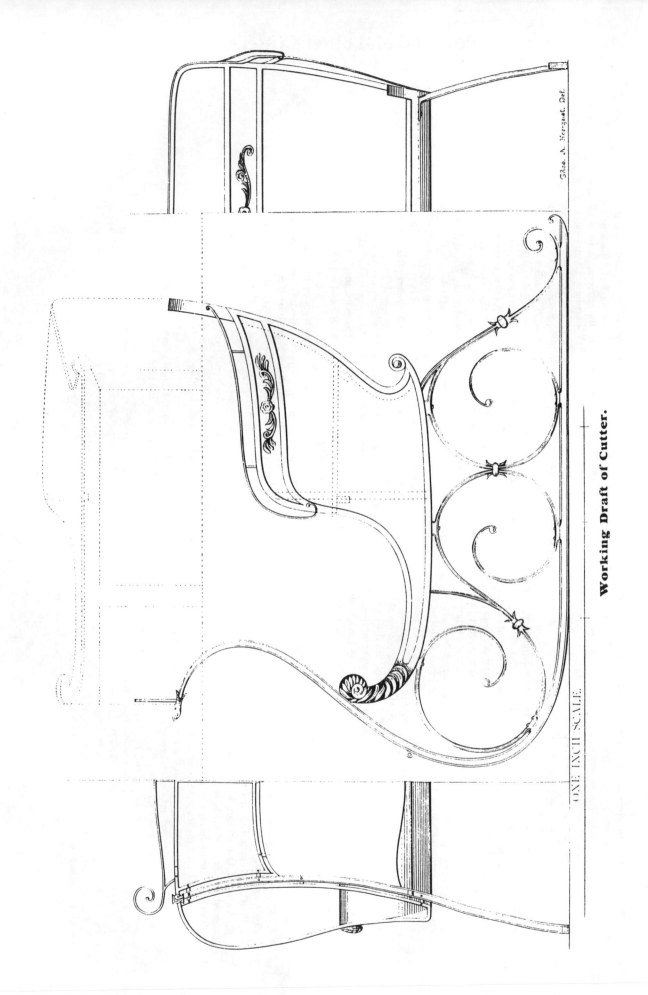

Working Draft of Cutter.

ONE INCH SCALE.

Geo. A. Hoogland. Del.

54

Working Draft of Cutter.

1-INCH SCALE.

While the construction of cutters is most simple, a few words about them may instruct those who are not experts at that work. Cutters generally have a bottom frame on which the entire body rests. The frame is made stationary to the runners; the body is set on the frame and fastened with two bolts passing through the bottom frame, and each tightened with a nut. We recommend this simplicity, but object to the joint between the bottom frame and the body, as, in most cases, the body does not fit to the frame, and daylight shows through the joints.

We have studied over this construction so as to improve its foundation, and not increase the labor. Why not use the same method as with buggy bodies? We will state right here that, on account of the curved front, a frame, as made by the old method, is not applicable, consequently a change in the construction is absolutely necessary. The sides of the bottom frame should be bent to the exact shape, as shown by the bottom line of body, and its size should be $\frac{3}{4}$ by $2\frac{1}{2}$ inches. It is necessary that these bottom sides should be bent, otherwise, when sawed to shape, the cross grain at the front end would be objectionable.

Framing by lapping the cross bars or tenons the same as a buggy frame; frame the side pieces into which the seat rail is fitted; also, join the back pillars to the frame. The back corner pillars must be bent also, and the upper cross bar is lapped to the pillars. The back panel is glued on the frame first, before it is tightened to the bottom frame. This practice is for convenience, as it is very easy to glue and handle it. When dry, clean the ends level with the pillars and glue to the frame. Of course, the back panel is cleaned off on the bench and not on the body.

Now glue the side panels. We prefer to clamp these panels, put screws in afterwards, and then put on moldings, and glue and brad them. Some will object to these moldings as unnecessary work, but they give shape and finish to the body, and, when striped, including the carving, look so well that the buyer is willing to pay the expense of the additional labor.

The carving, which is of a plain design, can be made more artistic, if made for a special customer, and moldings are rounded, to reduce the thickness of the upper edges of the body. Those builders who object to that can shift the moldings $\frac{1}{2}$ inch from the upper edge of body, showing the thickness of panel only. This does not detract any from its appearance. The seat rails are lapped and screwed directly against the pillars the same as is usually done in most factories.

The ironing, as illustrated, is very expensive compared with the wood knees and straight stays. They are made either entirely oval, or oval with a straight surface of $\frac{3}{16}$ inch on side elevation, which has a splendid appearance when those edges are striped, but involves much more labor. Others make them oval with but one sharp edge on the side elevation which looks well also. Generally the stays are made oval and striped either with one or two lines, producing the same effect as if the edges were left on the stays, and being decidedly less laborious. Those who object to these stays can replace them with wood knees, which are made in all shapes, but in our opinion the convex shape is the best for this style of body. If the body is made convex on top and concave at bottom, the knees should have the same shape.

The fender screens are different from those generally made. They are large side fenders the same as usual, and can be made with screens or covered with leather. In the center between the runners is a panel glued directly to and level with the runners; above this panel is another screen fastened between the runners, or instead, the iron frame is filled up with the screen and can be finished with leather the same as a dash. Those who do not like this can panel the entire space the same as usual. The dimensions of the body and runners are as follows: Across front top of scroll, 36 inches; across bottom, 30 inches; widest part of the body, 40 inches; at back above side panel, 38 inches; width of track, 38 inches.

For painting consult the July number, giving full explanation regarding it. To possess the appearance of the latest fashion these sleighs must be painted in party colors; for instance, the belt should be painted in pale blue and the main panels deep blue, carving deep blue, high-lighted with pale blue and yellow. Trimming blue cloth, mountings silver or gold

Carriage Monthly
August 1892
(diagram on previous page)

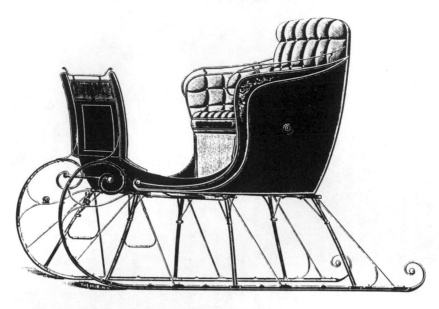

PLATE No. 15.   PORTLAND CUTTER.—SCALE, ONE-HALF INCH.

PORTLAND CUTTER.

—

SCALE, ½ INCH TO THE FOOT.

—

(See Fashion Plate No. 15.)

—

A FEW changes have been made in the outlines of this body, yet the original features of the Portland body have been retained. Sleighs of this design are usually intended for speeding purposes; therefore the whole should be light yet substantially constructed.

Portland cutters, as a rule, have curved or scroll dashers; the one introduced in this design is in harmony with the body; it is quite flat, and has leather wings at the side, and a wire screen on the top.

The runners are made of one bent piece, and are ⅞ x 1⅛ in.; shoes, ¼ in.; knees, ¾ x ⅞ in.; these should be left a little heavier at the center, say one inch.

The moldings on the sides of the body are all nailed on; the scroll work at the top can be painted on.

Width of body on top, 32 in.; and at bottom, 28 in. **Length** of body, 55 in. Height of body, 30 in. Track, measured outside to outside on the ground, 3 ft. 2 in.

Painting.—Body, medium shade blue; moldings, black, with fine line of yellow. Gearing, primrose yellow, striped black.

Trimming.—Blue cloth. Mountings, silver.

The Hub
June 1893

NEW STYLE COMFORT SLEIGH.

FIVE EIGHTHS INCH SCALE

PLATE NO. 4.

TWO PASSENGER SLEIGH.

(COMFORT STYLE.)

This design is similar to the "Comfort," but is not quite as heavy, has no round back corners and is molded, while the "Comfort" has generally been made with plain surfaces. The moldings on the side surfaces and front and back of body are ⅜ inch wide and rounded, with a round medallion in the center, on the sides and back panel.

Painting.—Body : deep green ; moldings, light green, no striping, and front of dash same as side surfaces of body ; the two stripes as seen are produced with ¼-inch stripes, ¾ inch apart, same color as moldings on body. Runners : deep green, striped two ⅛-inch lines, same color as dash, ⅜ inch apart.

Trimming.—Green cloth, style as shown in cut, carpet and rugs to match.

Finish.—Leather or wood fenders, screen line rail and body rail all silver.

———

Carriage Monthly
April 1894

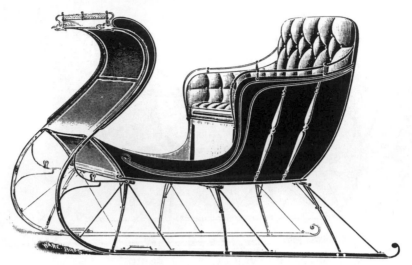

TWO PASSENGER SLEIGH.

FASHION PLATE NO. 6.—VOL. 30.—FIVE-EIGHTHS INCH SCALE.

PLATE NO. 6.

TWO PASSENGER SLEIGH.

This design is more pronounced in its characteristics, and is molded differently from the other designs. The side surfaces have a belt which is beaded on both sides and ¼ inch thick, a ⅝-inch wide molding at the bottom edge, and connected with two turned spindles. The same is done on the back panel, with four or five turned spindles. The body has convex surfaces, and so have the knees.

Painting.—Body: black; belt molding, yellow; beads, black, striped yellow. Spindles: yellow, touched up with black. Runners: yellow; striped one $\frac{3}{16}$-inch line of black, with one hair line each side, ⅜ inch apart. Dash panel: yellow, striped black.

Trimming.—Green cloth, and style as illustrated; carpet and rugs to match.

Finish.—Fenders, wood or leather; side rails, brass, and heavier than customary; a small screen for line rail also made of brass.

Carriage Monthly
April 1894

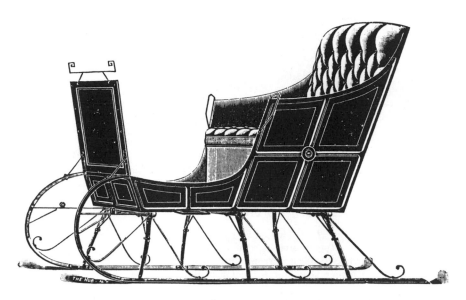

Plate No. 230. PORTLAND SLEIGH.—Scale, Five-eighth Inch.

IN all probability no one design of sleigh has passed through so many changes or become so universally popular as the Portland, and now after being in use nearly three-quarters of a century, a disposition is shown to return to the original pattern for such as are designed for general use. Fashion Plate No. 230 illustrates one of the patterns for the winter of 1896 and 1897. The body is made up of frame work, "express" style, and the panels are set in rabbets on the inside of the outer frame, grooved into the sills and against the cross seats so as to have a smooth finish inside. The corner parts should be 1¼ x 1½ in. square; sills, 1¼ x 2 in.; arm and front rail 1¼ in. square, the front rail of bent stock: cross moldings, 1¼ x ½ in.; medallion, 3 in. in diameter. Dash brackets and cross rails, 2½ x 1 in.; dash panel grooved in runners, 1¼ x 1 in.; knees, ⅞ x 1 in. at runner, and ⅞ x 1¾ in. at beams. Beams, ⅞ x 1¼ in.; width of body at the bottom, 32 in.; at the arm, 35 in.; at the tops of the back, 38 in.; tread of runners, 3 ft. 5 in.

Painting.—Dark olive green, champers and striping carmine.

Trimming—Green cloth; cushion and back squabbed, diamond arm quarters, and fall plain.

The Hub
June 1896

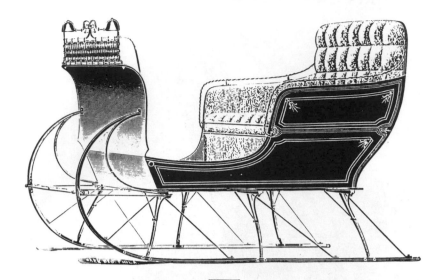

Plate No. 330.—Two Passenger Sleigh.

BUILT BY THE J. B. ARMSTRONG MFG. CO., GUELPH, ONT., CAN.

This plate shows one of the latest style of sleighs. It has very attractive trimmings, side rails with handles, screen above the dash, well shaped line rail, and furnishes abundant room for comfortable, riding.

Painting.—Body and runners, deep green, striped a light green.

Trimming.—Deep green plush, with carpet to match. Mountings of silver.

Carriage Monthly
September 1900

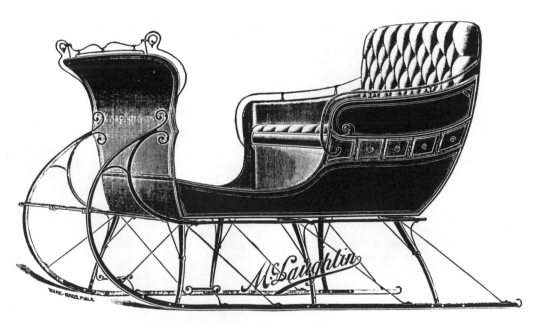

PLATE NO. 613.—TWO-PASSENGER SLEIGH.

Plate No. 613, a two-passenger sleigh built by McLaughlin Carriage Co., Oshawa, Ont., is especially roomy and comfortable. They are building cutters, gentlemen's driving traps and superb family sleighs. The quality and workmanship are always first class in this line of stock. The side surfaces on this sleigh are artistically molded and at center between moldings there are four turned spindles. Around the moldings and spindles are the stripings in various colors and which have a very pretty effect.

Carriage Monthly
July 1902

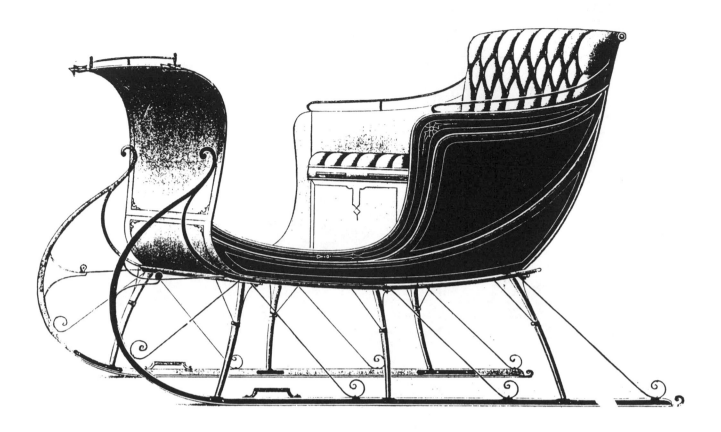

Plate No. 629.—Old Comfort Sleigh.

BUILT BY FULLER BUGGY CO., JACKSON, MICH.

This sleigh contains individuality of style, has distinguished attractions, is up to date in all respects, looks fresh and natty in appearance, and contains modern conveniences and comfort. The side surfaces are molded, one stripe on each side, with the exception of the moldings around the edges, which have one stripe only. The dasher is striped with one line, and has small ornaments at the corners.

Carriage Monthly
August 1902

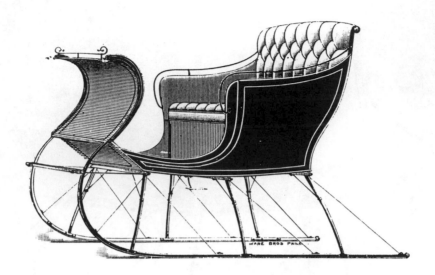

Plate No. 697.—Cutter.

BUILT BY L. C. GRAVES & CO., SPRINGBORO, PA.

Cutters are generally built with concave-convex back panel, the concave being at the lower part. They have a concave side panel, because one curve in opposition to another never works well. A bottom frame is made either ⅝ or ¾ inch thick, and about 2¾ inches wide. The panels are either built-up wood or poplar. The stripes shown are either very light beads or stripes. The striping is preferred, because it is less labor and looks just as well when properly done. The knees and runners are of the best hickory, and bent to shape. The braces are of light steel.

Painting.—Body, ultramarine blue, striped white; carriage-part, same color and same striping as on the body.

Trimming.—Blue cloth; back, blocks, full diamonds and pipes; cushion, blocks; plain cushion front; raisers on fall, and plain blue carpet.

Finish.—Rails black or nickel plated; rein rail nickel.

Carriage Monthly
May 1903

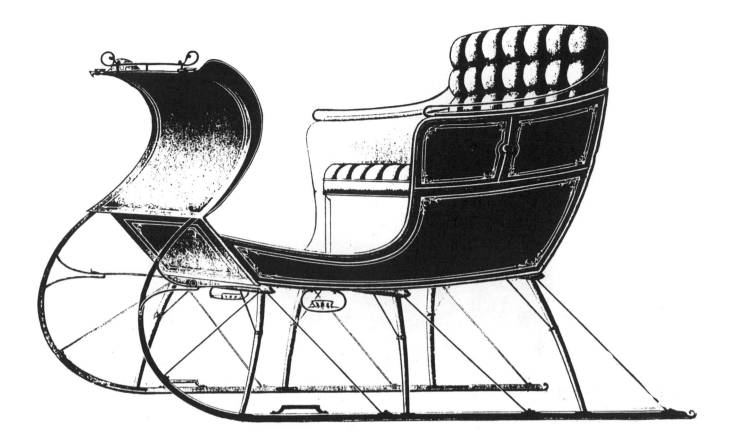

Plate No. 698.—Two-Passenger Sleigh.

BUILT BY FULLER BUGGY CO., JACKSON, MICH.

This company are known as extensive sleigh builders, and they build good work. The side surfaces are convex, including the back panel. The sides are molded around the edges; besides, there is a lengthwise molding dividing the lower from the upper, and the upper is connected with another, having a medallion in the center. The knees and runners are rounded, and this gives a splendid finish. When well painted, it adds to the beauty of the runners, if they are well curved. All braces are steel, clipped to the knees and screwed under the bolster.

Painting.—Body, deep green, striped cream; all corners a trifle ornamented. This is also carried out on back panel, heel and dash board.

Trimming.—Green cloth; style blocks; runners deep green, striped white; spring cushion; raisers on fall; carpet plain green.

Finish.—Steps black; side rails and dash rail full nickeled.

Carriage Monthly
May 1903

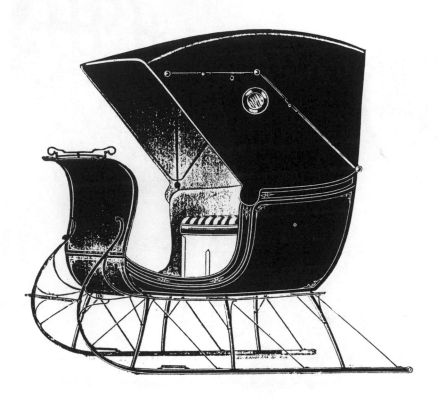

Plate No. 704.—Old Comfort, with Top.

BUILT BY JACKSON SLEIGH CO., JACKSON, MICH.

Old comforts are the most comfortable sleighs built for two passengers. Those with a close, three-bow top are even more comfortable. The belt on body is produced by two small moldings. Striping and ornamenting between makes it a very good finish. Imitation rubber cloth is generally used, and is especially used for tops for carriages and sleighs.

Painting.—Deep Indian red, striping and ornamenting black or white; runners, Indian red, striped white.

Trimming.—Brown cloth; style blocks; plain cushion fronts, and raisers on fall.

Finish.—Plated line rail; round beveled glasses; straight braces; curved dash.

Carriage Monthly
May 1903

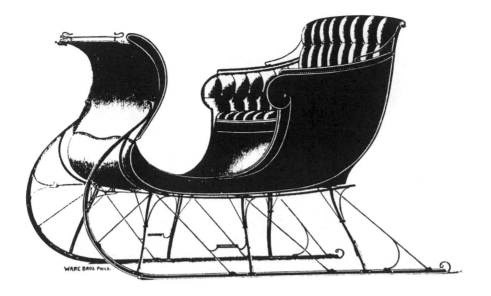

Plate No. 699.—Solid Old Comfort.

BUILT BY R. D. SCOTT & CO., PONTIAC, MICH.

Very few comforts are built with such beautiful outlines as seen in the plate. Note the main bottom curve from top of cushion to front of dash. It could not be better. The front wing pillar beaded on both sides, raised in the center, connecting with the arm-rail curve, cannot be surpassed. This same superior finish is observable outside throughout the side squabs, which are generally plain. They are heavily upholstered; the wings on the dash, the well-braced concaved-convex knees, including the side rails, show how well this is done.

Painting.—Body, Indian red, striped with a fine white line next to the moldings; runners, Indian red, a few shades lighter than the body, striped one hair line each side and a heavy line in the center.

Finish.—Side rail, black; rein rail, nickel; fenders, leather covered, and steps fastened to knees and braces.

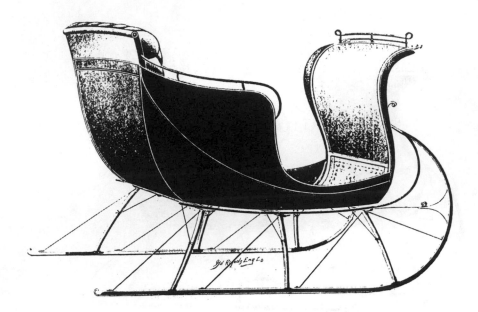

Plate No. 701.—Old Comfort.

BUILT BY SULLIVAN BROS., ROCHESTER, N. Y.

This firm are very well known, particularly through their large exhibits at the dealers' conventions. This old comfort is one of their latest. It is roomy, well trimmed, has spring cushions and back and is one of the most comfortable sleighs to be had. It will accommodate nicely two large people. The back corner curve is full toward the bottom, and turns into a slide concave toward the top and finishes with a roll across. It looks well, and the curved molding on the side surfaces is quite attractive.

Painting.—Upper part of side quarters, black, including moldings; lower part of side surfaces, back panel and dash, lemon yellow; molding striped ⅛-inch yellow line; runners, yellow, striped black.

Trimming.—Gray corduroy; style blocks; half diamonds and pipes for back; blocks for cushion, and raisers on fall.

Finish.—Rein rail and body rails nickel; carpet to match.

Carriage Monthly
May 1903

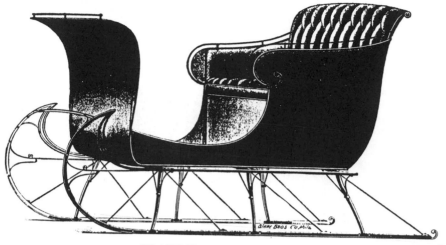

Carriage Monthly
June 1911

PLATE No. 1400. SLEIGH.

BUILT BY THE STURTEVANT-LARRABEE CO., BINGHAMTON, N. Y.

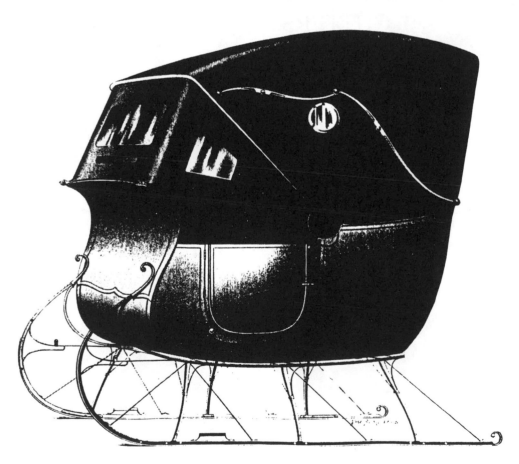

Carriage Monthly
November 1915

PLATE No. 1827. CUTTER, WITH STORM TOP AND FRONT.

BUILT BY THE AMERICAN CARRIAGE CO., KALAMAZOO, MICH.

SPEEDING
CUTTERS

BUFFALO SPEEDING CUTTER.

(See Fashion Plate No. 51, on this page.)

As a companion-piece to the " Portland Speeding Cutter " published in our July issue (Fashion Plate No. 27), we herewith present, in five-eighths-inch scale, an engraving of another peculiarly tasteful pattern of light cutter, designed and built by the Buffalo Carriage & Sleigh Wood-work Co., of Buffalo, N. Y., to whom we are indebted for the accompanying drawing and also for the following table of dimensions, which, in connection with the description of the Portland design above referred to, will be ample for the use of the draftsman or builder.

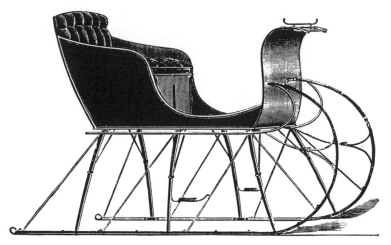

Dimensions.—Width of seat, 31 in. Height of gear, 22 in. Track, 42 in. Shoes, ¾ in. From where the steel shoe ends, to point of runner, ⅝ in. Fenders, ⅝ × ⅝ in. Piece between fender and body, ⅜ × ½ in. Knees, ⁹⁄₁₆ in. Beams, ¾ × 1¼ in., tapered at ends to the thickness of the knees. Corner molding at back, ⅝ in. on bottom, tapered to ½ in. at top. Width of body on bottom, outside, 25 in.; and on top, at the seat-pillar outside, 33 in.; across back on top, 32 in. Panels, ⁵⁄₁₆ in. The dash panel projects over on each side to form wings. A light bent bar connects the runners to the dash. A light sill is put in the body, 2¼ × ¾ in., and the body is screwed on the beams. On the side is put a light piece of hickory, ½ × ⅜ in., on the beams, between the fender and body.

Finish.—Painting of body, black, fine-lined with gold. Running-part, vermilion, fine-lined with black and gold. Trimming, black broadcloth or plush, with black tufts centered with red. Carpet, black, with red figures, or red with black figures. Mountings, gold.

Light Gentleman's Sleigh.

PLATE NO. 48.

EXHIBITED BY MESSRS. C. P. KIMBALL & CO., CHICAGO, ILL.

This is a very light, neat and well finished sleigh, exhibited in the white, showing original features worthy of imitation. The shape of the body is on the Portland pattern, very light at the front end, the side panels at the front but 1¾ inches deep; the back corners are convex top and concave bottom; the bottom curve has 1⅜ inches raise at the front, and ⅜ inch back. The back corners have ⅜ inch wide moldings, and are only ⅛ inch thick. The bottom frame, on which the body rests is only 7/16 inch full thick. The back corner pillars over which the back and side panels are glued are very light, as is also the frame on which the seat rests, being only ½ inch scant thick. Seat frame ½ inch scant thick by 2 inches wide for all four pieces, and caned between the four pieces. The side panels and also the back panel are ¼ inch thick, and its entire inside surfaces are canvased with fine muslin. The four back knees and the bolsters are ½ inch thick, knees ⅞ inch top and ⅝ inch bottom, and the bolsters 1⅛ inches deep, including the thickness of the iron. The side stays are 3/16 inch thick, and are bolted to the runners as usual; they pass over the outside surface of the knees. The clip is forged solid to the stay and clipped direct to the knee, and the upper end of the stay is bolted direct to the bottom frame of body. The inside surfaces of the knees and bolsters are plated with a continuous piece of steel, and corner stays are forged solid to it. These plates are bolted to runners, knees and bolsters, with diamond head bolts. This explanation has only reference to the two back knees.

The front is constructed different, as knees and bolster are made out of one bent piece, with sharp, round bent corners on each side, and are plated on the front surface, not under the lower surface, as explained, on the two back supports or knees.

The shaft irons are original; the front part is the same as usual, but back of the knee, bolted to knee, turning around in a circle and bolted again to the runner, and from the top of circle the stay branches out toward the body, and its end is bolted to the bottom frame.

The runners are ⅝ inch thick and 9/16 inch deep, but are tapered toward the front end from about ⅜ inch square. The shoes are ⅝ inch round-edge steel, ⅛ inch thick, bolted to the runners, and screws between the bolts. The front of the dash has a hickory molding rabbeted over the panel, to show joint only at the bottom of dash panel. Molding is rounded. Dash rail is only ⅛ inch full round steel, silver-plated, with four supports. Body rails 3/16 inch thick, round steel, silver-plated. Shoes at back end finish with a very light scroll, and front with a very light eagle head. The corner irons at the front where the foot board connects with the body are forged solid to the shoes, which makes a very neat finish.

Painting.—Body: filled in and varnished to show natural grain. Runners: same as body.

Trimming.—Green cloth; back trimmed plain and flat. Cushion made up in full squares; front facings are 1½ inches deep, finished with a ⅜-inch raiser. Fall plain, except ⅜-inch raisers ⅜ inch from its edges. Sides not trimmed. Carpet green, without figures.

Mountings.—Silver.

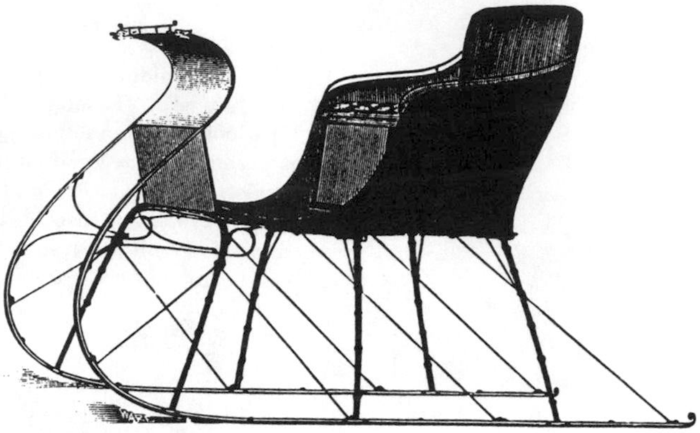

LIGHT GENTLEMAN'S SLEIGH.

HALF-INCH SCALE.

Carriage Monthly
October 1889

No. 34. SPEEDING SLEIGH.

KINGMAN, STURTEVANT & LARRABEE, BINGHAMTON, N. Y.

———

COLORED plate No. CXXXIX represents a speeding sleigh, manufactured by Messrs. Kingman, Sturtevant & Larrabee, of Binghamton, N. Y., who make a specialty of this class of work. The sleigh is very light, yet suitably constructed. A noticeable improvement is the front knees which are made of one bent piece. The shaft coupling is brought back on a line with the front knee, which permits the horse being hitched close to the shafts, which is the custom on speeding vehicles. There are no steps, the draw-iron being run back far enough to be used for that purpose. The sides of the body are swept same as at the back.

Painting.—Body, primrose yellow, with carmine stripe ; moldings, black; running part, carmine, striped black.
Trimming.—Green cloth. Mountings, silver.

The Hub
August 1891

Working-Draft of Gentleman's Sleigh.

EXHIBITED BY C. P. KIMBALL & CO. AT THE PARIS EXPOSITION.

This sleigh, probably the lightest ever made, weighing about fifty pounds with shafts and trimmings, differs in construction from those we have published before, and a working-draft of the details of construction will, no doubt, be appreciated by the trade.

Regarding the side elevation of the runners and body, *Fig. 1*, no novelty will be observed; the shape of the body is on the Portland style, and the runners are the same shape usually made. The bottom sweep of the body is curved very little at the back end, but raises the body considerably at the front. The bottom frame, on which the body

rests, is only $\frac{7}{16}$ inch thick toward the outside, forming a molding standing over the side panel $\frac{1}{4}$ inch scant. The back corner pillars are very light, made of ash, $\frac{1}{2}$ inch thick by $1\frac{1}{4}$ inches wide, top and bottom; to this add the side sweep (see back view, *Fig. 3*). The back and side panels are bass wood, $\frac{1}{8}$ inch scant thick, and are canvased on the inside with fine muslin. Another frame is made for the seat to rest upon, $\frac{7}{16}$ inch thick, and its shape can be seen from the front view, *Fig. 2*. The back corner moldings are $\frac{3}{8}$ inch wide on the side and back panels, and both moldings should be made out of one piece, avoiding the joint for the molding. If made this way, the panels can be glued and then braded, and the brad-holes covered with the molding, which makes good, strong work and good finish.

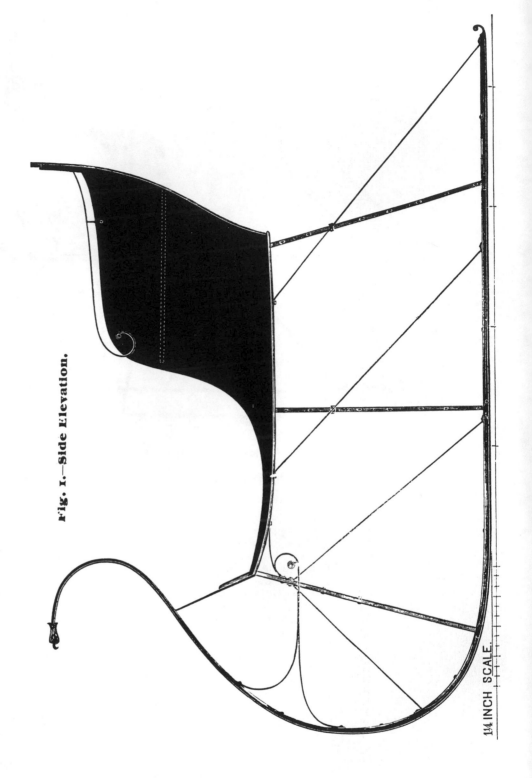

Fig. 1.—Side Elevation.

1¼ INCH SCALE.

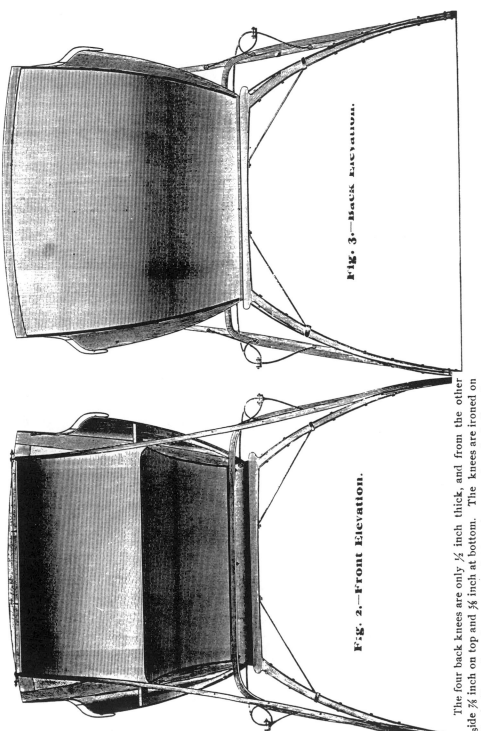

Fig. 2.—Front Elevation.

Fig. 3.—Back Elevation.

The four back knees are only ½ inch thick, and from the other side ⅞ inch on top and ⅝ inch at bottom. The knees are ironed on the inside surface from top to bottom in one piece, including the stays. The two back side stays are bolted to the runners, are clipped to the knees and also bolted to the body. The clip, when passing the knee, is forged solid to the stay after the inclination of the knees. The stays are made of ³⁄₁₆-inch round steel, and the clips welded to the stays are very light. The steel bands on the inside surfaces of the knees and bolsters are bolted to them, and the bolt heads are diamond shaped. The front knees and bolsters form one bent piece, with sharp round corners near the bottom of body. This bent piece is ironed vertically with a light piece of steel ⅛ inch thick and riveted to it. The shaft irons are also different from those usually made; they are taken also from ¹⁄₁₆-inch steel, and bolted back of bent knee and also to the body; for this see *Fig. 1*. The front knees are only ⅜ inch thick, ⅞ inch under body and ⅜ inch at bottom near the runner. The size of runners are ½ inch thick, ⅞ inch thick, but are tapered to ⅜ by ½ inch scant at front end. The scroll at the front ends of runners forming eagle heads are very light. The rein rail at the front is very light, has four supports and is only ⅛ inch

full thick. The body rails are ¹⁄₁₆ inch scant thick, well shaped and finished. On the original the front knees were level with the body, and a half round put on to cover the joint, but this is not necessary; the knees can be put ¼ inch in from the edge of the body, which will break the joint, or, in fact, the joint will hardly be seen and makes a lighter finish. The corner irons are welded to the shoes where the runners connect with the body. The size of the shoes are ⅝ inch round edge steel by ³⁄₁₆ inch thick. The front dash panel is ¹⁄₁₆ inch thick, rabbeted into the runners, and the joint covered with the shoes.

The widths of body are as follows: Across body, front, 20 inches; body bottom at center, 21½ inches; body back at bottom, 20 inches, giving ¾ inch round on each side for frame and bottom of body. Body back on top 27 inches, and full width of body 30 inches across the panels. Width of track front 36½ inches, and back 36¼ inches.

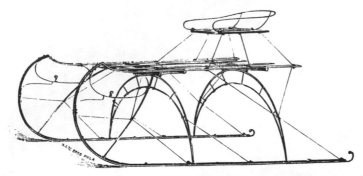

SULKY SLEIGH.

PLATE NO. 17.—VOL. 29.—HALF-INCH SCALE.

Carriage Monthly
June 1893

This is a very peculiar sleigh. We believe it is the first time that a style of such peculiar construction has been published. It originated with the Cortland Wagon Co., of Cortland, N. Y. We have made a few changes from the original by removing the bent braces, which were made similar to the two resting on the runners. We have replaced those bent stays with straight iron stays, as made on sulkies. The construction of the sleigh is very simple. The runners are bent as usual, but are very light, $\frac{5}{8}$ inch square, with steel shoes, $\frac{5}{32}$ by $\frac{5}{8}$ inch, and rounded toward the front. The inner edges of the runners are also rounded; in fact all the wood work is well rounded, with the exception of those pieces where the square surfaces must be preserved. The four pieces which constitute the two braces are bent circular, and are rounded from all sides, with the exception of the places where they meet at the bottom and where the cross bar rests on the top. The size of the braces, and in fact all the wood work on the sleigh, depends on the quality of the wood, and the quality of workmanship. We have seen the knees on a one man sleigh $\frac{3}{8}$ inch thick only, ironed from the inside, and ending with a stay under the bolster bar. In this case, on the two circular braces, the stays are dispensed with, and a T iron is placed on the runners, and extends far enough up, to run a bolt through the brace and the iron, and 2 inches above the bolt. At the end of the T iron, a screw only holds the T iron and two bent braces together. The stays between the bent pieces are simply straight pieces of steel wire, upset a trifle at the ends, to form a shoulder with a full $\frac{1}{8}$-inch bolt and screw at each end. The smith and finisher must use his own judgment as to the requisite sizes of steel wire and the tapering and upsetting for the various stays on this sleigh, because all the pieces, iron and wood, are so light, that $\frac{1}{16}$ inch increase in thickness of bolts would weaken the other part to such an extent, that it would effect the entire structure. Only experienced mechanics, with sound judgment should do such work. For further information in regard to the construction, see the Wood Department of this number. A 1-inch scale illustration will be found, showing in five different views, all the details needed in the construction. See also Figs. 1 to 6, giving the ends of stays. The illustration does not show a cushion, but a regular sulky cushion is used which is low in front, high at back end, with rolls on three sides and made up soft. The technical part of making a sulky cushion can be found on page 13, July number, 1891.

Painting.—These sleighs can be painted in any colors, as for example: maroon or wine color; lemon or orange yellow; deep or pale blue or green; vermilion, Indian red or carmine, and the color of striping to suit. In all of the colors mentioned above, the color of striping must be made to suit the color of the sleigh, and the striping is done with one or two hair lines only.

Finish.—Seat, caned; seat rail, silver plated. If the sleigh is to be increased in cost, all the stays for seat and runners could be nickel plated; in fact all the other irons should be nickeled.

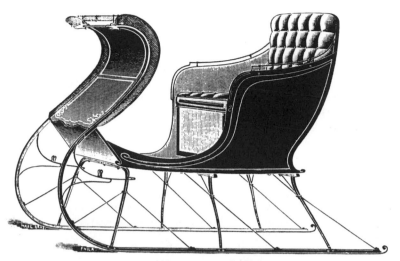

SPEEDING SLEIGH.

Fashion Plate No. 3.—Vol. 30.—Five-Eighths Inch Scale.

**PLATE NO. 3.
SPEEDING
SLEIGH.**

This plate represents one of the latest styles of speeding sleighs. It is light and graceful, and as it is hung 2 inches higher than the family sleighs, it should be from 15 to 17 inches from the floor. The back corner pillars are convex-concave, the bottom line a trifle curved, and the main upper curve to suit the style of the present fashion. These bodies have generally been made with plain surfaces and moldings, produced by broad stripes, but this is a thing of the past; and the explanation we have given, regarding the moldings on Plate No. 1, applies also in this case; also in regard to the back panel.

The runners for these sleighs are made ¾ inch, and sometimes less than that; knees, ½ inch, and the front one bent in one piece. The four back knees are convex-concave in shape, while the front one is bent a trifle outward from top to bottom. The stays, which are $\frac{7}{32}$ inch thick, are clipped different from the general method. The beauty of these speeders depends on the perfect workmanship, pleasing style and correct principle of the construction. The knees and runners should be tastily rounded, and the clips perfectly made. The runners should have perfect curves. There is also a great deal in the construction and finish of the body to add to its beauty. For information relative to the construction of the body, see working draft of four passenger sleigh, with ogee back corner pillars.

Painting.—Body: maroon; moldings, black; space between moldings, bright carmine; front of dash, maroon or carmine; moldings striped a hair line of carmine. Runners: maroon, striped two ⅛-inch lines of carmine.

Trimming.—Cloth, maroon color, and finish as shown in the engraving.

Finish.—Screen fenders, screen line rail, side rails on body, and mountings, silver.

Carriage Monthly
April 1894

Working Draft of a Sulky Sleigh.

1-INCH SCALE.

With this working draft we illustrate and describe a sulky sleigh, which is the first attempt in the construction of a sleigh for fast driving. It is constructed on the same principle as a sulky. The seat is exactly the same, and the arched braces are similar to those of the present style of sulkies. The entire construction is exceedingly light, as will be seen by the dimensions given in connection with this description.

This sleigh is illustrated by five different views: side, front and back elevations and top and bottom views. From these may be gathered all the necessary information relative to its dimensions, shape and construction.

SIDE ELEVATION.

The design of the side elevation is very simple, and has the same appearance as any other sleigh (especially the rear bob runners), with the exception of the seat, which is exactly as on a sulky. The runners are $\frac{5}{8}$ inch square, and the steel shoes are $\frac{1}{8}$ inch thick by $\frac{5}{8}$ inch wide, round edges on both sides. The tops of the runners are well rounded. The knees and bent arched braces are all $\frac{9}{16}$ inch thick. The shape of the front knee is shown on A, A, front and back elevations, and the bent braces are $\frac{9}{16}$ inch square, bent to shape as shown, and rounded top and bottom.

The bent braces are combined with six iron stays, $\frac{5}{16}$ inch thick, shouldered down $\frac{7}{32}$ inch thick, with a washer slipped over to make a good shoulder, and nut and screw at each end. The cross bars B, B are also $\frac{9}{16}$ inch thick, and the shape as shown. All the stays are made from round steel wire, $\frac{3}{16}$ inch thick. The bars C, C, running lengthwise, are $1\frac{1}{8}$ inches wide and $\frac{3}{8}$ inch thick, and bars D, D, are $1\frac{1}{2}$ inches wide by $\frac{1}{2}$ inch thick. The seat is $12\frac{3}{4}$ inches wide, and $14\frac{3}{8}$ inches long, caned as shown.

The width of track is 4 feet from out to out, and 10 inches wider than on regular sleighs, which are generally made 38 inches. This is purposely done to steady the sleigh for fast driving and for turning corners.

If steel wire is used for brace E, it must be upset to the size of a $\frac{5}{32}$-inch bolt where it passes through the brace knee and stay. This holds good for each end of the other braces, which must be upset and flattened. To show the construction of the stay we illustrate parts of it full size. Fig. 1 is part of a stay, as shown on F. The six stays resting on top of the runners and under piece D on each side of the sleigh, are finished as Fig. 1. Fig. 2 is put on E, top view, and is also seen on E, side elevation. Fig. 3 is seen on H, side elevation, or N, bottom view. Fig. 4 is the stay crossing the knee at K, side elevation. The clip fastens the knee at K and enters the two holes at Fig. 4, and is tightened with two nuts at the back of it. Fig. 5 represents the stay at L, side elevation; it is the same as Fig. 3, except that the shape from the side elevation differs from the latter. Fig. 6 is the stay shown on M. This is the most complicated, as it has three branches, and must stand in the proper position, without any twist. This can be very easily regulated by making a drawing as illustrated in Fig. 6, and welding the branches in the exact direction. This explanation will be sufficient for those who have practical knowledge of building this kind of work. If those who have not built sleighs would like to know more about the details of construction and will write us what they need, we will be pleased to explain more fully the necessary requirements in its construction. No doubt other improvements can be made by those who are familiar with this kind of work for the purpose for which it is intended. Many will consider the width of the track too wide for a one-man sleigh, but we have used the same width as made by the Cortland Wagon Co., the originators, and we feel confident it is right.

Carriage Monthly
June 1893

(diagrams on next page)

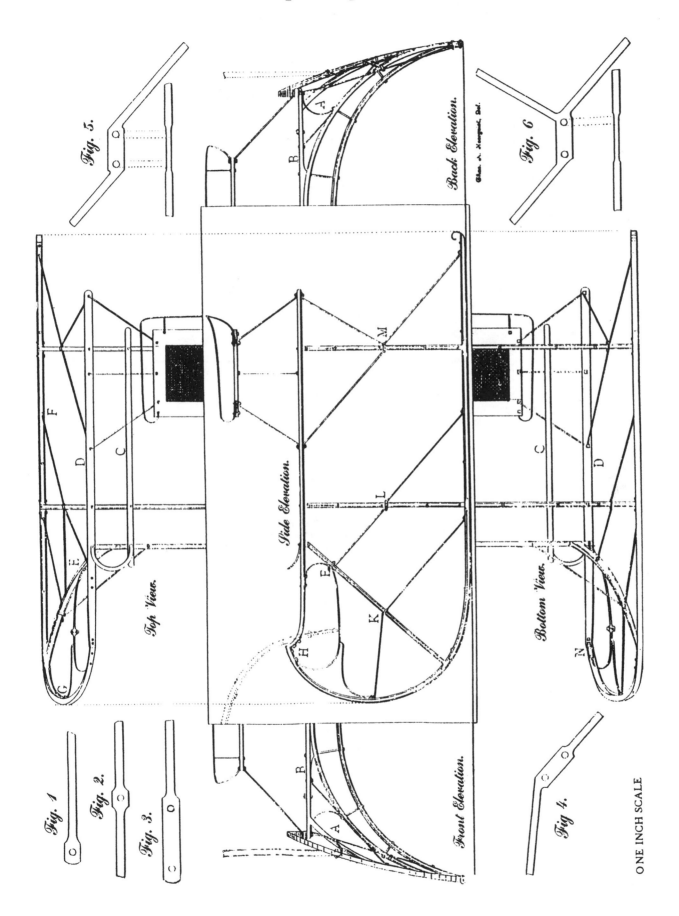

Fig. 5.

Fig. 6

Back Elevation.

Chas. S. Newport, Del.

Fig. 1

Fig. 2.

Fig. 3.

Fig. 4.

Top View.

Side Elevation.

Bottom View.

Front Elevation.

ONE INCH SCALE

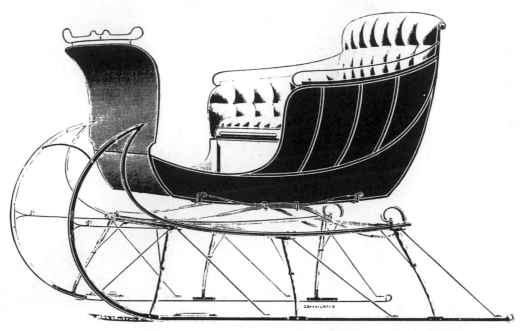

PLATE No. 733. SIDE SPRING COMFORT.

FIVE EIGHTHS INCH SCALE.

Plate No. 733.—Side-Spring Comfort.

This design represents a new style, and is a departure of the Prouty & Glass Carriage Co., worthy of note in sleigh construction. Springs have been put under sleigh bodies before, but not such springs as shown on this design. The front ends of side spring are fastened to the front bolster, and the rear ends are regular scroll ends. They not only look well, but take up the lengthening when the weight of two occupants settles the body, making one of the most comfortable riding sleighs ever used.

The runners and eve rails are well bent. The knees are concave-convex shaped and well braced, including the T-plates to strengthen the knees and runners. The body is molded around the edges, besides the other moldings, which gives character to the side surfaces, and which can be strengthened with the various colors to lift out this part of the body.

Painting.—Lower part of body, back and front panel inside of dash and moldings, black; front of dash and the four spaces between the moldings on each side, canary yellow; runners, canary yellow, striped black; dash also striped black.

Trimming.—Green cloth, style as shown.

Finish.—Dash and seat rail, nickel plated.

Carriage Monthly
November 1903

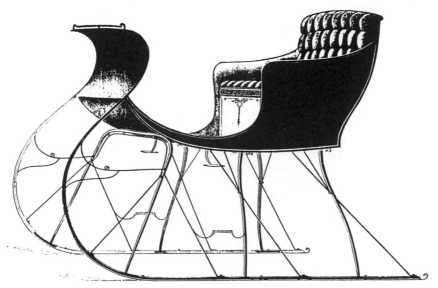

PLATE No. 769.—SPEEDING CUTTER.

The weight of this cutter is about 85 pounds; it has cane seat, concave-convex knees for rear and bent knee for front; straight braces, paneled dash, without fenders; two steps on each side, also braces on bolster bars. Paneled body with beaded edges, curved bottom, convex-concave back and side panels; built by the Sturtevant-Larrabee Co., Binghamton, N. Y.

Painting.—Body, Brewster green; runners, green or carmine; striped black, or any other harmonizing color.

Trimming.—Cloth or whip-cord, soft-spring cushion; size, 18 x 33 inches; height of back above seat, 19 inches; style as shown; lace cushion front and fall ornamented, Wilton mat.

Finish.—Nickel dash rail, front knee and beam bent in one piece; front knee, 28 inches from the floor; track, 48 inches.

Carriage Monthly
May 1904

Working Draft of a One-Man Speeding Sleigh.

ONE-INCH SCALE.

(See illustration in fashion pages.)

With this working draft we illustrate one of the lightest speeding sleighs yet made, and which is entitled to the designation of being an entire novelty in construction. Five views will be given. The entire length is 6 feet 1½ inches; width across the runners, 36 inches; length of frame, 4 feet 3½ inches on a straight line, including the foot board, which is 21 inches wide. From front of seat to dash,

28¼ inches, and seat 15¼ x 15¼ inches. From floor to top of frame, 26 inches, and from floor to top of seat frame, 10½ inches. The following dimensions will indicate the lightness of construction as one of the lightest sleighs that can be built.

The seat frame is ⅝ inch thick; the front and two side pieces, 2 inches wide; the rear piece, 2⅜ inches at center, and rear end curved ¾ inch. All the stays are made from ¼-inch round steel, including the seat stays. The seat rail is of 3-16-inch round steel. The dash is 10 inches wide by 20½ inches long, and is made of built-up wood, three layers 3-16 inch thick. The foot board is ½ inch thick, 9⅜ inches wide and 23½ inches long.

The main frame is 46 inches long and 21 inches wide; the side pieces ⅝ x 1⅝ inches. Five cross pieces are used, the front one being ⅝ x 6⅜ inches, 20 inches long. The step cross bar is ½ x 1⅞ inches, 20 inches long. The three other bars are all ⅝ x 1⅞ inches, 20 inches long. The runners are ⅝ inch square, bent circular at front and secured to the foot board near dash, and the ends to the main frame. The three cross bars on which the main frame rests are ½ inch thick, ½ inch at center, ⅜ inch at ends and ¾ inch 5 inches from center. The knees are ½ inch thick by ⅝ inch the other way, and bent in a single piece. The knee braces are ½ inch square, bent from a single piece and jointed to the main knees. The knees and knee braces are rounded, excepting on those places where the stays are fastened. The rear knees are strengthened with a cross stay, as shown on back elevation, to keep the runners from spreading.

Note the two center stays on side elevation. They are secured to the center knee in two places, forming a step on lower fastening, both doubly secured to front and back knees, runner and main frame, and is a study from a mechanical point of view.

Carriage Monthly
May 1904
(diagrams on next page)

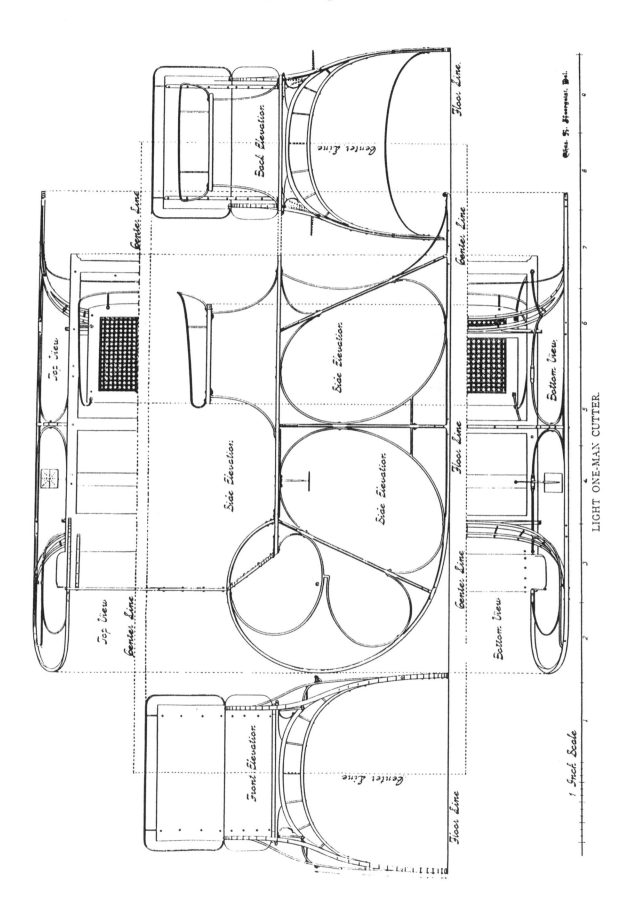

LIGHT ONE-MAN CUTTER.

Light One-Man Cutter.

ONE-INCH SCALE.

With this draft we give a light-constructed cutter comfortable and roomy for one person only and of the latest-improved construction. The length of the sleigh from out to out of runners is 5 feet 9 inches, the body is suspended from the floor 22 inches and supported on three bent knees. The supports heretofore have generally consisted of three pieces each, the bolster and two knees. On this design the three supports are bent, each made of one piece. The size of supports on side elevation is 9 inches, on back view 9-16 inch on runners. One inch on each short bend and 5⁄8 inch at center.

The size of runners is 9-16 inch square and on upper front end 7-16 inch; the front dash panel is 3-16 inch scant of built-up wood. The size of steel shoes is 3-32 inch by 5⁄8 inch, and size of stays ¼-inch steel. The body frame is 20 inches by 33 inches long; the side pieces are ½-inch thick and 2 inches wide. The end cross bars are 5⁄8-inch thick and 2¾ inches wide, and center cross bar 5⁄8 by 2 inches. The seat-rail supports are 5⁄8-inch thick and shape is shown on left side of back elevation. The corner pillars are shown by dotted lines on side elevation and back view. The upper back rail is 5⁄8-inch thick and 3½ inches wide; the seat rail ¾ by 1⅛ inches; the seat frame 5⁄8-inch thick and curved as shown on top view.

The widths of body are as follows: On widest part, 28 inches; on seat front inside of panels, 25¾ inches; across bottom edge of panels, 19¼ inches; across bottom frame, 20 inches; length of bottom frame, 33 inches; width across back at bottom of panels, 19¼ inches; width across top, 24 inches; width across runners at bottom, 30¾ inches. While this cutter is not as light as the one-man speeding sleigh, it is nevertheless built exceedingly light. The best and most improved feature is the bent knees. If bent, as illustrated on front and back views, with a short and graceful curve, and a trifle heavier at the short bend, the steel stays can be dispensed with. The rear knees are kept from spreading by a cross stay.

Carriage Monthly
May 1904
(diagrams on next page)

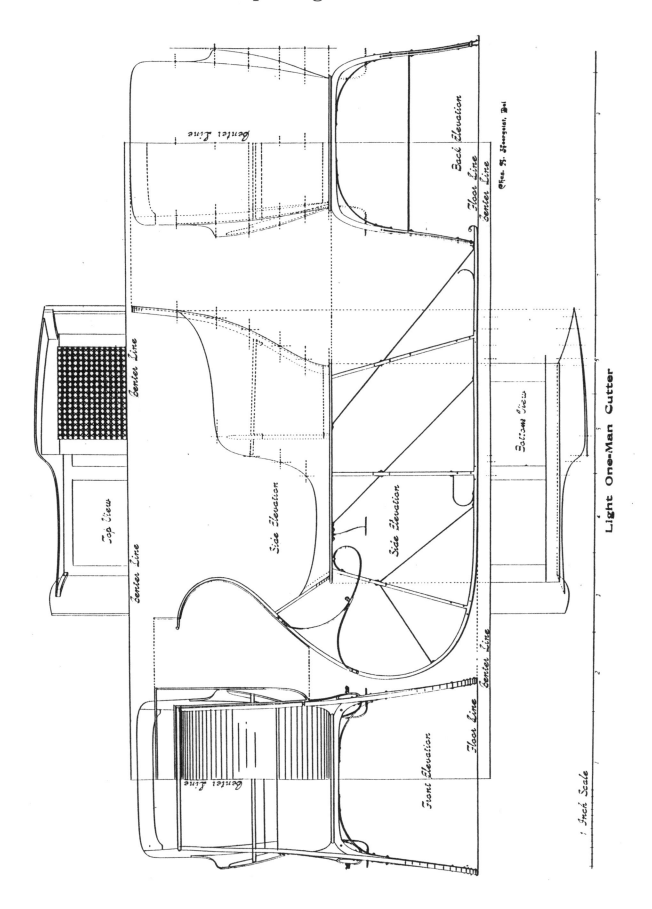

Light One-Man Cutter

FOUR-PASSENGER
SLEIGHS

No. 36. BOSTON PONY SLEIGH.—Scale, one-half inch.

This original and attractive pattern was suggested to us by Messrs. Kimball Bros., of Boston, Mass., and we have for this reason called it a " Boston " style. The lines of the body introduce a pleasing combination of a Canadian back-quarter with a style of front made quite frequently in New-England, which combination affords not only a cheap body, but one that is stylish. With the exception of the upright pillar, and the skirt, and two long square moldings at the bottom, the effect of the sides depends almost wholly upon the painting. The benches are secured by double iron rails.

Dimensions.—Width of seats, 38 in. Turn-under, 3½ in. on each side. Runners, 1 x ½ in. Knees, ⅞ x 1¾ in., tapered off to ⅞ x 1 in. Beams, ⅞ x 1¾ in. Shoes, ⅝ x 1½ in. Track, 3 ft. 6 in., out to out.

Painting.—Body and seats, dark green, striped as shown in cut, with gold and fine lines of red and light green ; runners, black, fine-lined with vermilion glazed ; bolt-heads, etc., gilded.

The Hub
August 1879

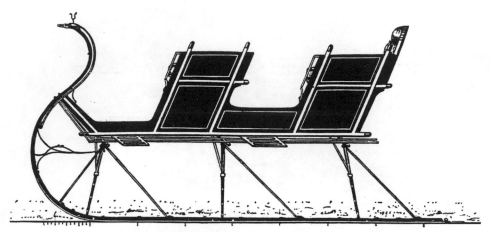

No. 59. FOUR-PASSENGER CANADIAN PONY SLEIGH.

SCALE, ONE-HALF INCH.

OF all the late patterns of Canadian Sleighs this is, without doubt, one of the handsomest in general appearance. Its plain outlines are relieved to good advantage by the four upright pillars or standards, and by the skirt or bottom molding, made square, with round tips at the ends, either gold or silver-plated. The striping shown on our cut may be made in a bright color on dark panels. City makers mostly put square, double side-rails on the finer classes of sleighs of this description. The following are the principal dimensions : Width of seats on top, outside, 39 in. Turn-under, on each side, 2 in. Runners, $1\frac{1}{8}$ x $1\frac{3}{8}$ in. Knees, $1\frac{1}{4}$ x $2\frac{1}{8}$ in. on top ; $1\frac{1}{8}$ in. square at bottom. Beams, $1\frac{1}{8}$ x $2\frac{1}{4}$ in. Shoes, $1\frac{1}{8}$ x $\frac{5}{8}$ in.

Painting.—Body panels, umber brown, made by adding to burnt umber a very little Indian-red. Frame (shown in the engraving by wide white lines), dark olive green, made by the mixture of yellow ochre and black with a drop of red. Chamfers on frame, black. Stripe on panels, $\frac{1}{8}$-inch gold, edged with straw color and vermilion. Runners, vermilion, glazed with carmine, and striped with fine lines of gold bronze ; bolt-heads, steps, etc., black.

Trimming.—Brown plush or velvetine, tufted with crimson tufts, and corded with patent leather. Mountings, silver.

The Hub
October 1879

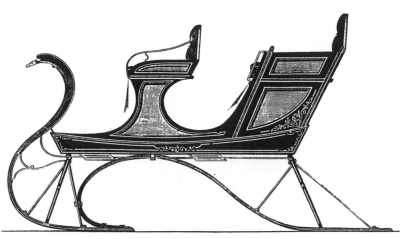

No. 73. PONY SLEIGH, WITH BRYANT'S IMPROVED SLEIGH-RUNNERS.

SCALE, ONE-HALF INCH.

To the Editor: The feature of the accompanying design is the application of Bryant's new sleigh-runners, which were fully described in your last number, page 307.

Dimensions.—Width of seats, 38 in. Turn-under, 3½ in. on each side. Runners, 1 x ½ in. Knees, ⅞ x 1¾ in., tapered off to ⅞ x 1 in. Beams, ⅞ x 1¾ in. Shoes, ⅝ x 1⅛ in. Track, 3 ft. 6 in., out to out.

Painting.—Paint the parts shown in tint with crimson lake ; and all other parts, shown in black, with dark ultramarine blue ; scroll work and broad stripes in gold, edged with fine lines of cream color and vermilion, one on each side. Paint the runners with vermilion glazed, and fine-line with bronze or imitation gold. C. W. V.

BRYANT'S IMPROVED SLEIGH-RUNNERS (*UNPATENTED*).

To the Editor.—Dear Sir: I inclose a sketch of J. L. Bryant's Improved Sleigh-runner, Hillsdale, Mich. The one he first used it on is a four-passenger, piano-box style. The hind runner of this sample job is in one piece, and has a double curve. It is bolted to the knee, as shown by Fig. I, and jointed to the front runner. He used two knees in the form of a trestle leg, as shown, but I think one would be sufficient, as shown by Fig. II. The bent runner is bolted at the center bench or cross-bar.

Mr. Bryant devised this as an improvement on the usual bob-sleds, from which he conceived the idea of non-continuous runners, fastened rigidly. He first used one of this style in the

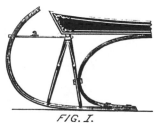

FIG. I.

winter of 1878-79, and says he found it far superior to the old style, especially on rough and rutty roads. With it, inequalities in the road were scarcely perceptible. As regards beauty, it is claimed that the double-curved runners add graceful sweeps, and in fact the very line of beauty, and if the lines of the body are made harmonious, the vehicle as a whole should be tasteful and attractive.

The construction is identical with the old style of runners, excepting the attachment of the forward part of the back runner, which is bolted to the front knee and to the front runner, near its heel. It is not patented.

I will endeavor to prepare for you a drawing of a Boston Pony Sleigh, fitted with this new runner, in time for your next, or November, number. Very truly yours, · C. W. V.

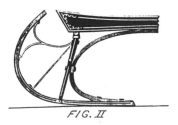

FIG. II

The Hub
November 1879

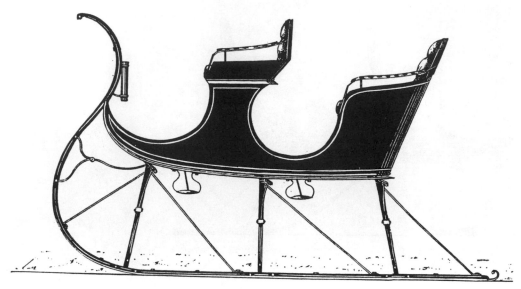

NO. 55.—FOUR-PASSENGER PORTLAND SLEIGH.—BUILT BY PRICE & SHAW, OF ST. JOHN, N. B.

SCALE, ONE-HALF INCH.

No. 55.—FOUR-PASSENGER PORTLAND SLEIGH.

THE accompaning design, kindly furnished us by Messrs. Price & Shaw, carriage and sleigh-builders, of St. John, New Brunswick, was accompanied by the following description, which they thus modestly introduce : "We do not have any draftsman with us, and therefore our sketches of the sleighs do not look any too well. We have consequently written out the description of each as fully and accurately as we can, and hope they will answer for you."

The height of the dasher is 4 ft. 4 in. Width of dasher, 2 ft. 3 in. Space between dasher and front of seat, 19 in. Width of panel under front seat, 12¼ in. Height of panel under front seat, 17½ in. Width of panel at back seat, 15¼ in. Height of panel at back seat, 17½ in. The space between the front and back seat, 20½ in. The panel is cut down in front of seats to 4¼ in. The panel of front seat is 5½ in. at front and 8 in. at back of seat, with a top back 7½ in. deep. The front seat is 15½ in. wide, and is fastened with three hinges, and turns to the front. There is an outside rave which is 1⅝ in. from the body at the front bench, 2 in. at the center bench, and 1½ in. at the back bench. The width of the body is 2 ft. 11 in. from outside to outside on the bottom, and flares to 3 ft. 10 in. outside at seat. The front seat-riser is 3 ft. 3⅜ in. across the top.

The front bench is 19¾ in. high, and 14½ in. from bend of runner. The middle bench is 19¼ in. high, and 2 ft. 1 in. from the front bench on top, and 2 ft. 4 in. from it on the runner. The back bench is 20¼ in. high, and 2 ft. from the middle bench on top, and 2 ft. 3½ in. from it on the runner. The runner projects 14½ in. back of the back bench.

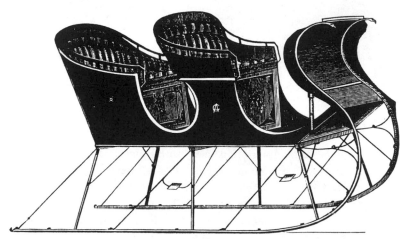

No. 68. FOUR-PASSENGER PORTLAND SLEIGH.

BUILT BY A. P. MARSHALL & CO., OF LANCASTER, N. H.—SCALE, ONE-HALF INCH.

THE accompanying plate represents a standard style of four-passenger sleigh, of the Portland pattern, which Messrs. A. P. Marshall & Co., of Lancaster, N. H., are now building in preparation for the coming winter's trade. Our engraving has been reproduced fac-simile from a drawing made for us by Mr. Marshall's own hand, and we cannot but add that he has reason to be proud of his skill in this direction.

The drawing is made carefully to the scale of one-half inch to the foot, and the principal dimensions not shown in our cut are as follow : Width of body at bottom, 30 in. Width of body at seat-rail, 38 in. Runners, 1 x ⅞ in. Dash, 24 in. Track, 40 in.

Painting.—Panels, a deep shade of bottle green ; moldings, Indian red, glazed with carmine. Runners, vermilion glazed, striped with dark green, similar in shade to the panel color.

Trimming.—Dark green cloth or morocco, and plain carpet of same color. Mountings, silver.

The Hub
September 1881

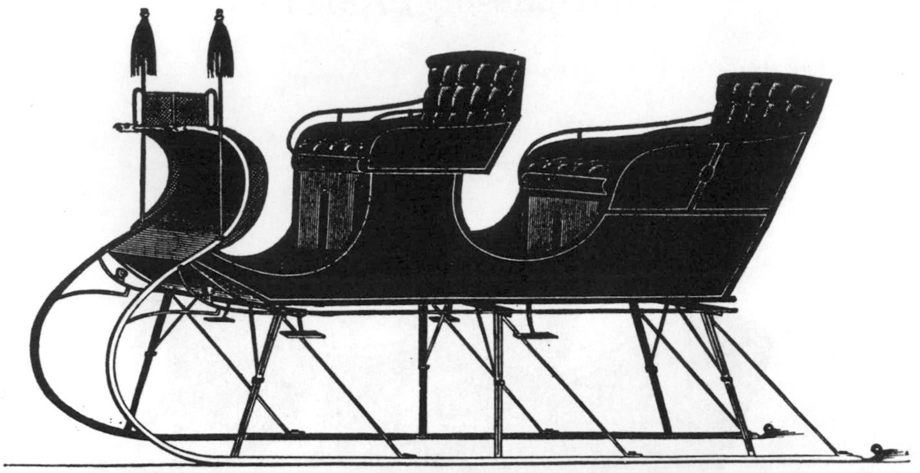

Plate No. 39. FOUR-PASSENGER PORTLAND SLEIGH.—Scale one-half inch.

FOUR-PASSENGER SLEIGHS of this description met with universal favor last year, and will no doubt retain their popularity during the coming season. The Portland pattern, as a whole, is not an elaborate one, but is characterized by simplicity and strength. It should be remembered that all such sleighs, with plain body and running-part, require great skill and taste in finish; and first-class material and exquisite taste in the trimming department, combined with excellent painting, will be requisite to give this sleigh the elegant appearance necessary to make it attractive.

If preferred, the body can be shortened one or two inches, and in that case the front seat must be hinged to the body, and so arranged as to admit of being lifted to give sufficient room when entering the sleigh. The front seat should preferably have round corners, as this finish will not only give more room in entering, but will also serve to prevent tearing the dresses of lady passengers, which is more likely to occur with sharp corners.

The frame-work is made up in the usual way. The bottomsides are $1\frac{1}{2}$ in. deep, by $1\frac{1}{4}$ in. thick; and the corner-pillars $1\frac{1}{4}$ in. square. The front pillars on the hind seat run up to the top of the side panels. The seat-rail is mortised into the pillars. The pillars are $\frac{7}{8}$ in. thick, by $\frac{7}{8}$ in. wide at the bottom, and $1\frac{1}{4}$ in. at the height of the seat-rail. From the top of the seat they are then lightened to $\frac{1}{2}$ in. at the top of the side panel. The seat-rail is $\frac{7}{8}$ x $1\frac{1}{2}$ in. The supports for the front seat are $\frac{7}{8}$ in. thick and $\frac{7}{8}$ x $1\frac{1}{8}$ in. wide. The top cross-bars are $\frac{7}{8}$ x $1\frac{3}{8}$ in.; and the cross-bars connecting the bottomsides are $1\frac{1}{2}$ in. thick by 2 in. wide. All the uprights are either rounded on the inside, or chamfered between the seat-rails and bottomsides, the first-named method being preferable, as it gives a better finish. The panels are $\frac{7}{16}$ in. thick, and mitered at the corners. Round corners for the body will also look well. In this case, the back should have from $\frac{3}{4}$ to 1 in. swell. A slightly swelled back-panel will look well for a square-cornered body. The moldings around the body are $\frac{3}{4}$ in. wide by a full $\frac{1}{4}$ in. thick, and rounded on the outside $\frac{1}{16}$ in. To make a good job, the moldings must be glued and clamped wherever the clamps can be applied; and then, after being cleaned off, receive a few nails. This will take a little more time than if the panels were glued and nailed without the use of clamps, but the result is more satisfactory. If preferred, the moldings may be entirely omitted, where extreme plainness or economy is desired.

Dimensions.—Width of body on top, at the hind seat, 40 in.; and at the bottom, 32 in., from out to out. Width of body on top, at the front seat, 34 in. Width of the front seat at the bottom, $34\frac{1}{2}$ in., and at the top, $38\frac{1}{2}$ in., from out to out. The seat-frame extends outside of seat panels $\frac{3}{4}$ in. The runners are 1 x $\frac{7}{8}$ in. The uprights for the benches are $\frac{7}{8}$ in. thick by $\frac{7}{8}$ in. wide at the bottom; and $\frac{7}{8}$ in. thick by $1\frac{1}{8}$ in. wide at the top. The cross-pieces are $\frac{7}{8}$ in. thick by $1\frac{1}{4}$ in. deep, and all made of hickory. The shoe for the runner is $\frac{7}{8}$ x $\frac{5}{16}$ in., steel. The side-stays are made of $\frac{1}{2}$ in. round iron. The cross-stays are $\frac{7}{16}$ in. round iron.

Finish.—Painting: Body panels, black, with a carmine fine-line, $\frac{1}{2}$ in. from the molding, on all the panels. Runners, carmine, with double fine lines of black, $\frac{5}{8}$ in. apart, centered with a heavier fine line of gold. Bolt-heads and nuts, touched with gold. Trimming, red plush throughout. The carpet should match the color of the plush; and the figures, if possible, should match the striping of the running-part. Yellow plumes will look well. Mountings, brass.

The Hub
August 1883

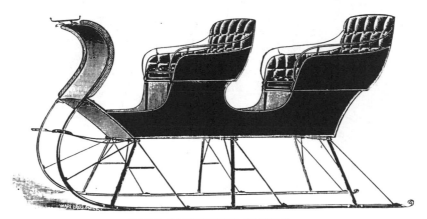

FOUR-PASSENGER SLEIGH.

PLATE No. 30.—HALF-INCH SCALE.

With this plate we illustrate a style as made by Messrs. J. L. Spencer & Co., Oneida, N. Y., who kindly furnished us the drawing. It is a well-proportioned four-passenger sleigh, and will compare favorably with other styles. The sides of the body and seats are molded with ⅝ by ₁³⁄₁₆-inch moldings, which are slightly rounded. The runners, knees, bench bars, stays and braces are as usual, all straight.

Painting.—Body and seats, black. Moldings striped a fine line of yellow. Runners: yellow, striped two hair lines, ₁³⁄₁₆ inch apart.

Trimming.—Claret plush. The backs are of the plaited block pattern, with buttons to match. The seat squabs are made in diamonds, also plaited. The cushions have plaited block tops, with 2-inch front facings and 1-inch raisers; these raisers are also applied to the falls, which are fastened to the cushions. Rugs, red carpet, bound with leather. The dash has wire screens of brass or silver.

Mountings.—Silver.

Width across the bracket-front, 26½ inches; across the bottom, 27 inches; across the top, 30 inches; this will give 1½ inches turn-under each side of the body. Width across the seat at bottom, 33 inches; across the top, 38 inches. Seats not contracted, but it will be found, when the seats are not contracted, that they will be wider across the back than across the front, and should be contracted at least ¾ inch on each side. No rocker plates. Track, 38 inches. Runners, ⅞ inch deep by ¾ inch thick.

Carriage Monthly
July 1885

FOUR–PASSENGER SLEIGH.

PLATE No. 30.—HALF-INCH SCALE.

Sleighs of this style have been made by Messrs. Emond & Quinsler, Boston, Mass., we making a few alterations to the upper sweep of seat. The sides of the body are straight, flaring out on top. The seats have full paneled backs, and the sides are slightly contracted. Moldings are nailed to the sides, and also to the seats, but they can be worked on solid on the seats. The knees are slightly curved, and the runners bent the usual shape.

Painting—Body: black. Runners: green, striped ¼-inch black line ; body striped a fine line of green.

Trimming.—Green plush. The full back is of the plaited block-and-pipe design, tufted with green plush buttons. The trimming for this sleigh is made comparatively light. The cushions have plain block tops and leather welts ; the fronts are plain plush, and about 1¾ inches high. The falls are as plain as possible, the edges being hemmed ; they have plain raisers around the edges and stitched ; they are sewed to the cushions. The rugs are green carpet, bound with fringe.

Mountings.—Silver. ———

Body: across bottom, 34 inches ; across top, 38½ inches. Seats: across bottom front, 40 inches ; across top, 42 inches ; back at bottom, 39 inches ; back at top, 41 inches. Amount of turn-under of body each side, 2¼ inches ; of seats, 1 inch, and contracted ½ inch each side. Runners: track, 40 inches, out to out. Runners, 1⅛ inches thick by 1⅛ inches deep. Shoes, ¼ inch by 1¼ half round edges. Width across top, 30 inches. Ovals, 17 inches deep, out to out, taken from ¾ by ½-inch oval iron. Center braces, ½-inch round iron. Shaft braces, 1⁷⁄₈-inch round iron.

Carriage Monthly
July 1886

Plate No. 37. FOUR-PASSENGER SURREY SLEIGH.—Scale, three-quarters inch.

THIS design of a four-passenger sleigh is original in many of its features, and should prove one of the most salable patterns of this character.

It is made with three knees and three beams on each side, as usual. The construction of the body is plain, being straight on the bottom, with a slight swell and turn-under. It has a large bracket front, and each rocker should consequently be made in two pieces. The bracket projects ⅜ in. over the rocker, to allow for the thickness of the panel. The panel is ⅜ in.

There are two uprights framed under the front seat to the sill, with a cross-piece framed on top, dressed up on the outside with a ¼-in. swell, to give the necessary fullness to the side.

At the front of the rear seat, a pillar is framed to the sill, extending nearly to the top of the panel. From the top of the seat this pillar is lightened out to a feather-edge. From this pillar, at the bottom of the back seat, a piece is framed to the back corner-pillar, the back end being 1 in. lower than the front, this being the pitch of the seat. There is also a bar framed at the back, to support the back end of the seat, and one in front to support the front end. A board seat is used, with a lid. The front seat is made similar to a buggy, and separate from the body, with the moldings worked on, ¾-in. whitewood being used. There is also a box under the front seat. The bottom rests on the cross-beams, and has a strap underneath the bottom.

Dimensions.—Width of body on top, 39 in.; ditto at back, 38 in.; ditto at bottom, 36 in. The front seat projects 1¼ in. over the side. Runners, 1 × 1⅛ in. Shoes, 1 × ⅜ in. Track, 38 in., from out to out.

Painting.—Sides and rear portion of the body, dark green; and moldings, black, striped with a fine line of carmine. Runners, carmine, striped with two lines of black.

Trimming.—Green cloth, made up for the back, cushions and quarters in square blocks. A cord welt is used on the cushions. Carpet, plain green. Mountings, silver

The Hub
August 1887

FOUR-PASSENGER SLEIGH WITH SLAT SIDES.

The sides of the body are swelled both lengthwise and vertically, for the better display of the painting and varnishing. A short plate may be fastened to the inside of the front end of the bottom sill. The uprights and corner-pillars are let into the bottom-sill, and a ½ in. panel is glued over the framework. The slats may be either imitated by painting or be worked on. The moldings are both glued and nailed on. To avoid weakening the panel where the slatwork is introduced, this part is strengthened by gluing a light extra panel to the inside of the side panel, with the grain of the inside panel crossing that of the outside one. The rear panel is either mitered to the side panel, or glued over the joint, and then covered by the side moldings.

The sides of the seats are made of thick whitewood, and the moldings are worked on. To increase the attractiveness of the sleigh, the seats are made to project over the sides about 2 in. in front and ½ in. at the rear, which will give the seats a contraction of 1½ in. on each side. The sides are glued to the corner-pillars and seat-frame pieces, and the rear panel is then fitted between the sides.

To produce the scroll which projects over the top of the seats at the front end, a piece of hard wood is halved to the inside of the sides, with a shoulder at the top end. This shoulder is of such depth as to bring the piece within ¼ in. from the outside of the moldings. The runners terminate at the front end of the body, and are secured there by plates.

The ironwork of such a sleigh should always be drafted on the blackboard before beginning the work, and the position of every bolt and the proper position for fastening it to the runners should then be indicated. In forging the irons, the lines thus laid down on the draft will be found to greatly facilitate and expedite the work; and the irons can then be forged, finished and bolted to the runners, and the body placed on top of the stays and bolted to its place without unnecessary fitting. On the other hand, without such a draft, the body will need to be placed on trestles of the proper height, with the runners held in position meanwhile, and the irons must then be fitted in the best way possible. This latter is an awkward and slow method, and the result is seldom entirely satisfactory.

Dimensions.—Width of body on top, 37 in.; ditto at bottom, 33½ in.; ditto seat on top, 46 in.; and ditto at bottom, 41 in. Runners, 1 and 1¼ in. Shoes, 1 × ½ in., cast-steel. Side-stays, ½ × ¾ in., oval. Cross-stays, ⅝ × ¾ in. Track, 40 in., from out to out.

Finish.—Painting of body and moldings, black; and seats, slat-work and front of the dash-panel, dark green, striped with carmine. Runners, carmine, striped with two round lines of black. Trimming, green cloth. The backs and cushions should be made full and soft, and the figures used should therefore be of good size, especially for the backs and cushion tops; while similar figures, but of smaller dimensions, may be used for the side quarters. The cushion fronts and falls are faced with broad-lace. Carpet, green, with red figures. Mountings, silver. Plumes, black, red and green.

The Hub
July 1886
(drawing on next page)

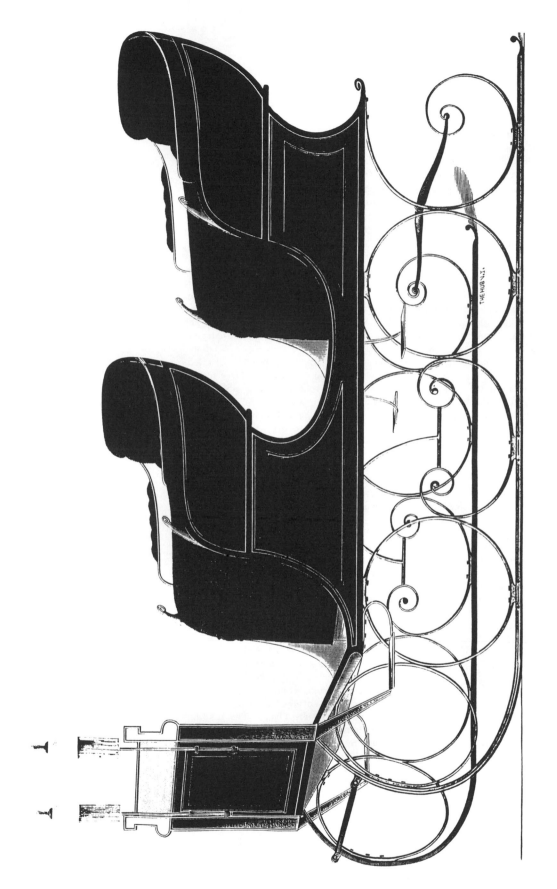

PLATE NO. LXXIII.   FOUR-PASSENGER SLEIGH WITH SLAT SIDES.

SCALE. ONE INCH.

FOUR-PASSENGER SLEIGH WITH OGEE BACK.

WHILE this sleigh is by no means plain, it demands much less labor than those preceding. The sides are straight lengthwise, but inclined sidewise, and the finish on the sides is produced by the moldings only.

The rockers of this job are made of one piece on each side, and provided with a plate on the inside. The thickness of the rockers is $\frac{7}{8}$ in., and $2\frac{3}{4}$ in. high as far as the front boot-pillar; and, from that point, the height is regulated by the top and bottom lines of the toe-board rocker. The side panels have a thickness of $\frac{1}{2}$ in., and project $\frac{5}{8}$ in. over the rear panel.

The side molding at the rear corner-pillar is on a line with the rear corner, which makes the molding inclosing the rear panel $1\frac{3}{8}$ in. The rear panel is fitted between the side panels and glued to the corner-pillar. The top cross-molding at the rear of the body is curved upward about 3 in., and is somewhat heavier in the center than at the ends. Another molding is nailed at the back, on a line with the center molding of the sides. The introduction of a thin panel of course requires further framework than the rear corner-pillar.

The middle pillar and arm-rail are also made of hard wood. A thickness of $\frac{5}{8}$ in. is sufficient for the arm-rail, while $\frac{7}{8}$ in. is required for the middle pillar. If, however, it is preferred that the rear or molded portion of the body be swelled, then thick whitewood should be used, about $2\frac{1}{4}$ in., which will prove sufficient for producing a nice swell. The thin panel is then retained, but it does not extend further than where the line of the panel intersects with the molding of the sides. The thick whitewood pieces are then glued to the sides, and cleaned off when dry. The moldings are worked on. The front or scroll end should not project less than $\frac{7}{8}$ in. outside of the thin panel. The thickness of the sides at the rear is $\frac{3}{4}$ in., and these form the moldings for the back. In this, as in the first-mentioned method, the rear panel is fitted between the sides and glued to the corner-pillars.

The front seat is made like a buggy seat, and with either curved or square corners. The runners are finished at the top with a scroll. Wooden trestles are used, and these are strengthened by straight side-stays. T-plates are placed at the inside of the runners at the bottom, to strengthen the uprights. On top, the trestles are strengthened by cross-stays as usual.

Dimensions.—Width of body on top of the middle pillar at the rear quarter, 42 in.; ditto at back, 39 in.; ditto under the front seat, 35 in.; and ditto at bottom, 33 in. Width of front seat on top, $40\frac{1}{2}$ in., and ditto at bottom, 36 in., exclusive of moldings. Rocker-plates, $2 \times \frac{3}{8}$ in., fastened with $1\frac{1}{2}$ in. Nos. 14 and 16 screws. Runners, $1 \times 1\frac{5}{16}$ in. Shoes, $1 \times \frac{3}{8}$ in., cast-steel. Side-stays, 3 in., round iron. Cross-stays, $\frac{7}{16}$ in., round iron. Track, 39 in., from out to out.

Finish.—Painting of side and rear panels of the back portion of the body, dark green; and moldings and boot panels, black. The moldings are striped with a fine line of carmine. Runners, carmine, striped with two round lines of black. Trimming, green cloth. Squares are used for the upholstery of the back, cushions and quarters. The front of the cushion is left plain, being merely finished at the top and bottom edges with a cloth-covered cord welt. The falls are finished with one raiser. Carpet, plain green. Mountings, silver. Plumes, black, green and red.

The Hub
July 1886
(drawing on next page)

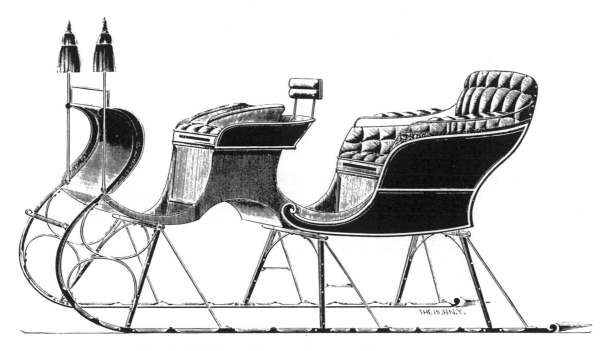

Plate No. 28. **FOUR-PASSENGER SLEIGH WITH OGEE BACK.**—Scale, five-eighths inch.

FOUR-PASSENGER BOB-RUNNER SLEIGH.

(See Fashion Plate No. 38.)

THIS attractive and comfortable pattern of bob-runner sleigh, built by the Fisher Mfg. Co., Limited, of Homer, N. Y., is known by them as their "Russian Portland Sleigh," deriving that title, no doubt, from its Russian dasher. It is fitted with their "improved patent bobs."

The bobs are substantial in construction. The beams are made of bent wood, two in the front bob and two in the rear, and the beams are bent so as to form half the knee and also the inside stay. At each side of this beam is a steel plate, that runs clear across the body and continues to the runner, forming a double stay, which also answers for the continuation of the knee. At the end of the beams, the wood is diminished and the thickness of the steel increased, thus retaining throughout the same thickness of the beam. At the intersection of the two stays which form the knee, is a stay intersecting with the straight portion of the beam and supporting the same.

The raves are made of bent wood, $\frac{3}{4} \times$ 3-in. oak, screwed to the beams; and, in front, they intersect with the runner, and are fastened on top of the runner. The shoe of the runner is made to fit on top of the rave, about 6 in. on the front end, and riveted to the rave, which forms a substantial corner. The rave is shaved out on the inside the thickness of the runner, with a very little swell on the outside.

The front bob is hung in the usual way, with a fifth-wheel and a swivel king-bolt; but the top fifth-wheel is provided with two small pulleys attached to the body, at each side, directly over the bottom fifth-wheel, which assist the front bob to work easily. The rear bob is also hung, as usual, being required to work only one way, and to always keep parallel with the body.

The construction of the body resembles that of carriage-bodies of this class, although, as a rule, sleigh-bodies are of course made with somewhat less labor. The following hints will prove ample for the instruction of the body-maker.

The sills are made of $1\frac{1}{4} \times$ 3-in. oak, of the best quality. The bracket is made to halve on to the sill. There are two pillars framed to the sill, directly under the front seat, with a connecting piece framed on top. Each of these pillars should have a slight swell, to give a good appearance to the side. Underneath, the back seat is framed in a similar way, except the corner-pillar, which is made thick enough to form the molding into which the side-panel and the back panels are grooved. The panel in the bottom is grooved into the sill, and set in with white-lead. The sill projects in the rear to form a scroll. All the other moldings on the body are glued on.

The seats are made separately and fastened on afterward. The seats are made of $1\frac{1}{4}$-in. whitewood, with a hard-wood pillar glued on the back corner, forming the back molding, and made high enough to take the high back. The sides are lightened out as much as practicable. The pillar at the seats is glued on with a miter joint, which prevents the panel from checking, and is finished on top with a scroll. The seat projects $1\frac{1}{2}$ in. over the side.

The body is hung 22 in. from the ground.

Dimensions.—Width of body on top, front of seat, 36 in.; and on bottom, 30 in. The sides are concaved. The bottom is straight. Width of seat on top, 45 in.; and on bottom, 39 in. Depth of seat inside, $18\frac{1}{2}$ in. back; and 18 in. front. Seat-room inside, 35 in. Height of dash, $18\frac{1}{2}$ in. Size of runners, $1\frac{1}{4} \times 1\frac{3}{8}$ in. Shoes, $1\frac{1}{4} \times \frac{7}{16}$ in., steel. Track, 37 in.

Painting.—Body, black, with a fine line of straw-color around the moldings. Seat-panels, green. Moldings, black, striped with a fine line of straw-color. Running-part, maroon, striped with two lines of carmine.

Trimming.—Maroon cloth, made up in blocks, three rows; and cushions to match. The fall is trimmed plain, with broad-lace around the edges, and a star in the center. Carpet, maroon, with red figures. Plumes, green, brown and red. Mountings, silver.

The Hub
August 1887
(drawing on next page)

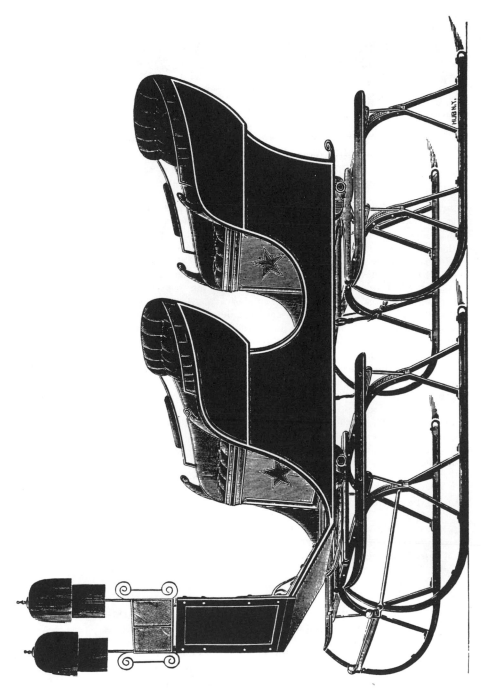

Plate No. 38. FOUR-PASSENGER BOB-RUNNER SLEIGH.—Scale, three-quarters inch.

FOUR-PASSENGER SLEIGH.

PLATE NO. 28.—VOL. 24.—HALF-INCH SCALE.

The outlines of this body are an imitation of the present style of surrey body, with the exception of the front, which, of course, is made heavier to give it the characteristics of a sleigh body. The sides of the body are concave, but only slightly. The construction of the body is the same as the regular surrey body; bottom-sides 1¾ inches deep by 1½ inches thick; back and side panels ½ inch thick, glued against the frames. The back corner joint is mitered when made without moldings, but when molded the back panel can be made to pass over the side panels, and the corner molding will cover the end-wood. The seats are constructed the usual way; the seat frame is made out of four pieces; the side quarters are solid, and the moldings worked on, with the exception of the center molding and medallion. The back panels are glued against the corner pillars; they are only a ⁵⁄₁₆-inch panel, and are not mitred at the corners, but the panel is placed direct against the molding. When better work is desired, a light groove can be put into the side quarter moldings the depth of ⅛ inch, which will obviate the joint. The knees are slightly curved, which is done on almost all sleighs at present. The runners have a well-formed curve, and for size, track, and widths of body see dimension page.

Painting.—Body: black. Runners: deep carmine, striped two ³⁄₁₆-inch lines of black. Body striped a full, round line of carmine inside the moldings on seat and body panels.

Trimming.—Green cloth. The backs are made diamond shape, tufted with buttons, covered with green cloth, and are made heavy to be comfortable. The cushions have block tops, plaited with 1¾-inch high front facings, and 1-inch plain raisers. The falls are fastened to the cushions, and have 1-inch plain raisers. Rugs, green carpet, with yellow figures.

Mountings.—Silver. ———

Width across bottom of body, 30 inches; across top, 33 inches. Across seats at bottom, 36 inches; on top of seats, front, 42 inches. Sides of seats slightly contracted toward the back, to give less width across the back. Runners: width of track, 38 inches, from out to out. Thickness and depth of runners 1 by 1⅛ inches. Shoes, 1 by ⁵⁄₁₆-inch round edge steel. Knees: convex, and ¾ inch scant thick, rounded with the exception of the flat part of stay. Stays, ⁵⁄₁₆-inch steel.

Four-passenger Sleighs

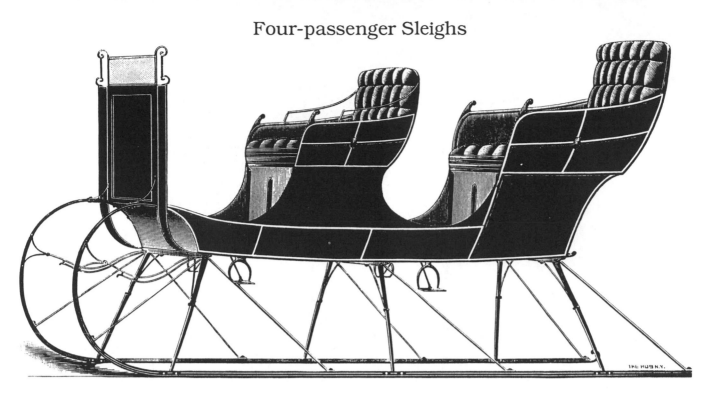

PLATE No. 37.   FOUR-PASSENGER SLEIGH.—SCALE, THREE-QUARTERS INCH.

WE are indebted to Messrs. H. A. Worthen & Co., of Dover, N. H., for this design of four-passenger sleigh, which is quite new in outline.

The sills of body are ash, $1\frac{1}{4} \times 2\frac{1}{4}$ in., with a slight sweep to the bottom, and a $\frac{1}{4}$-in. swell to the sides. The end-sills are the same thickness. At the rear of body a corner-pillar is framed to the sill and extends to the top of the body. At the front of the rear seat is a post framed to the sill and extending to the top of the body. A piece $1\frac{1}{4} \times 1\frac{1}{2}$ in. is framed from the corner-post to the center, to which a seat is fastened. The back end of body is concaved, and the back seat projects $\frac{3}{8}$ in. over the rear of the body, the seat forming a $\frac{3}{8}$-in. molding. At the front of body under the front seat are two posts framed to the sill and extending to the top of the body. A piece is framed across, the same as the rear of the body, which the seat is fastened to. The runners are $\frac{3}{4} \times 1\frac{1}{8}$ in. and extend to the front sill of the body, and where it intersects with the top of panel it is sawed out $\frac{3}{8}$ in. from the face of the runner and $\frac{3}{8}$ in. wide, the thickness of the side-panel. The side-panel is set in and clamped fast to the runner. The molding in center of body is glued on, this molding forming a true sweep with the runner. The knees are mortised into the beams and runners. The beams and knees are $1\frac{5}{8} \times \frac{7}{8}$ in. at the thickest part, with $\frac{7}{16}$-in. stays on the inside from the knee to the beam. Center moldings in the body and seats are glued on.

The seats have solid sides and project $1\frac{1}{2}$ in. outside the top of the body. The seat-frame forms the bottom molding. A hardwood piece is glued on the inside of the body, and forms the scroll in front. A hardwood piece is also glued on the back corner and extends to the top of high back. The moldings in the rear of seats are made to match the sides. The stays are made of $\frac{3}{8}$-in. round iron. The shoes are $\frac{3}{4} \times \frac{5}{16}$-in. iron. At the front of seats a molding is glued on flush with the outside of seats, and finished with the center moldings of the body, forming a concave at front of seats. The inside of the body is partitioned off under the front and back seats, forming a large box. The dash is wood, with leather wings at each side, with silver mountings.

Dimensions.—Width of body on top, 29 in.; and at bottom, 26 in. Width of seat on top, 38 in.; and at bottom, 33 in. Track, 39 in.

Painting.—Body, black, with a fine line of carmine; running part, dark green, with a carmine stripe.

Trimming.—Dark green cloth is used throughout, made up in blocks for the cushion and back. The sides are trimmed plain. Carpet, green. Mountings, silver.

The Hub
August 1888

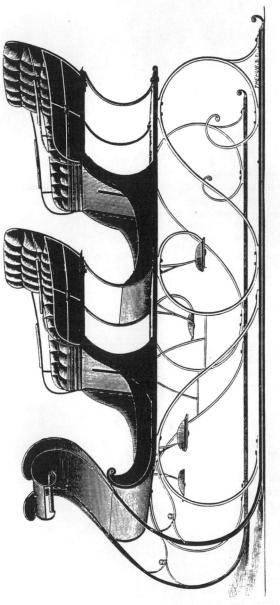

THE HUB, N.Y.

PLATE No. 35. FOUR-PASSENGER TOBOGGAN SLEIGH.—SCALE, THREE-QUARTERS INCH.

THIS plate represents a new style of toboggan sleigh. It is similar to a four-passenger ordinary sleigh. Its principal changes are the style of the body, which represents a toboggan. Together with the running part, the lines are all in harmony and present an elaborate four-passenger sleigh. The body is made separate from the running part and is bolted to the runners with $\frac{5}{16}$-in. bolts. The sills of the body are $1\frac{1}{4} \times 3$ in., and extend the full length of the body, with a cross-bar at the front and back of the same size. There are also two in the center at equal distances apart, which are mortised into the side sills, thus forming a solid sill for the body.

At the front of each seat is a pillar framed to the sill and extended to the bottom of the seat-frame. At the rear of seats is a stay, $\frac{3}{4}$-in. oval iron, bolted to the sill and to a piece at the bottom of seat-frame which is framed to the front pillar.

At the front of the sill a curved piece is framed to the same, and extends up to the neck of the runner as shown in design, and forms a continuous molding of the sill to this point. The molding is $\frac{1}{2}$ in. thick, and at the inside of the molding a panel is glued on, and a light piece of ash is glued on the top edge from the pillar to the front of body. A scroll is worked on the top edge from the pillar to the top edge of the panel. A $\frac{1}{2}$-in. plate is screwed on the top edge of the body. The back portion of the body is made in the same manner. The bottom is screwed on lengthwise with the body, level with the top of the sills.

The seats are made of ash, $\frac{7}{8}$ in. thick and 4 in. wide. The frame projects 2 in. outside the top of the body and the skirt is finished up according to taste. The seat-panels are $\frac{3}{4}$-in. whitewood with a light swell on the outside. The outside moldings are glued on. The center ones can also be glued on with a medallion in the center. A hardwood piece is mitered in the back corners and extends to the top of the high backs. The back panel also extends to the top; a molding running across the back on a line with the top molding of the side, with 2 in. arch. The moldings on the low panel at the back are molded to match the sides. The rear seat is done in the same manner.

At the inside of the body are four stays, two on each side, extending from the center cross-piece to the top of the pillar; this stiffens the body and prevents it from swinging. The runners are $\frac{3}{4} \times 1\frac{1}{4}$ in.

The shoes are $\frac{3}{4} \times \frac{5}{16}$ in. The stays are $\frac{3}{4}$-in. oval iron. The steps are made fast to the body.

Dimensions.—Width of body on top, 28 in.; and at bottom, 26 in. Width of seat on top, 38 in.; and at bottom, 31. Rocker-plates, $2 \times \frac{3}{8}$ in., fastened with No. 16, $1\frac{1}{2}$-in. screws. Track, 39 in.

Painting.—Body, dark green, with a yellow stripe.

Trimming.—Green cloth is used throughout, made up in blocks. Carpet, green. Mountings, silver.

The Hub
August 1888

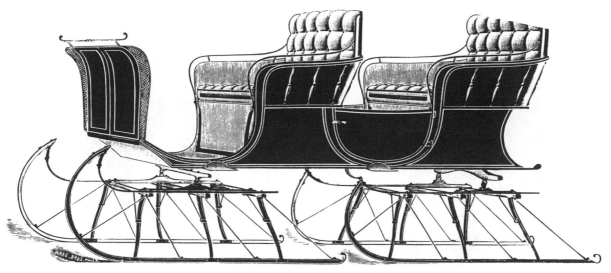

FOUR PASSENGER BOB SLEIGH.

PLATE NO. 26.—VOL. 28.—FIVE-EIGHTHS-INCH SCALE.

PLATE NO. 26. FOUR-PASSENGER BOB SLEIGH.

The body is constructed with straight surfaces, flaring out only on top, and is molded as shown, with ¾-inch wide moldings, which are rounded on top surface. The door joint is covered with the upper molding, and lower hinge must be bent backward to allow the door to open square. The bottom sides are 2 inches square, beveled from the outside for side flare. The upright and the upper pieces are 2½ by ¾ inch, and panels glued over the entire frame, and canvassed from the inside. The moldings are glued and bradded. The back corner molding is solid—that is, a corner is cut out of a square piece, avoiding the angle joint. The seats are constructed from 1½-inch thick planks, and the corners are jointed with corner blocks, as is usually done on such seats for carriage or sleigh bodies. The moldings can be worked or bradded on. The runners are made in the usual way, with knees, either convex concave, or convex only, and ironed with straight stays.

Painting.—Body and seats, black ; space between moldings on seats and body deep blue, and moldings striped light blue. Spindles, deep blue, high lighted with light blue. Runners, deep blue, striped light blue. If striped three lines, make two lines light blue and center line yellow. If center line is striped yellow, high light the spindles on body with yellow, in connection with blue.

Finish.—Dash of wood, and striped, brass wire fenders each side ; seat rails, dash rail, and door handles gold plated.

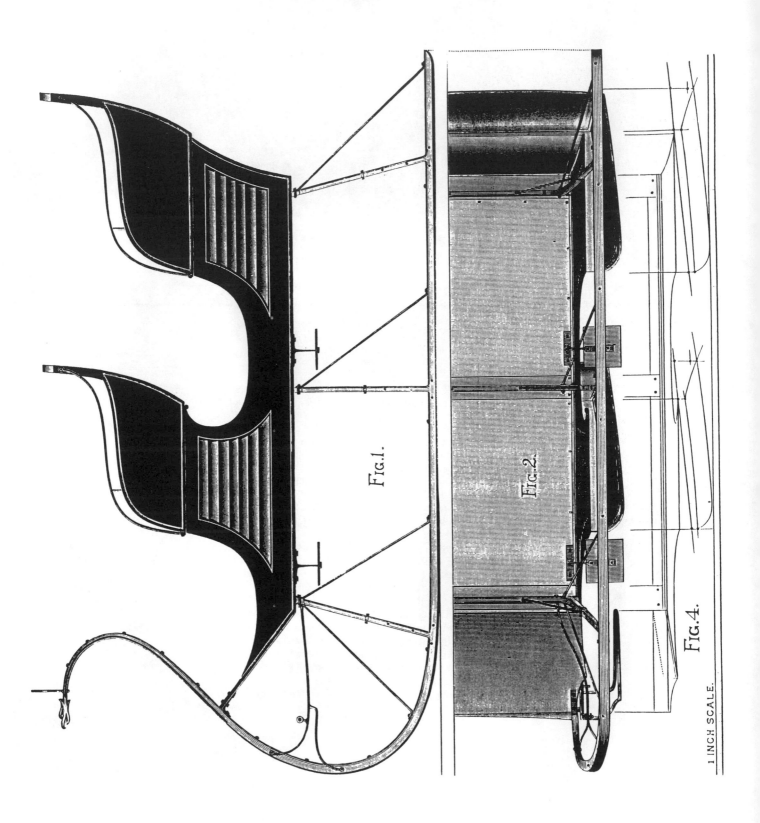

FIG. 1.

FIG. 2.

FIG. 4.

1 INCH SCALE.

Carriage Monthly
August 1889
(continued on next page)

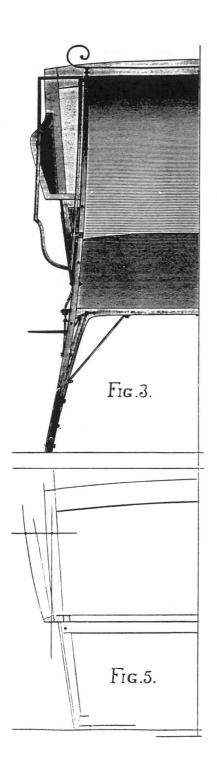

FIG.3.

FIG.5.

Working-Draft of a Light Four-Passenger Sleigh.
ONE—INCH SCALE.

The style of this four-passenger sleigh is shown in plate No. 29, July number of the MONTHLY, and while it is not particularly new, we illustrate it more on account of the details of construction, of which we give five different views.

Fig. 1 is the side elevation; Fig. 2 the bottom view; Fig. 3 the front elevation; Fig. 4 the working lines, showing the horizontal view of the body, and Fig. 5 showing the working lines from the front elevation. These bodies are built very light, and differ a great deal from other designs shown in the illustrations of sleighs in this number. The body is made the same as a surrey body for carriages, and in all cases is paneled. The bottom sides are 1½ inches thick by 1¾ inches deep; seats ¾ inch thick and 1¼ inches wide on top, and the cross-bars are given the same size. The back bottom cross-bar is 3 inches wide and 1¼ inches thick, and the front and also the middle cross-bars are also the same size. These bars must rest on the bolster bars, as shown on the bottom view, Fig. 2. The bottom boards are of poplar, and are ½ inch thick, while the cross-bars are made of ash. The slats are imitation, and are worked on to the panels.

The moldings at the bottom and back edges are glued and braded the center on both ends. The ends are rounded and very short, see Fig. 2. The stays, when made of steel, are ¼-inch round steel, and when iron $\frac{5}{16}$ inch.

Now for those who do not understand how to construct sleighs, we illustrate, Figs. 2 and 3, the details of construction, which can be seen by following the parts and shades. The upper panel between the runners, Fig. 3, is rabbeted into the runners, is $\frac{5}{16}$ inch thick on very light sleighs, or only ¼ inch, and the joints covered with the iron, which stiffens the runners. The shape of the fenders can be seen at Fig. 3, but the shape of the front end is best seen in Fig. 2. The shape of the bench bars and knees is best seen at Fig. 3, but the stays and shaft irons are best seen on Fig. 2; in fact, the bottom view, Fig. 2, gives those who have never built any of these sleighs, a very good inside view of the construction.

In the interest of the body maker, we illustrate Figs. 4 and 5. Fig. 4 gives the horizontal view, or the working lines of the body, without a center line, but it can easily be drawn into it by taking the center width from the body from Fig. 5.

Fig. 5 shows the working lines essential in constructing the body; it gives the turn-under and inclination of seats, the inclination of the back pillar and inclination of the sides of body; in fact the lines complete for constructing the body.

Carriage Monthly
July 1889
(continued on next three pages)

Working Draft of Four-Passenger Sleigh.

ONE-INCH SCALE.

With this illustration, we give a new style of four-passenger sleigh, new in both outlines and construction, and which will be a very good pattern to copy from ; for this reason we show four different views to better understand all the details.

Fig. 1 represents the side elevation, illustrating the new style of body, graceful runners and stays. *Fig. 2* is the bottom view of the body, without the runners ; we have left these off purposely, as they would cover those parts we particularly desired to show. *Fig. 3*, the front view, showing to advantage the width and shape of the runners, fenders, rails, body and stays. *Fig. 4*, the back view, with all the details above mentioned viewed from the back, including the finish of the back panel.

The body is constructed separately from the seats, which facilitates its construction, and its widths are as follows : Body at bottom, at outside of panels, not counting the shell sides, 31 inches ; body on top, outside of panels, 34¾ inches ; amount of flare for each side of the body, 1⅞ inches. Width of body at bottom at shell sides, 34 inches. Width of seats at front, at bottom, 39 inches ; at bottom back, 36¼ inches ; at top back, 40 inches, and at top front, 43½ inches. By these measurements it can at once be seen that the body is straight, top and bottom, and one width back and front. The shell part has side sweep, and also turn-under, and the seats have side sweep and also turn-under. The sides of the body can be made out of ¾-inch poplar boards, and the size of the rocker is about 2 by 2 inches, for a good foundation to bolt the stays to. The shell parts are made of poplar planks, and the shells worked out of the solid. These pieces are marked after a pattern, and dressed after the inclination of the sides of the body, and are glued against the sides before the shells are worked on. The sides of the seat can be framed as illustrated in *Fig. 3 ;* panels with strainers, or its sides of solid poplar planks, and the back panels ⅝ inch thick. In both cases when paneled or solid, the center moldings on the side panels are put on, glued and braded, after the surfaces have been cleaned off.

The bottom view of the body, *Fig. 2*, will give the body-maker a very good idea of its construction ; *A*, the front panel, which is bent around the scroll ; *B*, the bottom bar, to which the panel is fastened, and also the bottom board *C ; D*, the hard wood cross-bar, on which the stays are bolted ; *E*, the bottom boards ; *F*, the cross-bar on which the back stays are bolted, see back view, *Fig. 4 ; H*, the back bar ; *K*, the back panel and back top cross-bar ; *L* is the rocker ; *M, M*, the shape and thickness of the poplar planks on which the shells are worked, and *N, N*, the side quarters. All the widths can be taken from that view, by doubling the amount from the center line, or can also be taken from the front view, *Fig. 3*, or the back view, *Fig. 4*.

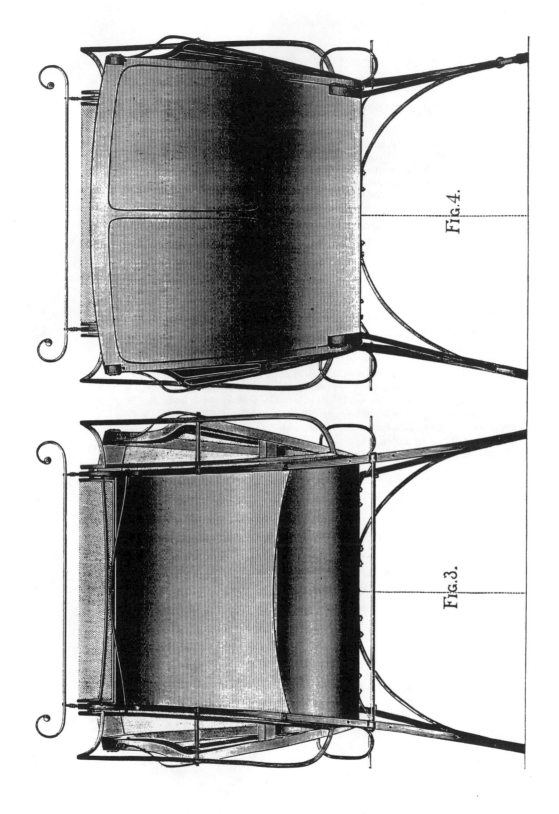

Fig.4.

Fig.3.

WORKING DRAFT OF A FOUR-PASSENGER SLEIGH

WORKING DRAFT OF A FOUR-PASSENGER SLEIGH

The finish of the side quarters, and back panel, if well done, has a very good appearance when varnished. The front end of the body, and the top of the back pillars of the seat, are carved as shown in the illustration.

The runners are bent as shown in the side view, *Fig. 1*, and the front view, *Fig. 3*. It is very essential to the beauty of the sleigh that these runners should be well bent, that is, have artistic curves, and the width across the runner at the front top should not be too wide; the width shown being a very good one. The fenders, seen best on the front view, *Fig. 3*, are of the regular, full size fender iron, and covered with either patent or brown leather. The screen can easily be traced to its size by the wire screen which is cross lined. The rein rails are shaped as illustrated, and have standards which are bolted to the runners. If plumes are used, an extra socket should be provided for them.

The general dimensions are as follows: Width of body across bottom, 31 inches; on top, 34¾ inches; amount of turn-under, 1⅞ inches. Width across the shell sides at bottom 34 inches, and across the seat front at bottom, 39 inches, which gives 2½ inches turn-under each side for the shell part. Width of seat at the front top, 43½ inches; at the back bottom, 36½ inches, and at the back top, 40 inches. These cross widths result in 2½-inches turn-under for each side, 1¾ inches contraction top of the side quarter each side, and the contraction of the seat at the bottom is 1¼ inches on each side. For amount of contraction, we mean here outside contraction, not the inside surfaces of the side quarters. Width of track: 40⅜ inches front, and 40 inches back. Size of runners: 1½ inches thick by 1⅝ inches deep, tapered toward the front ends. Size of stays: ¾ by 1 inch on the top, tapered toward the bottom. Rails on side quarters, front and back, and also the rein-rails, are silver or gold-plated, according to the general finish of the sleigh.

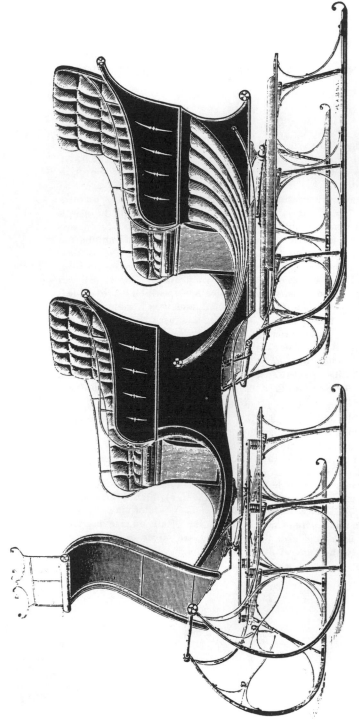

PLATE No. 24. FOUR-PASSENGER SLEIGH HUNG ON BOB RUNNERS. SCALE, THREE-QUARTERS INCH.

The Hub
June 1890
(description on next page)

Four-passenger Sleighs

FOUR-PASSENGER SLEIGH HUNG ON BOB-RUNNERS.

This design of sleigh is well adapted for family use, and is consequently quite roomy, as indicated by the dimensions named below.

The shell is made out of 1¼-in. whitewood, and concaved to ⅝ in. at the bottom. The duster under the front seat is 1¼ in. thick, tapering to ½ in. at the front end of the bracket, and it should be bent from one piece of hard wood. The boot and back sills are set and framed up to the inclination of the sides, and beveled on the top and bottom edges to a horizontal line; use 1⅜ × 3 in. ash and join to the toe-bracket, which should be 1¾ in. thick and framed up square in order to bring the point of the bracket to the width of the boot at the bottom, afterwards dressing it to a wind and to the inclination of the boot sills. A light rocker-plate is used, 1½ in. wide by $\frac{5}{16}$ in. thick, extending to the center of the rear seat.

The front pillars are 1 in. square. The pillars under the back corners of the seats are made to conform to the shape of the sides, and are 1¼ in. thick. The front edges of the pillars are vertical, and they should be 2 in. wide at their narrowest point. The bearings for the seats are made of 1½ × 1¼ in. thick ash, united with cross-bars 1¼ in. thick by 2 in. wide on top. A panel ⅜ in. thick should be screwed against the front pillar of the front seat, extending the full height of the body, to protect occupants of the back seat from a draught. A ½ in. board, 4 in. wide, is screwed to the front pillar of the rear seat at the bottom, forming a convenient receptacle for parcels. A panel 6 in. wide is glued to the rear pillar of the front seat at the top edge of the body, and finished with a molding at the bottom edge, ½ in. wide, half round.

The side panels are made of ⅜ in. whitewood, and extend beyond the back panel 1 in. at the top and ½ inch at the bottom, rounded on the back edge. The back panel should be glued on first. This method breaks the joint at the bottom of the seats; and, besides being a quick method, presents a good appearance. The same method can be employed in constructing the seats. The moldings are glued and bradded. The backs of the seats are finished the same as the sides, with turned spindles, faced off on one side, and glued and bradded.

The dash is made of ⅜ in. basswood, and ironed both rear and front sides with 1 in. half-oval iron. At the top and bottom an ear is formed, and to this is bolted the wing, which can be made either of bent elm, with the grain of the wood running in a vertical direction, or an iron frame can be made and covered with leather. The outside pillars of the screen dash pass through the top ear and the wing ear, and a nut on the bottom securely fastens both. An iron fender extends the whole length of the body and forms steps at the point of entrance.

Dimensions of Body.—Width of body on bottom under back seat, 31 in.; ditto on top both front and back seats, 34 in. Width at the toe-bracket, 31⅜ in. The sides are inclined at the height of the rear seat, 1½ in. on each side. Height of body, 15 in. Seat-frames, 37 in., and contracted ½ in. on each side. The seat sides are convexed, and have a width on top of 43 in.

Dimensions and Construction of the Bobs.—The front bob is framed 14 in. high; and the back bob, 12 in. high. Runners, ¾ × 1 in. deep. Shoes, ¾ × ½ in. Beams, 1½ × 1 in. thick. Knees, 1½ in. at the top by ¾ in. thick; and these should be made of bent wood. Track, 3 ft. 2 in., outside. Raves, 1 in. wide by ¾ in. thick, and spread upon the beams 32 in. outside. The center knee is framed 32 in. outside on top. Fenders, ¾ in. square, and mortised to the beams. Distance between the raves and fender, 2½ in.

The bobs should be made of second-growth hickory, or first-quality black hickory, which latter is stiffer and not so much affected by moisture. The whole should be handsomely rounded where required, and ironed in the best possible manner. Care should be exercised in the lay-out of the gear, and the different bevels should be correctly obtained in order that the tenons on the knees entering the runners may not split the mortices.

Finish.—Painting of body, dark green; and bobs carmine, striped with fine lines of black. Trimming, green cloth. Mountings, silver.

FOUR PASSENGER CORTLAND.

PLATE NO. 28.—VOL. 28.—FIVE-EIGHTHS-INCH SCALE.

PLATE NO. 28.

FOUR PASSENGER CORTLAND.

This design of four passenger sleigh has different characteristics from those manufactured in past seasons, and is pleasing in its entire appearance. It is decidedly heavier than last year's style, imitates the fashions in carriages, and has also some carving on the front bracket, which can be increased to advantage on stanhope pillars, as is done on cabriolets and victorias at the present time. The construction of the body may be changed to suit the manipulations in the shop in regard to seats and the body. Some builders prefer to separate the body from the seats, while others prefer building the seats stationary to the body. It is, of course, handier to have the seats separated, but in this case we prefer the seats stationary, if the joints on stanhope pillar are to be avoided. The construction, to give different results, depends also on the taste of the builders. Some prefer a convex turnunder on top and concave at bottom; also side surfaces level, with the exception of the molding thickness, while others have the seats convex, the same as first mentioned, but below the seats the body surface is sunk from 1 to 2½ inches, which improves its appearance. That part of the body in imitation of the wheelhouse is set in the thickness of the molding only. The stanhope pillars are beaded from both sides, ending with both of the front brackets. The moldings can be beaded or rounded on the inside surface. The bottom sides are 2 inches deep and 1½ inches thick, without any plate. The lower part of the body is framed and paneled if made separate from the seats, and the seats are made of 1½-inch thick boards. If the seats are made stationary, the body and seats are framed. The runners are 1¼ inches square; shoes 1¼ by ¼-inch round edge steel; knees, ⅞ inch thick, and iron stays 1⅛ by 1⁷₁₆-inch iron.

Painting.—Seat panels, deep green; moldings and body black; beads on moldings striped a fine line of pale green; wheelhouse, imitation cane; carving touched up in pale green and yellow. Runners, deep green, striped pale green and yellow.

Trimming.—Green cloth; style, blocks. Both backs have a 2-inch roll on top, with four rows of blocks. Cushions, block tops and ⅞-inch raisers on cushion front; same on falls. Carpet, deep green, with pale green and yellow figures.

Finish.—Dash and seat rails silver plated; fenders, bent wood.

Carriage Monthly
July 1892

Four-passenger Sleighs

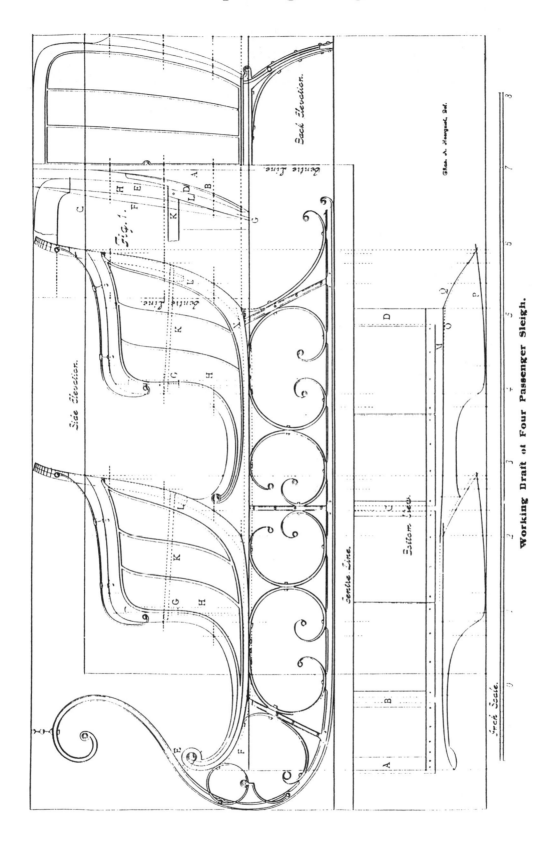

Carriage Monthly
April 1894
(description on next two pages)

Working Draft of Four Passenger Sleigh.

The fashionable features of two and four passenger sleighs, with the exception of some built by a few houses, are plainness and simplicity of construction. The character of the sleigh is heightened by the application of moldings and by painting them in various colors, consequently the labor and expense of producing bodies for first-class sleighs is considerably reduced. The object in view is to give a pretty style which is pleasing, attractive, of good proportions and constructed with the least expense. Note the style and characteristics of the four passenger sleigh with convex-concave back panels published also in this number. While some of the outlines approach this style, other outlines are decidedly different, and the application of the moldings is entirely different.

The bodies of those styles having imitation wing pillars are painted one color and the wing pillar another color, as is done on victorias and cabriolets. The runners are painted either the color of the wing pillars or the other colors of the body. Either way is correct. With such styles as the one shown in this illustration it is different. The space between the outlines of the body and the moldings is generally painted a dark color, mostly dark green, moldings black and space between moldings some bright color, such as pale green, pale blue, lemon, orange, yellow lake or any other suitable color; or the entire body can be painted one color and the moldings a bright yellow, to set them out. The trimming is drab cloth for expensive sleighs; corduroy, green and blue cloth or plush for medium priced sleighs.

THE CONSTRUCTION OF THE BODY.

The construction of the body is very simple. The foundation consists of two side pieces, ¾ inch thick by 3 inches wide, and bent to shape. There are four cross bars, shown at A, B, C and D, bottom view. The front bar is lapped on the bottom sides as shown on E, side elevation; bars B, C and D are mortised into the bottom sides, and rest on the knee bars, each bolted with two bolts, which keep the runners solid with the body.

To save work and labor the bottom boards are screwed directly to the bottom surface of the bottom sides without any rabbet. The thickness of the bottom boards is shown by dotted lines: they are ½ inch thick. The board at F at the front of body is ⅜ inch thick only on account of its curve, and is canvassed from the inside. The bottom boards in each case run over the cross bars and against the brace bars. The seat rails are shown at G, G, and the upright pieces H, H, are shown in dotted lines on the side elevation; so are the seat boards resting on seat bars G, G, at front and I, L, at back. These cross bars, I, L, are worked to shape as shown, and are screwed against the back corner pillars.

With Fig. 1 we illustrate the working draft as used in practice. It represents a sectional view divided by a center line, indicating one-half the width of the body. Line A represents the outside of the body; line B is the turnunder line, and must intersect with line A at the height at C. There is another turnunder line at D, which is used for the back corner pillars only, to create a straight line at M, bottom view. If the bottom line of the body was straight at N, side elevation, we could dispense with turnunder line D, but the raise at N increases the width of the body, and consequently creates a curve as shown by dotted lines O. To avoid this and have line M as shown, we obtain it by making turnunder line D, and take all points from A and D, while for the rest of the body we use turnunder line B.

Line F, Fig. 1, representing the rear corner of the back corner pillars, is created by discounting the amount of turnunder from A to D, Fig. 1, carrying it over to the bottom view and placing it between lines P and Q. Transfer line Q, bottom view, over to line F, Fig. 1, which is created from line Q. For those who do not know how to place these lines, it is best to make a draft of this kind and then transfer all the prick marks and compare with our draft. The size of back corner pillars is shown by dotted lines on the side elevation, and its thickness is shown from line E to F. Line F is the inclination of the pillar. The pillar must be dressed after line E, otherwise the surfaces will not range with the straight edge across the body.

We have shown the prick marks to prick off the pillar from F to E, but the bevel must be added for the side sweep of the body, which is shown at P, bottom view, and the thickness of panel must be discounted from line E. After this is done, make the tenon as shown on G, which enters the bottom sides and make the lap for upper cross bar. The pillar is lightened as shown on H, Fig. 1. The shoulder for the upper cross bar must not be cut after line F, but after line H; the same is done with the shoulders of cross bars L, L, shown on side elevation, which must also be cut after line H, Fig. 1.

The length of the seat rails is taken as shown on K, Fig. 1, of which line L is the shoulder. If all the lengths of cross bars are taken from the draft they will be all alike, and one sleigh will not be narrower than the other. The pillars H, shown by dotted lines on side elevation, are also mortised into the bottom sides the same as the back corner pillars. The seat rail shown on K, Fig. 1, has a tenon and a lap, and is drawn tight with an iron draw pin, and glued together on the bench; the same is done with the bottom sides, also the entire back, including the seat bar.

After all is done they are glued into the bottom sides, and the panels are glued over them. It must be understood that the panels must be bent to the required shape before gluing them over the frames. Note the side sweep P, bottom view, and turnunder line B, Fig. 1, which are considerably curved, and would occasion too much strain if not avoided. Forms should be made sufficiently strong to bend four or six panels at one time. The panels should be steamed and kept in the dry room to prevent shrinking after the panels are glued on the frame.

(see previous page)

PLACING MOLDING ON THE BODIES.

In all cases when moldings are glued and bradded to bodies, and are finished to all shapes and sizes, they must be worked to shape, as they cannot be bent except they are made very light ; $\frac{3}{8}$ by $\frac{1}{8}$ inch full are the lightest, but they are made as large as 1 inch wide by $\frac{1}{4}$ inch thick. The shape of moldings is made to suit the builders' taste. The oval shape is accepted as the prevailing style, but other shapes are made and look as well. The square beaded molding on well shaped bodies always looks well, and when striped with a fine line has a better appearance than the oval moldings. The $\frac{3}{16}$ or $\frac{1}{4}$ inch round beads on each side of the moldings look exceedingly well, and more so when each of the beads is striped with a very prominent hair line. The back view will give the shape of the moldings as applied, to correspond with the side elevation.

THE RUNNERS.

In all cases the runners are bent to shape, and the size is 1 inch square for the lightest four-passenger sleighs. Some builders make them $1\frac{1}{4}$ inches square. This is done occasionally only, and $1\frac{1}{8}$ inches is the medium size used generally, but they must be lightened toward the front from both sides. The knees for medium sized sleighs are $\frac{3}{4}$ inch thick, and the shape is shown on back elevation, and corresponds with the shape of turnunder on body. The size of the knee on back elevation must correspond with the size of the runners. If the size of the runners is 1 inch, the base of the knees must be 1 inch also.

The upper part is always somewhat heavier, as shown on the back elevation. The knee bars are the same thickness as the knees, and are $1\frac{1}{4}$ inches deep for four-passenger sleighs. Some builders make them $1\frac{3}{8}$ inches, and if they are ironed as illustrated, this is sufficient. All the ends on the knee bars have well finished scrolls, turned upward instead of downward. The stays in this case are all curved and made separate from each other, and bolted together in two places, and the rest are bolted to knees, body and runners. The knees and runners, when made with the least labor, are finished with a chamfer only, while for better work they are rounded, which looks considerably better than chamfers. The size of iron stays is $\frac{5}{8}$ by $\frac{3}{4}$ inch in the center, and tapered toward the ends.

WIDTHS OF BODY.

Across front	$31\frac{3}{8}$ inches.
Across bottom	28 inches.
Widest part of body	$41\frac{1}{2}$ inches.
Upper part of back	$38\frac{5}{8}$ inches.
Lower part of back	28 inches.
Amount of turnunder	$6\frac{3}{4}$ inches.
Width of track	$39\frac{3}{4}$ inches.
Size of shoes, round edge steel	$\frac{5}{16}$ by $\frac{1}{8}$ inch.

(see two previous pages)

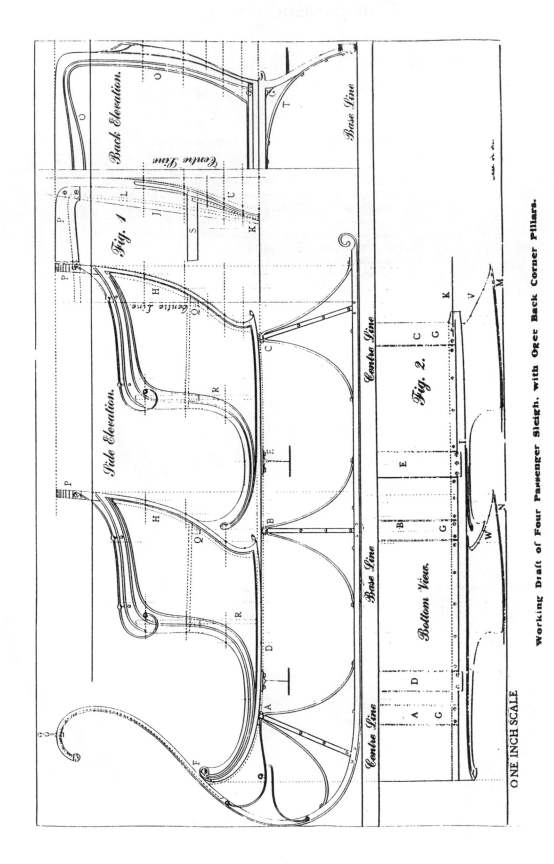

Working Draft of Four Passenger Sleigh, with Ogee Back Corner Pillars.

ONE INCH SCALE

Carriage Monthly
April 1894
(description on next two pages)

Four-passenger Sleighs

Working Draft of Four Passenger Sleigh, with Ogee Back Corner Pillars.

THE BODY.

Sleighs as built in this country are marvels of simplicity and lightness of construction. Nowhere else is this carried to such extremes as in the United States. The body consists of a very light frame for its base, back corner pillars, seat rail pillars, and is then paneled over. The base or frame is ¾ inch thick by 2½ or 3 inches wide, with three cross bars under the knee bars, which are mortised into the side pieces and shown on A, B and C, side elevation, and also on bottom view, A, B and C. There are two more cross bars on D and E, 1¼ inches thick, or ⅜ inch thicker than the bottom sides, having short tenons ½ inch long only, which are lapped over at bottom surface and secured with two screws on each side, as shown on D and E, side elevation.

There is another cross bar at the front end on F, which is made of poplar, lapped to the bottom sides and finished to correspond to the shape of the scroll. The space from this cross bar F to cross bar A, is covered with a $\frac{5}{16}$-inch panel, which is rabbeted into the bottom sides or glued directly over the bottom surface of bottom sides and bars. The frame is bolted to the knee bars through the cross bars, as seen by the bolt heads at G, back elevation, and G, G, G, bottom view. The back corner pillars, H, H, on side elevation, are 1⅜ inches thick the entire length, excepting at their bases, where they are lapped over the bottom sides shown at base, Fig. 1. The bottom sides are bent to shape and dressed square. The outside surfaces are dressed after shape I, and the bevel which is created by the turn-under line.

The back corner pillars are dressed after line J, Fig. 1, and K, Fig. 2. The outside surface of this pillar is shaped to line L, Fig. 1, and is beveled to the side sweep of body M, Fig. 2. The bevel on the front corner pillar on top is the same as the side sweep N, while at the bottom it is parallel with line I, Fig. 2. The back panel is rabbeted into the back corner pillars, and its joint is covered with the molding shown at O, O, back elevation. The side panels are either mitred or pass over the pillars. Mitreing those corners involves a great deal of labor, and it requires very particular work to fit and glue them to their place. A better way, at least less laborious and more durable, is to bevel the pillars, leaving the thickness of the panel off, and glue the panel over the entire thickness. To hide the joint, bead it the entire length. This looks neat and at the same time rounds off the corners nicely, and gives a pleasing finish.

The upper back bars, P, Fig. 1, are 1 inch thick, lapped over the pillars as shown on P, P, side elevation, and the back panel is rabbeted into it, as on the back pillars. Two other bars are shown on Q, Q, side elevation, shaped as shown by dotted lines, and screwed against the corner pillars, the seat board resting upon it. The seat rails are 1 inch thick by 1¾ inches; the pillars, R, R, into which they are mortised, and shown in dotted lines, are ⅝ inch thick, and the ¼ inch which the seat rail is thicker than the pillars, is lapped over the pillars, as shown by dotted lines on the side elevation in front of pillar. The shape of the pillar and also the rail is shown on S,

Fig. 1. The rail is mortised into the pillar, and the shape of pillar is as shown. The pillars at the lower end are mortised through the bottom sides, and the side panels are screwed to the pillars.

The panels have considerable side sweep and a great deal of turn-under, which is concave-convex shape. To avoid the strain of these panels, they should be bent to the exact shape before they are glued

(see previous page and next page)

to the frame, and should be bent in such a manner that they retain the shape. It is best to make a form strong enough to bend four panels at once. The panels should be steamed and left in the dry room until they are dried sufficiently to avoid checking. The front side panels are glued on first, and the rear side panels afterwards. The front ends of these panels enter into grooves on the back corner pillars. The moldings on the side surfaces, also on the back panel, are made of two pieces to save stuff and to avoid the cross grain. A pattern must be made to the shape as shown, and its moldings shaped to the pattern and glued to the side surfaces after the panels have been cleaned off to shape. The beads on moldings are made after they are glued on.

THE RUNNERS.

The runners are bent to shape, and made to order to conform to the desired shape, but many sleigh builders have their own plants for bending, and consequently make their own forms and give their own sizes for runners and knees. The sizes for knees on light passenger sleighs are generally ⅝ or ¾ inch thick, the cross pieces are the same thickness, and 1¼ inches deep. The runners are ¾ or ⅞ inch square, tapered slightly toward the front. The shoes are ¾ or ⅞ inch round edge steel, and ¼ inch thick. Toward the front the steel is rounded, and is also tapered considerably to suit the proportions of the front part, and is screwed to the runners. On account of the lightness of the runners and knees, double braces are shown on the side elevation, and a brace is also shown on T, back elevation, which keeps the runners from spreading.

Sleighs of this kind are generally well finished with side rails, side fenders, screens and line rails. Wooden fenders are occasionally made, because they are cheaper than screens, but screens improve the appearance. This is also true of the screen line rail. When sleighs are hung as low as in this design, and when the bodies are cut down as low as 14 inches from the bottom line, steps are dispensed with. Sleighs, however, should be made with steps. Their shape can be made to suit the builders.

WIDTHS OF BODY.

Across front 30	inches.
Across bottom 28	inches.
Across back, on top 37	inches.
Across back, at bottom 29	inches.
The widest part of body 40	inches.
Amount of turnunder 5¾	inches.
Width of track 40	inches.

Runners 1⅛ inches square, and tapered toward the front.
Thickness of knees and knee bars, ⅝ inch.
Shoes ¼ by 1¾ inches, round edge steel.

Two Different Turnunder Lines on One Body.

We call special attention to the two turnunder lines on the working draft of four passenger sleigh, with ogee back corner pillars published in this number. The side elevation of the front part is exactly like the back part, but there is considerably more turnunder on the back corner pillar than on the back corner pillar on the front part of the body, while both amounts of turnunder are the same at R, R, on the side elevation. This is caused by the contraction of the bottom sides at the rear end. Examine line I, Fig. 2, and see how that line is contracted toward the center line, and consequently gives some swell at the bottom of the body, which looks well, and is better than if the body was straight. Those who want a straight sill, and use one turnunder for both bodies only, may take dotted turnunder line U, Fig. 1. The difference will be that line I will be straight to the back end, and line V will have the same shape as W, Fig. 2.

(see two previous pages)

PLATE No. 96.   FOUR PASSENGER SLEIGH.—SCALE, FIVE-EIGHTH INCH.

FASHION PLATE No. 96 is another four-passenger sleigh, built by Willoughby, of Rome, N. Y. The body is neatly decorated by shell work and spindles. The front hanging is the same as that of No. 95, but the back is hung upon half elliptics and scroll body loops. The sides, when worked to the shell pattern, are of 2½ in. whitewood. This is ann uusually neat and attractive pattern. The dimensions are the same as those of No. 95.

Paint the body black ; the shell work claret, shaded with black and touched up with gold; gear, carmine, striped with black and gold.

Trimming, claret cloth; plumes, black and claret.

The Hub
July 1894

PLATE No. 519. DOUBLE FOUR-PASSENGER SLEIGH.

THREE-QUARTER-INCH SCALE.

PLATE No. 702.—FOUR-PASSENGER SURREY SLEIGH ON BOBS.

Carriage Monthly
top, December 1901; bottom, May 1903

120

BOX-BODY
SLEIGHS

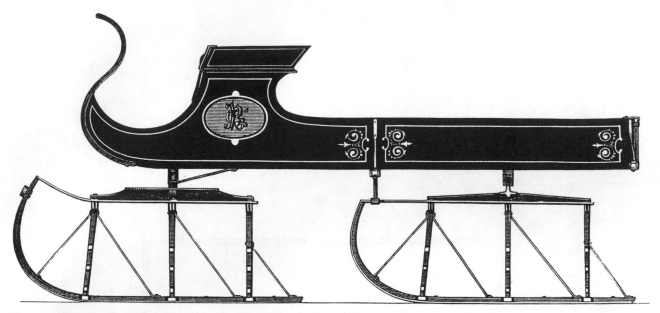

No. 77. BUSINESS SLEIGH.—Built by Brigham, McRay & Co., Ayer Junction, Mass.—Scale, three-quarter inch to the foot.

THIS well-engraved design represents, in three-quarter-inch scale, a practical and attractive style of Business or Store Sleigh now built by Messrs. Brigham, McRay & Co., of Ayer-Junction, Mass.

The side-panels are framed on the inside of body, with solid panels ½ in. thick, the seat-riser and sides being all in one piece. The front or dash is framed with the panel inside, and the frame outside or forward, dividing the surface of the latter into three smaller panels. The curved outlines of the body are very graceful. The seat is paneled. The running-part consists of two bob-sleighs, made in the ordinary manner, with straight braces.

Principal dimensions as follow: The body is 40 in. wide, and the extreme length 7 ft. 9 in. Side, 16 in. high under seat. Dash, 2½ ft. high. Runners, ⅞ x 1½. Posts, 14 in. between shoulders; 40 in. wide on ground outside.

For painting Mr. Gardner suggests the following: Body, japan brown or lake all over, with striping and flat scrolling in gold; running-part, a clean-looking cream color, striped with black and vermilion fine lines. Bolt-heads, either black or vermilion.

The Hub
October 1877

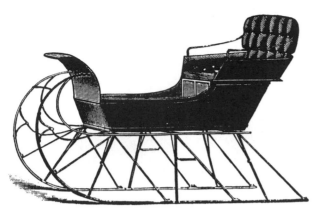

PHYSICIAN'S SLEIGH.

PLATE NO. 42.—HALF-INCH SCALE.

Physician's Sleigh.

PLATE NO. 42.

The body of this design is flared front and back, as shown in the drawing, and has 1½ inches flare on the sides. The seat is also flared to correspond with the sides. The back corners of the body and seat are rounded, and the moldings on the body are braded on.

Painting.—Body: black, striped with a medium line of gold on the molding, with a fine line of green on each side. Runners: dark green, with two fine lines of green.

Trimming.—Dark green or red plush, plain, with patent-leather cord welts. Carpet to match.

Mountings.—Silver.

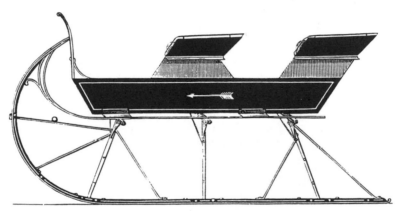

No. 70. GRANGER CUTTER.—SCALE, ONE-HALF INCH.

This design represents a Western style of inexpensive four-passenger sleigh, specially adapted for use in the country. It has a regular wagon body, and its general appearance is very plain, but by no means objectionable.

Dimensions of the body: Width of seats on frame, 37 in. Width of body on top, 36 in. Turn-under of sides, 1¼ in.

Dimensions of the under-part: Runners, 1 x 1½ in. Benches, 1 x 1⅞ in. Knees, 1 x 1⅞ in. Track, 42 in.

Painting.—Body and seat panels, light brown; seat-risers, dash and edge of body, dark brown. Molding and seat skirts, black, with fine line of carmine. Running-part, straw color, striped with vermilion and black. *Trimming.*—Brown cloth; oil-cloth and rug to match.

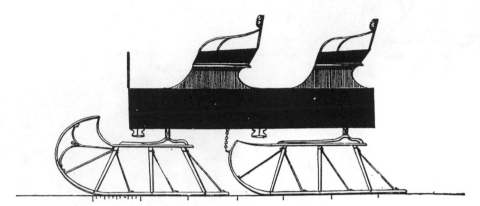

No. 37. BOB-RUNNER PUNG.—Scale, one-half inch.

WE here represent an inexpensive design of Sleigh very popular throughout New-England for business purposes. The pattern illustrated was built by Mr. J. M. Barber, carriage and sleigh-maker, of North Adams, Mass., who has furnished us with the following list of dimensions. No special description of the Bob-runners is necessary, as we have so recently illustrated and described the so-called "Hub-runners," which, with the exception of the hub attachment, are very similar in construction. See February *Hub*, page 588.

Dimensions.—Length of body, 6 ft. 3 in.; width of same, 2 ft. 10½ in ; height of side panels, 9½ in. Dash, leather, 12 in. high. The knees and beams are made of the best hickory, ¾ × 1⅝ in., and the runners are shod with steel tire, ⅞ × ½ in. The fenders (not visible in our cut) are made of ½-inch round iron.

Finish.—Painting : body, black ; gearing, red, striped black. Trimming, black leather ; lazy-backs with double arm-rails.

The Hub
July 1882

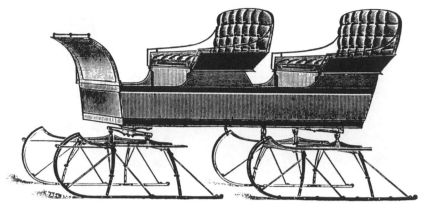

BUSINESS SLEIGH.

PLATE NO. 30.—VOL. 24.—HALF-INCH SCALE.

Width across bottom of body, 30 inches; across the top, 31 inches. Across the bottom of seat, 34 inches, and across the top of seat 39 inches. Flare of body, ½ inch each side, and flare of seats 2½ inches each side. Bob runners, with two braces each side, shape convex. Width of track, 34 inches for both bobs. Thickness and depth of runner ⅞ by 1 inch deep. Shoes ⅞ by 1 5/16-inch steel. Stays 5/16-inch round steel.

These sleighs are used for business and pleasure; are inexpensive when manufactured in large quantities, and as a consequence a great many are used, particularly for business purposes. The sides, front and back of the body have raised panels, which are obtained by routering down the upper and lower edge of the panel; ⅛-inch thickness relieves their plainness of the panel and looks very good. The risers are plain, but are generally striped or ornamented to relieve their plainness. The seats are plain board seats, mitred at the corners and strengthened with corner blocks. The dash is a bent panel, fastened with two stays running up the dash and down to the sills of the body, forming a square corner and bolted to the sills. The bob runners are of the simplest construction, the bent knees and coupling the most improved and strongest. The spring attachment to the bob runners is another of these valuable improvements which gives comfort to the riders and strength to the bobs.

Painting.—Body: black. Runners: black, striped ⅛-inch line of green; body striped a fine line of green if desired.

Trimming.—Blue cloth. The backs are block backs, with plain blue tufts. The entire job has patent-leather finish around the edges. Fall plain, finished with patent-leather welts. Carpet plain, bound with cloth.

Mountings.—black. ———

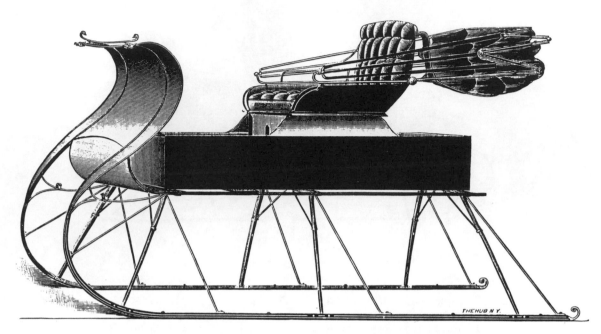

PLATE No. 27. PIANO-BOX CUTTER. – SCALE, THREE-QUARTERS INCH.

THIS design consists simply of a square-box buggy body, mounted on appropriate sleigh runners, which are plain but serviceable.

The knees have a slight swell on the outside, and are ⅝ × 1¼ in. at the beam, and at the runners ⅝ × ¹¹⁄₁₆ in. The runners are ¹¹⁄₁₆ × ¾ in. and extend to the top of the dash. The shoes are ¹¹⁄₁₆ × ⁵⁄₁₆-in. steel, and are bolted to the runners and stays. The knees are mortised into the beams, and on top of the beams are two raves extending the full length of the body, and perfectly straight, upon which the body rests. The beams project outside of the body 4 in., and a fender is fastened on the ends, 4 in. outside the line of the body, and tapering in to the runner at the bottom line of the dash. From the front beam to the bottom of the dash, a curved panel is set in, and this butts up against the dash.

At each side of the dash is a leather wing, tapered at the top and bottom. The stays are made of ⁵⁄₁₆-in. round iron.

The body is made similar to that of a square-box buggy. The sills are ⅞ × 1⅛ in., the corner posts 1 in., and the center posts, ⅝ × ¾ in., extending to the top of the riser. A ⅜-in. panel is used for the sides and ends. The seat-frame is made of ¾-in. ash, and is mitered at the corners to avoid as much end grain as possible. The seat-panels are made of ¾-in. whitewood.

Dimensions.—Width of body on top, 24 in.; width on bottom, 23½ in.; and width of runners on bottom, 36 in.

Painting.—Body, black, and running-part, dark green, with a carmine stripe.

Trimming.—Green cloth throughout. The cushion is tufted in diamond pattern. The back is made up in blocks of small size. The fall has a cloth finish. Carpet, green. Mountings, silver.

The Hub
July 1888

126

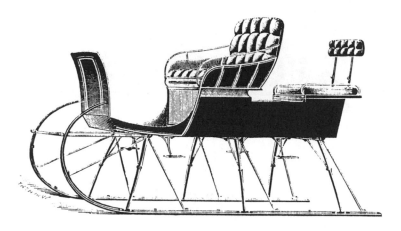

PLATE No. 11. TURN-OVER SEAT CORNING-BODY SLEIGH.—SCALE, ONE-HALF INCH.

THIS style of sleigh is well adapted both for business and pleasure purposes. It is provided with a seat at the rear, which works on hinges screwed to a piece 1¼ × 2 in., which extends across the body. The front seat is also hinged at the front and must be raised up to allow the rear seat to be turned down. The sides of the body are cut down to the thickness of the rear seat-board, so that, when the seat is down it will leave a flat surface at the rear. There is ample room in the body for carrying articles of various kinds. The sides of the body are comparatively plain, and have a swell of about ½ in. The molding, extending from the bottom of the seat to bottom of body, is worked off in a convex-concave shape, and extends to front of body. A light plate is fastened to the inside of rockers. The seat is made of 2-in. whitewood with the moldings worked on solid.

Dimensions.—The body is 28½ in. wide at the top, and 25 in. at the bottom; the seat is 35½ in. wide at the top, and 30½ in. at the bottom. Runners, ¾ × ⅞ in. Knees, ⅝ × ¾ in. Shoes, ½ × ¾ in. Track, 38 in.

Painting.—Body and moldings, black. Seat-panels, deep lake. Moldings striped with fine line of carmine. Gearing, carmine, striped with fine lines of gold.

Trimming.—Maroon cloth. All ironwork black.

The Hub
May 1889

PLATE No. 13.   ROAD CUTTER.—SCALE, ONE-HALF INCH.

THE design herewith introduced is light in construction and is well adapted for speeding purposes. The seat is high and gives good control of the horses. The body is constructed similar to that of a spindle wagon. The sides and backs of the seats and body are open with enameled dash-leather nailed to the framework from the inside, with a line of stitching around the inside of molding ; but, if panels be deemed preferable, they may be easily introduced. The front-pillar, extending from the top of the seat to the bottom-sills is made of bent wood and is mortised into the sills. The rear corner-pillar of the seat is mortised into the seat-frame and lapped to the top-rail of the seat. The seat-riser is made of ⅞-in. whitewood. It recedes ⅛ in. from the outside of top-rail, and is grooved into the top-rail and front-pillar. Two cross-rails are let into the top of the riser, ⅛ in. from the outside. Light corner-plates should be used for both the body and seat, at the rear corners. A wooden dash is used with two iron plates on the inside, to which the dash is bolted. These plates extend down to the front cross-piece. Chime-bells are used in front as in the cut. Wire screens are placed all around the dash.

Dimensions.—Width of body on top, 31 in.; and at bottom, 27 in. Width of seat on top, 35 in.; and at bottom, 31 in. Extreme length of body, 49 in. Height of body, 10 in. Runners, ½ × ⅝ in. Knees, ½ × ¾ in. Shoes, ⅜ × ½ in. Track, 38 in.

Painting.—Body and dash, black, with two fine lines of yellow on dash to form a panel. Fine line of yellow around molding. Gearing, chrome yellow, striped with gold.

The Hub
May 1889

128

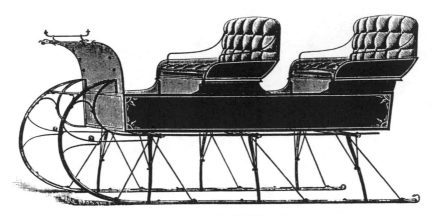

BUSINESS SLEIGH.

PLATE No. 31.—VOL. 25.

Sleighs as illustrated in this design, are usually used for business purposes. The back seat is removed when not wanted, and the front seat is shifted in the most desirable position. The body is plain, but can be made with moldings, or can be striped as shown. The seats have moldings, which are worked on solid, and the side pieces are convex, the same as shown on back end. The knees are concave-convex, and are braced with straight stays which are $1\frac{5}{6}$ inch thick.

Painting.—Body: black; seats and risers also black, striped light geeen. Runners: generally black, but if some contrast is desired, deep green, striped black, is the rule.

Trimming.—Green cloth, backs and cushion square blocks; falls, $\frac{7}{8}$-inch raisers.

Mountings.—Black.

BUSINESS SLEIGH.—Body: Length of body, 5 feet 6 inches at bottom, but are made any length to suit the requirements. Width across the bottom, 30 inches; across top $31\frac{1}{2}$ inches; flare each side, $\frac{3}{4}$ inch. Seats: width across bottom, $33\frac{1}{2}$ inches, and on top, 39 inches; flare each side, $2\frac{3}{4}$ inches. There is not any contraction on seat frame. Dash is of bent wood and stands over the body $\frac{1}{2}$ to 1 inch on each side. Runners: width of track, 36 inches over all. Size of runners, $1\frac{1}{8}$ by $1\frac{1}{4}$ inches. Shoes, $1\frac{1}{8}$ by $\frac{5}{16}$ inch. Knees concave convex, $\frac{5}{8}$ inch thick scant, and $1\frac{1}{4}$ inches wide on upper ends.

———

Carriage Monthly
July 1889

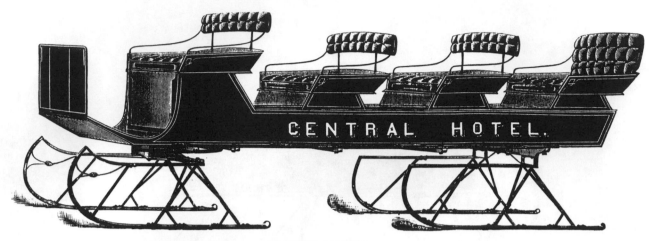

DEPOT SLEIGH.

PLATE No. 32.—VOL. 25.

DEPOT SLEIGH.—Body: 10 feet 7 inches long; 40 inches wide; side panels 9 inches deep. Number of seats, four; height of driver's seat from bottom edge to under seat, 18 inches: other seats 12 inches. Depth of seats at bottom, 15 inches; space between seats, 15 inches. Driver's seat stationary, and the other three seats moveable, secured to the body with Lamb's seat fasteners. Runners: B. M. Wentworth's independent traverse steel gear, with wide track, and full fifth-wheel.

This sleigh was furnished us by one of our oldest subscribers, Jeremiah J. Livengood, of Elk Lick P. O., Pa., who sent us the following description: Driver's seat stationary, and the three other seats movable, secured to the body with Lamb's patent seat fasteners. The B. M. Wentworth independent traverse steel gear is used; wide track. The dimensions are on preceding page.

Painting.—Body: black, striped a ⅜-inch line of pea green; distant fine line, dove color; lettering gold, shaded with carmine.

Runners.—Deep English vermilion, striped ⅜-inch line of black; distant fine line of black.

Trimming.—Moquette plush; hind seat, full back; fall sewed in the cushion. Other seats, open backs without falls. Dash covered with patent leather.

Mountings.—Black.

Carriage Monthly
July 1889

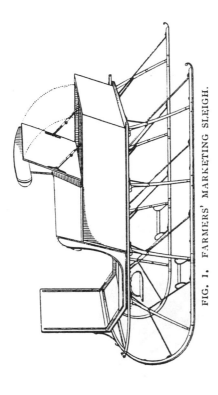

FIG. 1. FARMERS' MARKETING SLEIGH.

FIG. 2. DRUMMERS' SLEIGH.

A FARMER'S MARKETING SLEIGH AND A PEDDLER'S OR COMMERCIAL TOURIST'S SLEIGH.

FEW men have contributed more fully to trade journals than J. I. H. Mosier, including technical matter for the advanced workman, instruction for the apprentice, and original designs and novelties for the trade in general. In keeping with his custom, he has furnished the two novelties in the way of sleighs which we illustrate and describe herewith.

Fig. 1 represents a sleigh for the use of the farmer in marketing small wares, and in bringing from town such material as is needed for consumption at the farm. Because of the extra length of the sleigh, I place four posts and beams to prevent "hogging" between the posts, Make the top of body two, three or more feet longer than the usual every day heavy cutter, as occasion may require, the extra length being back of the seat; usual wood, dash, seat and lazy back.

The illustration shows a single lid, held in position when open by two top joints, $\frac{1}{2}$ x $\frac{1}{2}$ in. knuckles, the lid being hinged onto back bar of seat. This part on the lid may be made in two pieces, divided at the center, the fore section to turn up and spring-lock to back of seat, the back section to be furnished with falling back and side rails, and made to turn back, and thus form a convenient extra seat.

Fig. 2 is designed for the use of peddlers, drummers or commercial tourists. The back is built up to the full height of the back of the seat, and has an upper and lower compartment with door or gate to each to let down, these being held horizontal by chains. It is also furnished with a rail on top, to which to secure parcels. Make the rail of $\frac{7}{16}$ or $\frac{1}{2}$ in. round iron, and secure to top of deck and back of seat with $\frac{5}{16}$ in. bolts, the nuts of the bolts resting on the legs of the rail. Make the three front, side and post stays of $\frac{1}{2}$ in. round iron or steel; those of the back post, beam and side of $\frac{9}{16}$ in. round iron or steel. The three post stays all may be secured with $\frac{5}{16}$ in. bolts, the back one with $\frac{3}{8}$ in. bolts. Use a 1¼ x $\frac{3}{8}$ in. or 1¼ x $\frac{1}{2}$ in. Bessemer steel shoe, and secure with ¼ in. bolts; the back ones and all the stays at runner connection, with $\frac{5}{16}$ in. bolts, the other iron-work comparatively stronger.

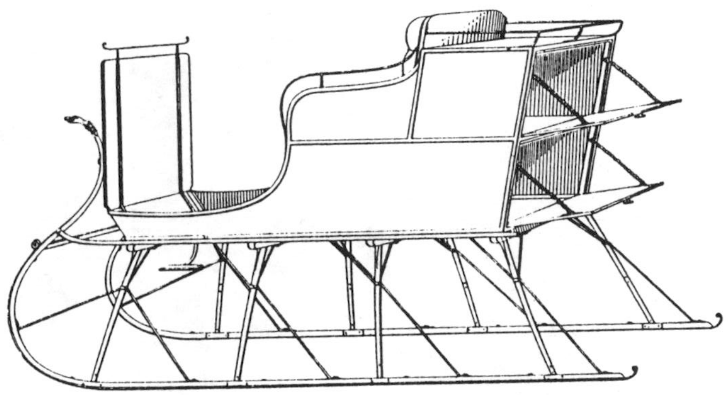

The Hub
July 1895

PLATE No. 992. TWENTIETH CENTURY PLEASURE BOB.
BUILT BY CARTIER, CHAPMAN & CO., LUDINGTON, MICH.

Carriage Monthly
August 1906

TRAPS
and
SPORTING SLEIGHS

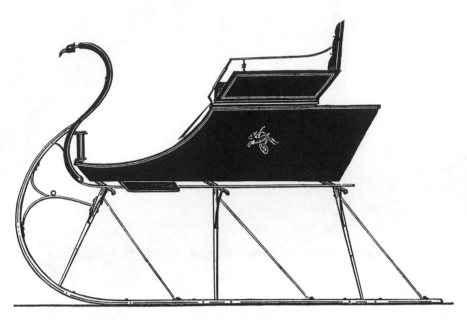

No. 76. WHITECHAPEL PONY-SLEIGH. SCALE, THREE-QUARTERS INCH.

THE Whitechapel is another favorite pattern at this time, and does well for use in the form of a sleigh. It is still plainer than the Surrey, having no stanhope-pillar, and being, in fact, as cheap a body as can be made. The corners of the body and seat are made square in our design, which is characteristic of this style. In order to relieve the otherwise plain sides, we have placed a light molding on the seat and body, or a similar effect may be obtained by striping simply.

The dimensions for this pattern are as follows:

Width of seat, 32 inches.
Turn-under of sides, 2¼ inches.

Track, 3 feet 4 inches.
Runners, ⅞ inch square.
Shoes, ⅞ x 5-16 inch.
Benches, ⅝ x 1½ inches.
Knees, 1¼ x ⅝ inch.

Painting: body, black; seat blue, striped with fine line of gold; running-part, ultramarine-blue, striped with one line of gold.

Trimming: blue cloth; cushions tufted in the manner described for the Goldsmith No-top Speed-wagon, which appears in this number of The Hub, page 189.

The Hub
October 1874

SURREY PONY-SLEIGH.

(See illustration on this page.)

THE Surrey-Wagon has met with greater success than any other new style of light vehicle introduced for several years past. The style of body is not very expensive, and its adoption as a sleigh-body seems to us a good idea, the more so as the present variety, in styles of single-seat sleighs, is but small. By reference to our illustration, it will be noticed that the general lines of the body are not different from the ordinary Surrey-Wagon, but the box is shortened six inches behind the seat, which is necessary, as the body hangs low to the ground, and would otherwise look too long. The number of slats is reduced to four on each side, and the same number in the back part of the rail, and in the cross-bar behind the seat. The construction of the body is the same as that of the Surrey illustrated on page 8 of the present volume of The Hub, only that the body is made wider in order to comfortably seat two persons.

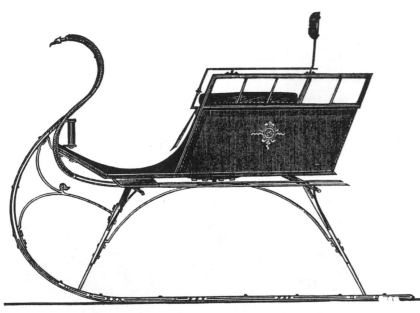

No. 75. SURREY PONY-SLEIGH. SCALE, THREE-QUARTERS INCH.

The principal dimensions are as follows :

Width of seat, 32 inches.
Width of body on top, 30 inches.
Width of body at bottom, 25 inches. Track, 3 feet 4 inches. Runners, ⅞ inch square. Shoes, ⅞ x ⅜ inch. Benches, ¾ x 1½ inches. Knees, 1½ x ⅞ inches.

Painting : body, black ; seat-rail and stanhope-pillar, English red ; slats of seat, black ; running-part red, striped black. Ornamenting seems to be out of place for this style of body.
Trimming : black cloth, with red buttons.

The Hub
October 1874

135

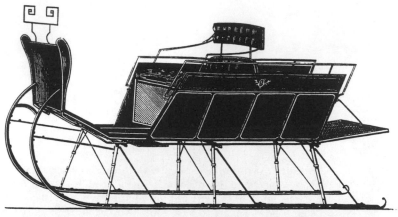

No. 6ɔ. SURREY PONY SLEIGH.—Scale, one-half inch.

The Hub
September 1880

THIS handsome design of a convertible two and four-passenger sleigh is one of the so-called Canadian patterns, which for a few years past have been favorably received in the United States, and have, in some measure, eclipsed the Portland and Albany patterns, which once held exclusive sway.

Our illustration hardly needs any explanation, as the perspective view gives a clear idea of the whole arrangement. The tail-board, which serves also as a toe-board for the hind seat, is closed by spring hooks on either side. The front has a wooden dash, against which the runners terminate. Sheet-iron or wire wings are placed to the outside of the dash.

The principal dimensions are as follow: Width of body, 30 in. on seat-rail. Turn-under, ¾ in. on each side. Runners, ¾ x 1 in. Beams, 1 in. x 1½ in. Knees, 1 in. Track, 41 in.

Painting.—Body panels, dark bottle green; ribs, black, striped with fine lines of gold; runners, black, striped with "full stripe" of bright lemon yellow; bolt-heads ornamented with same color.

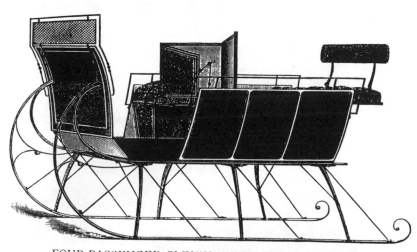

Carriage Monthly
August 1885

FOUR-PASSENGER SLEIGH, WITH TURN-OUT SEAT.

The special feature of this sleigh is its turn-out seat, originated and patented by P. A. Lariviere, of Montreal, Canada. Half of the front seat slides back and turns in to admit passage to the rear seat, the driver remaining seated. This seat can be applied to all styles of carriages as well as sleighs.

Painting.—Body: black. Runners: carmine, striped three fine lines of black, ⅜ inch apart. Body moldings striped a fine line of carmine.

Trimming.—Green cloth. The front seat has a plain one-roll back, finished with lace. The cushion has a plaited diamond top, with a plain front facing; the welts are of seaming lace. The driving cushion is made soft and has lace welts. The rear seat is trimmed perfectly plain, of green cloth also. The rugs are plain green carpet, bound with lace.

Mountings.—Silver.

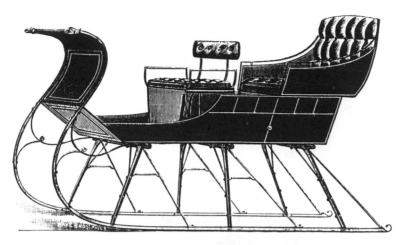

LIGHT FOUR–PASSENGER SLEIGH.

PLATE No. 31.—VOL. 23.—HALF-INCH SCALE.

This style represents a light, inexpensive sleigh. J. D. Harper, of Christiana, Pa., furnished the original. They can be supplied with jump-seat irons, thus making a two-passenger sleigh. The sides and back panel of body are molded with $\frac{1}{2}$ inch by $\frac{3}{16}$-inch thick moldings, and are glued and braded. The sides on seat are of solid poplar, and moldings worked on. The runners are of the old kind, and knees are straight.

Painting.—Body : black. Runners : black, striped fine line dark green.

Trimming.—Red plush. The full back is a block and pipe back, finished with leather welts; the front back is an open plain back with four or five tufts inserted to relieve it. The cushions are made with plain block tops and $1\frac{3}{4}$-inch high front facings with plain 1-inch raisers. The falls are attached to the cushions and have a plain raiser around the edges. The rug is maroon carpet with attractive figures.

Width across body at bottom, 30 inches ; at top, $36\frac{1}{2}$ inches ; seat across front, top, 42 inches ; across back, 40 inches. Front seat, 33 inches, and 14 inches deep ; made from $\frac{7}{8}$-inch ash. Sides of seat, 2-inch poplar, swept from both sides, and when finished is only $1\frac{1}{8}$ inches thick. Sides and back panel for body $\frac{1}{2}$-inch poplar, and bottom sides, $1\frac{1}{8}$ inches deep by $1\frac{3}{4}$ inches thick. Width of track, 40 inches from out to out. Runners, $\frac{7}{8}$ inch by $1\frac{1}{8}$ inches deep. Shoes, $\frac{7}{8}$ by $\frac{1}{4}$ inch. Knees, $\frac{3}{4}$ inch thick, and at bottom, $\frac{7}{8}$ inch, and top, $1\frac{1}{4}$ inches wide ; bench bars, $1\frac{1}{4}$ by $\frac{3}{4}$ inch.

Carriage Monthly
July 1887

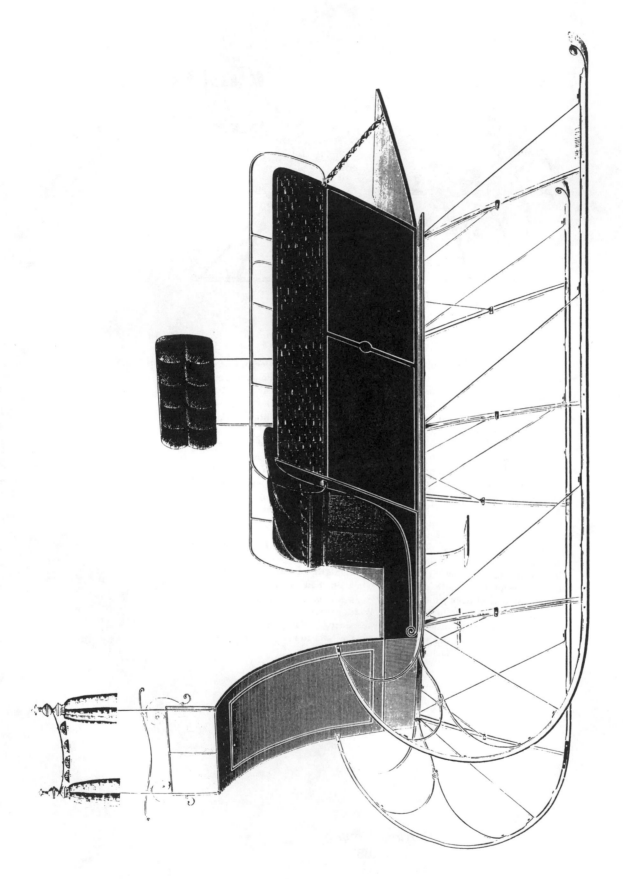

PLATE No CXXI. SURREY SLEIGH.

The Hub
May 1890
(description on next page)

SURREY SLEIGH.

(See Colored Plate No. CXXI.)

OUR Colored Plate this month represents a new design of surrey sleigh. It is intended for four passengers, and is provided with a tailboard at the rear, which gives easy access to persons occupying the rear seat. This is comparatively new on a surrey sleigh, and does not necessitate the front seat being made in two parts. The back of rear seat is made to lie down, and the seat is hinged. The construction of the body is similar to that of a surrey or gentleman's driving cart. The bottom of the body is straight, and the sides have a throwout of 2½ in. The sills are 1¼ × 2 in., framed to the end sills with tenon and mortise. There are three upright pieces framed into the bottom sills which extend to the top of body. A piece 1 × 2½ in. is framed lengthwise to the body on which the seats rest; the front seat is made stationary. The panels are of ⅜-in. whitewood, the moldings are glued and clamped on, and when finished should be secured with fine brads. If preferred, the moldings could be worked on solid; in that case, it would be necessary to use ½ in. whitewood panels. The upper panel is of imitation basket-work. The stanhope-pillars are of 2½ in. ash, and extend to the sills; a piece of whitewood is glued on to form the continuation of the same with a scroll worked on the end. The dash-frame is screwed to the sills, and a bar framed across at the top edge of panel and also at the extreme top, the dash is tapered to ⅝ in. at the top. A ¼ in. panel is glued on from the inside, showing the framework from the outside forming a molding. The running-part is composed of six knees, ⅞ × 1½ in. at the thickest part. The runners are 1⅛ × ⅞ in. and extend to the intersection of the raves, and are spliced and bolted together. The raves are ¾ × 2½ in., and are let into the beams ⅛ in. The shoes are ⅞ × ½ in. The stays are of ⅜ in. oval iron.

Dimensions of Woodwork.—Width of body on top, 38 in.; and at bottom, 32 in. Length of body, 4 ft. 4 in. Height of body, 18 in.

Painting.—Moldings, black, striped with fine line of orange; lower panels, bottle green; imitation basket-work, stained green; running-part, orange, striped with fine lines of black.

Trimming.—Green cloth, made up in large squares. Carpet, plain. Mountings, silver.

NOTE.—In this design and the four Fashion Plates which immediately follow, the plumes and chimes are drawn from some of the latest novelties and styles kindly furnished by the Chapman Mfg. Co., Meriden, Conn.—ED.

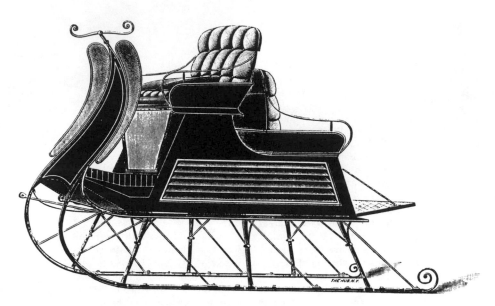

PLATE No. 8.   DOG CART SLEIGH.—Scale, one-half inch.

Scale ½ in. to the foot.

FASHION Plate No. 8 represents a Dog Cart Sleigh; the original was built at J. Dixon's Carriage and Sleigh Works, at Toronto, Ont., where this style is very popular. The front view shows the shape of the dash. The fenders are of wicker work. The portion of the bracket shown, with a series of vertical lines, represents a box 3½ in. deep, which keeps the robe well in around the feet. The sides of the body are straight. The " blind " work is painted on.

Dimensions of Woodwork.—Width of body, 35½ in. Width of seat on top, 41 in. ; and at bottom, 39 in. Length of body, 5 ft. 8 in. Height of body, 24 in. Runners $1 \times 1\frac{1}{8}$; shoes, $1 \times \frac{3}{8}$ in.; knees, $\frac{7}{8} \times 1$ in., rounded on the outside ; beams, $\frac{7}{8} \times 1\frac{1}{8}$ in.; stays, $\frac{3}{8}$ in. round iron.

Painting. Body and seats, vermillion; running part yellow, striped carmine.

Trimming.—Blue cloth; mountings, brass.

The Hub
May 1892

140

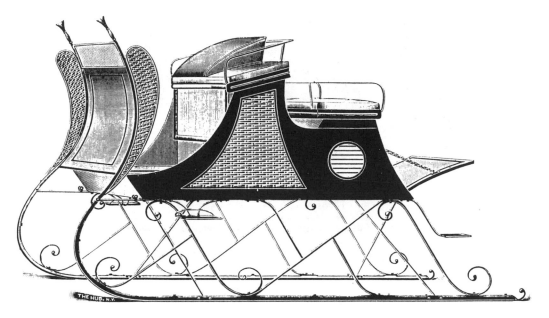

PLATE No. 160. TANDEM SLEIGH.—SCALE, FIVE-EIGHTH INCH.

SCALE, ⅝ INCH TO THE FOOT.

(See Fashion Plate No. 160.)

THE lovers of the tandem, four-in-hand, and other specially made-up teams are gradually growing to a liking for sleighs that are suited to the purpose as well as wheeled vehicles, and each succeeding winter sees more and more of such rigs. A sleigh for tandem driving must be constructed to meet all the well-known requirements. It must be compact, high, and the front seat so placed that the driver will occupy the same position as when in the tandem cart, and the "tiger" must be provided for at the back. Fashion Plate No. 160 represents a tandem sleigh in which all the requirements have been studied and provided for. The body is deep, and the heavy appearance has been relieved by an imitation cane panel at the front, and a round slatted ornament at the back. The dash is high, but is lightened by a wire screen panel at the top. The wings, which are sufficiently large to protect the driver from the snow balls from the horses' feet, are wicker work. The under work is of straight and S braces, artistically combined, so as to secure the maximum of rigidity and strength.

Dimensions of Woodwork.—Body: width across top, 28 in.; across bottom, 26 in. Width at seat, front, 32 in.; back seat, 26 in. Runners, 1¼ x 1½ in.

Painting.—Body, black; seat risers, slats, and front of dash and moldings, carmine; cane work, light buff; runners and ironwork, carmine, striped black.

Trimming.—Front seat, buff Bedford cord; back seat, black; seat rails covered with black rail leather.

The Hub
June 1895

Plate No. 232. TRAP SLEIGH.—Scale, Five-eighth Inch.

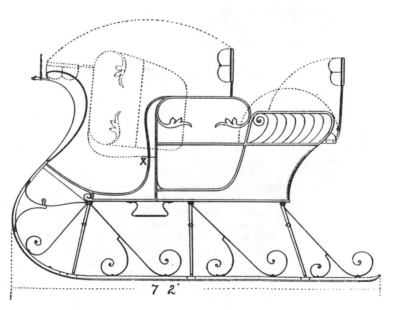

TRAP SLEIGH, SHOWING MOVEMENTS OF SEATS.

The Hub
June 1896
(description on next page)

TRAP SLEIGH.

SCALE, ⅝ INCH TO THE FOOT.

(See Fashion Plate No. 232.)

TRAPS in summer and traps all the year round are the popular fad. We herewith introduce a very novel and exceedingly attractive two-seat trap sleigh, Fashion Plate No. 232, that is bound to be a seller if artistically and carefully constructed and finished in good shape.

The characteristic features of this design are its compact form, being only a 7 ft. 2 in. runner, and also the convenience of a side entrance from either side which affords easy access to rear seat. When not in use, the back seat is so constructed as to fold forward and close up, and is then a one-passenger sleigh.

The front seat hinges at point X and one-half of seat and side goes forward (see dotted line) with the greatest possible ease, by simply tilting it forward.

The side quarter at rear seat is handsomely carved in the form of shell work, which, when blended and striped in the proper manner, lends much to the general attractiveness of the outfit. The ends of runners at dash have carved eagle heads and wings on the side of each runner bent out of $\frac{5}{16}$ in. soft elm.

The iron-work braces are shaped into simple scrolls when they join the runners. This helps to fill up on the gear part and balances the rest of the sleigh.

Track, 40 in.; shoe, ⅞ x $\frac{7}{16}$; length of cushions on front seat, 37 in. The cushions are made up solid on each seat and nailed to same. Not detachable.

Mounting.—Plated rein rail and screen for dash.
Trimming.—Green cloth or Bedford cord.
Painting.—Gear, carmine or maroon. Body, pea green. Gold stripes.

CANADIAN
SLEIGHS

A large Canadian sleigh drawn by a unicorn team.
The sleigh has solid wooden runners with the body set low to the ground.

Harper's Weekly
February 1887

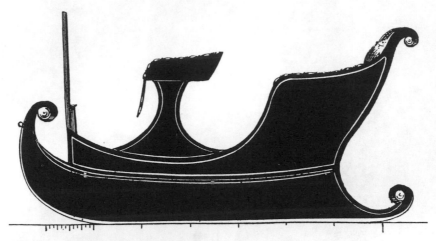

No. 57. RUSSO–CANADIAN SLEIGH.—SCALE, ONE-HALF INCH.

RUSSO–CANADIAN SLEIGH.

(See Plate No. 57.)

THE accompanying plate represents one of the numerous variations from the typical Russian patterns of sleighs which have been developed in Canada; and then introduced to the American public, to a greater or less extent, through New-York and Boston. This shows one of the varieties least known at present; but a single enterprising builder of Canada feeling inclined to work the New-York market, or a single example imported from Canada by some railroad magnate, is liable at any time to bring this or any other Canadian sleigh into sudden popularity; and we are therefore glad to put it on record, and Mr. Chas. A. Francis will please accept our thanks for securing the sketch. We are also indebted to his hand for the following description of its mechanical features:

Dimensions.—The runners are made of $1\frac{1}{2}$ in. ash; three bars are framed into them, and they are well stayed by braces under the bars. The body is made of $\frac{1}{2}$-inch panel stuff, bent on a framework. The body at the arms has a $4\frac{1}{2}$ inch flare.

The driver's-seat is made for one person, and is twenty inches wide on the seat-frame. The boot for driver is built up from the inside of framework of main body; and being narrow on top, more room is allowed for admission to the back seat. Sometimes the front seat is made for two persons, and it is then well to hinge the front seat. The dash is made narrow on top, and wings are fitted on each side, with fine wire netting covering them.

The scroll at top of back is made of thick whitewood. The scrolls on the runners are of the same thickness as the runner; they must be securely fastened and well ironed, or otherwise they are liable to get broken off.

The panels are made high at the points of entrance, to give room for sufficient wrappings, as the Canadian winters are very severe. Fenders, extending the full length of the body, and standing out $4\frac{1}{2}$ inches, form a step, and offer a place to scrape snow from the feet.

Finish.—Painting, dark carmine; striping, black. Trimming, fur.

No. 53. RUSSIAN SLEIGH.—Scale, one-half inch.

BUILT BY LARIVIERE, OF MONTREAL, CANADA.

SLEIGHS of typically Russian design are much in use in the Lower Canadian Province, principally in the cities of Montreal and Quebec; and many examples of this pattern are now owned in New-York City. The driver's-seat lifts out, it being fitted into a socket, and made fast by means of a thumb-nut. It has a knuckle each side, which allows the top of seat to be thrown forward, to admit persons more readily to the back seat. The seat is high, the driver being almost in a standing position when driving. The runners are sawed out of ash plank. The body is made with $3\frac{1}{2}$ in. flare at top of cushion, the back being 4 inches narrower than the body at front of seat. It is made much after the manner of a Portland cutter. A rail of $\frac{1}{2}$ in. iron stands out 6 in., forming a fender or guard.

Dimensions.—Width of body, on top of cushion, $39\frac{1}{2}$ in. The dash has a wire netting on top, and also a driving-rail, both silvered.

Finish.—Painting: light vermilion, glazed with carmine, on both body and runners; all ironwork black. Stripe with $\frac{3}{8}$ in. line of black, on panels of body and runners. Trimming: red velvet or plush; plumes, red.

The Hub
August 1882

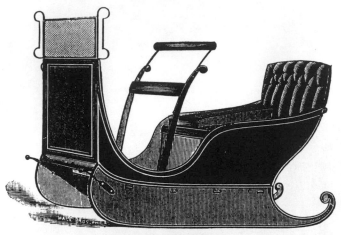

CANADIAN SLEIGH.

Canadian Sleigh.

PLATE NO. 31.

There are characteristics in this plate not to be found in other sleighs. They are, we believe, of Russian origin, but are now made in the Eastern States, and extensively so in Canada. The runners are cut from a solid plank, 1½-inch stuff, and framed upright with four cross-bars, its tenons showing from the outside. The sides of the body are made from a solid poplar plank, which is planed to shape to have side swell and turn-under, to give it the appearance of a coach body. The back is paneled and glued to the back pillars, the latter glued against the sides. The front seat is more to lean against than for setting on, being simply a trimmed cross-bar, 3 inches wide, and when not used is thrown forward. The dash is framed to the body, and gives it the support from the front. The iron rail starts from the upper part of dash, and ends at the upper extreme back on top of sides, supported with two braces as shown. This sleigh was obtained from the warerooms of Messrs. W. P. Sargent & Co., Boston, Mass.

Body : width across front of dash, 33 inches; across bottom of body, 33 inches ; above top of seat, 39 inches ; across back top of side panels, 40 inches ; turn-under of body, 3½ inches each side. Runners : width across, out to out, 32 inches. Thickness of runners, 1½ inches. Shoes, ¼ inch by 1½-inch steel.

Painting.—Body : black. Runners : black, striped a fine line of red, runners and body.

Trimming.—Green cloth. The back is trimmed in plaited diamonds, tufted with plain green tufts ; a narrow roll is applied across the top. The cushion has a plaited diamond top ; cloth welts, 1⅝-inch front facing, with plain 1-inch raiser. The fall is sewed to the cushion, and is simply hemmed ; it has a plain raiser around the edge. The rug is a green carpet, with red figure, and is bound with cloth or fringe. Sheep-skin mats are often seen in these sleighs.

Mountings.—Silver.

Carriage Monthly
July 1886

CANADIAN SLEIGH.

PLATE NO. 39.—VOL. 24.—HALF-INCH SCALE.

Messrs R. M. Bingham & Co., of Rome, N. Y., furnished us with this design of Canadian sleigh, which will be placed on the market the coming season. The novelty shown is in the shape and finish of the dash, which heretofore has been made straight, while here it has a gentle curve, adding much to the general appearance. Also the center molding, including the medalion on the sides of the seat, adds to its finish. The back panel has a molding in the center, also a medalion to correspond with the side panels. The front seat is hinged at the bottom of the body to facilitate entrance to the seat.

Width of body across bottom, 36 inches; across front on top, 36 inches; in the middle of the body, 41 inches. Front seat. 28½ inches. Turn-under, 2½ inches each side. Runners: width of track, 36 inches; thickness of runners, 1¼ inches; size of shoes, 1¼ by ½-inch steel.

Painting.—Body: light claret, striped a fine line of primrose yellow. Runners: primrose yellow, striped a broad and two fine lines of black. Outside of dash painted yellow and striped black; inside of dash light claret, striped yellow.

Trimming.—Maroon cloth, diamonds for back, sides and cushion. Front seat trimmed plain, strap for lazy-back, dog-cart style. This seat works on hinges, so as to swing forward, or it easily can be removed and used as a two-passenger sleigh only. Rug, maroon color, with primrose figure. Rail on front dash silver-plated.

Mountings.—Silver.

———

Carriage Monthly
August 1888

RUMBLE-SEAT
SLEIGHS

No. 56. PONY SLEIGH WITH RUMBLE.—Built by Price & Shaw, of St. John, N. B.

SCALE, ONE-HALF INCH TO THE FOOT.

No. 56.—PONY SLEIGH WITH RUMBLE.

This design, also furnished by Messrs. Price & Shaw, is described by them as follows :

The height of the dasher is 4 ft., and the width is 2 ft. 3 in. The width of the body is 2 ft. 8 in. on bottom. The width of the body on the outside of the panels is 3 ft. 8 in. The front of the body is 14 in., and is made for a child's seat, which is fastened with hinges, and trimmed.

The panel is 20 by 8 in. with a top back almost any depth (we make them about 12 in). The benches are all 14 in. high, and are 18 in. apart. The dickey-seat is 28 in. from the runner ; and the runner projects 2 ft. 2 in. back of the back bench.

Painting.—Dark brown or lake, striped with fine gold lines.

Trimming.—Crimson plush is well adapted for this sleigh.

Note: The wishbone attached to the seat is a trident used for supporting the reins while the sleigh was driven from the rear seat.

The Hub
August 1881

Plate No. 29. VICTORIA SLEIGH, WITH RUMBLE.—Scale, one-half inch.

(Drawn and Engraved expressly for "The Hub.")

THIS attractive pattern represents one of the very latest New-York styles, the outlines of the body being similar to those applied to Victorias at the present time.

The sides are full, giving ample seating capacity. The lower portion of the body, as the drawing shows, is open; but if preferred, this could be closed; the panel then, as on a carriage body, forming a recess. The bottomsides are each made out of one bent piece. Solid sides are used for the upper half of the back quarter, for which 2-inch whitewood will answer. The back panel is grooved in. A pillar is framed into the bottomsides, within 1 inch of the outside. This pillar is connected with the back corner-pillar or bent bottomside, by means of a rail about 1¼ x 1¼ in. in size, even with the bottom edge of the molding. The side panel is mitered to the back edge of the bottomside. The lower part of the side, forming the center pillar, is glued to the inside frame piece referred to above. It will be advisable to bridge the joint over at the connection which the center pillar forms with the side panel, in order to keep the joint from showing. Light rockers are screwed on the inside of the bottomsides, from the center pillar to the front, and these are connected with the runners by means of corner-plates.

The rumble, as will be noticed, consists of a top and bottom frame. The seat, or top frame, is supported by iron stays; while the front of the rumble, or toe-board, is connected with the body by two iron stays. The center of the body rests on a wooden bench, strengthened crosswise by means of stays. The side-stays are secured to the uprights of the bench by two bolts. Considerable skill and care will be required on the part of the blacksmith in forming the side-stays, which, if not made properly, are very apt to spoil the good appearance of the sleigh.

Dimensions.—Width of body, at the center of the arm-rail, 42 in.; ditto at the back, at the arm-rail, 38 in.; ditto at the front, 32 in. Turn-under, 3¼ in. The runners are ⅞ in. square. The shoes are ⅞ x 1/16 in. The side-stays should be made out of ¾ x ½ in. oval iron. Track, 40½ in.

Finish.—Painting: Panels, medium shade of green; moldings, black, edged with a fine line of vermilion, deep shade. Runners, vermilion, striped black. Trimming, green plush. The back and cushion on the body are laid off in diamonds. Raisers on the fall, 1 in. A plain box-cushion is used for the rumble, with fall the same as on the body. Carpet, to match the trimming. Plumes, red, with silver tops. Mountings, silver.

The Hub
July 1883

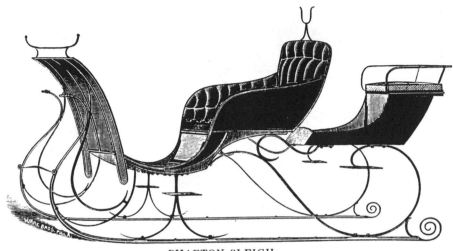

PHAETON SLEIGH.

PLATE NO. 66.—HALF-INCH SCALE.

Phaeton Sleigh.

PLATE NO. 66.

This design was kindly sent us for publication by Henry Hooker & Co., of New Haven, Conn., and represents one of their neatest styles.

The dimensions as received are as follows: Seat 38 inches, back 35 inches, turn-under 3½ inches, rumble 22 inches, and height of body 17 inches.

Painting.—Body: panels dark green, moldings black, rumble black, striped; moldings edged a fine line of carmine. Runners: bright carmine, striped with fine line of black.

Mountings.—Silver.

Carriage Monthly
November 1883

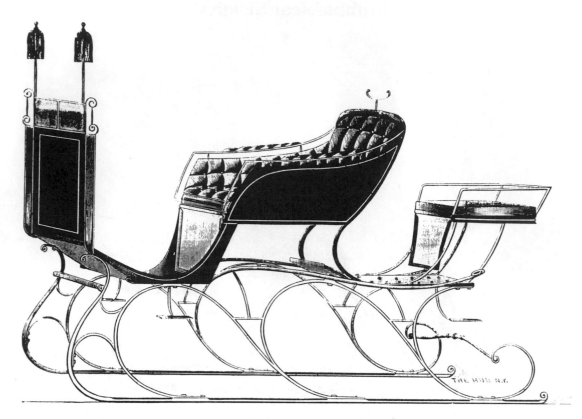

Plate No. 38. SPIDER-PHAETON SLEIGH.—Scale, three-quarter inch.

As a rule, latterly almost universal, the bodies of the heavier classes of sleighs now follow very closely, in outline and general finish, those of wheeled vehicles; and we think the experiment, here suggested, of adapting the body of a Spider Phaeton to use on runners will prove satisfactory.

The body should not have as much side-swell as if placed on a carriage, but may otherwise be built the same as usual. The upper section of each side is either made of solid whitewood, or of frame-work, and in the latter case a thin panel is used, and put into a groove. If solid sides are used, 2½ in. whitewood will be sufficient. The corner-pillars are made of bent wood. For the bottomsides bent wood will also be preferable, at least from the back of the middle pillar, and it is then spliced to the front part. A plate is screwed to the inside, and rounded at the outside. The pillar and bottomside, if of bent wood, can be made very light, or considerably lighter than on a carriage, as the iron side-stays give great support. The middle and back corner-pillars are framed into the bottomside. On the middle-pillar, if solid sides are used, the sides are halved to the pillar, and mitered to the back corner-pillar, the same as mentioned in the description of Fashion Plate No. 27, page 252.

The rumble consists of a bottom and top frame combined by four upright stays, which are bolted to the frames. The back of the rumble is supported by the back stays of the running-gear, and the front rests on two stays, forming a T, and bolted to the bottomside. Near the bottomsides of the body a lap is welded to the bottom plate of the bottomsides, and the rumble stay is welded to this lap. The runners are bolted to the toe-board bracket, and further strengthened by two stays welded to the side-stays.

Dimensions.—Width of body on top of the middle-pillar in front, 44 in.; ditto back, on top, 39 in.; and ditto bottom, 30 in. Width of dash, 28½ in. Turn-under, 6½ in. Runners, ⅞ × 1 in. Shoes, ⅞ × ⁵⁄₁₆ in. steel. Side-stays, ⁹⁄₁₆ × 1⅛ in. oval. Cross-stays, ½ × ¾ in. oval. Track, 39 in., from out to out.

Finish.—Painting of the side and back panels, blue, not too dark; and moldings, black, with a fine line of gold. Running-part, light blue, with two lines of gold. Trimming, blue cloth throughout. Carpet, blue, with yellow figures. Plumes, yellow. Mountings, silver.

The Hub
August 1884

TWO–PASSENGER SLEIGH (with Rumble).

PLATE NO. 29.—VOL. 23.—HALF-INCH SCALE.

The body of this sleigh is of the latest improved design for proportion and style. The upper panel is plain, but molded with ¾ by ¼-inch oval round moldings. The lower part of body represents shell, ending with a scroll front. The body can be constructed in two separate parts, comprising seat and lower part of body. When body is made out of solid sides, it is laid out in such a manner as to give the sides the least possible thickness for the round and turn-under of the body. It is planed to the shape and moldings, and shells worked out of the solid stuff. In case the seat is made out of two parts, the upper part is made exactly as a phaeton seat, and lower part the same as when sides are made in one, with the exception that less thickness of stuff is wanted. There is no labor saved, and one method is about as much work as the other. The rumble is plain, made of ⅞-inch thick board. The runners are bent differently from the regular style. They are short, and well curved upward front, both runners running together in an Indian head. The dasher is of silver-plated wire and plated frame. The iron stays consist of three separate pieces each side, which are very easily made by any blacksmith. The front steps are solid on front stays, and back steps for rumble are dispensed with, the end scroll serving for a foot-rest on entering the rumble.

Width of body at front, 32 inches ; at center, 44 inches, and across back panel 38 inches. Amount of turn-under, each side, 6 inches, only convex shape. Width across rumble at bottom, 22 inches; at top, 24 inches ; at seat frame, 26 inches ; depth, 14 inches. Thickness and depth of runners, 1⅛ by 1⅜ inches, bent to shape. Width of track, 40 inches. Width across dash at bottom, 36 inches ; at center, 48 inches, and across top, 44 inches.

Painting.—Body : upper panels blue, lower part of shells and rumble black ; shells outlined with fine yellow lines ; also molding on seat. Runners : blue, striped two fine lines of yellow, ¼ inch apart.

Trimming.—Blue silk plush. The full back is trimmed in blocks, plaited, and tufted with blue plush buttons; the cushion has a plaited block top with plain front and fall, which is attached to it; the welts are of plain seaming lace to match in color.

BERLIN VICTORIA SLEIGH.

PLATE No. 27.—VOL. 25

With this plate we give an original style, designed by Mr. Paul Steinbeck, draftsman for Messrs. R. M. Bingham & Co., Rome, N. Y. The body is made the same as the regular Victoria or cabriolet sleigh, with solid sides and $\frac{5}{16}$-inch thick back panel. The moldings on the body are worked on solid, also the carving and shell. The carving and shell part must be well finished to look good. If the front scrolls on the body were made larger, or a tiger's head substituted for it, it would look much richer for an expensive sleigh. The rumble is a plain board seat without a back, supported on iron stays, and is made but for one man only. The combination of the curves for the stays show some originality, and have a good appearance. The dash panel is cut down on top, which looks well on these sleighs, and is well curved down toward the sides. The fenders are of patent leather.

—Body : Width across front, 36 inches ; width at lion's heads, 45 inches ; back on top, near scroll, 39 inches. Amount of turn-under, 5 inches on each side and its shape is convex only. Rumble : width across bottom, 21 inches ; across top, 26 inches, giving 2½ inches flare for each side. Seat frame, ⅞ inch thick, back and side boards, ⅝ inch thick. Runners : width of track, 40 inches from out to out, ⅜ inch wider front than back ; width across front on top 28 inches. Size of runners, 1⅝ by 1¾ inches ; shoes, 1⅝ by ⅜-inch round iron. Stays, ⅝ by ⅞-inch oval iron.

Painting.—Body: side and back panels, deep blue, dark panel the same color, and moldings black. The front part of the sleigh, comprising the three small ovals and the shells are painted light blue in contrast with the main panels. Rumble blue, same as the main panels.

Runners.—Deep carmine, striped two $\frac{3}{16}$-inch lines of black, ½ inch apart. Body striped a heavy line of carmine around the edges of the moldings. Winged lion heads on body and dragon heads on runners, are picked out in black and yellow.

Trimming.—Blue cloth; finish, squares and blocks for back, cushion and sides. Falls plain, except ⅞-inch wide raisers. Carpet deep blue, with black and red figures.

Finish.—Body rails, rein standard and rein rail, including the bells, gold plated; plumes, egret feathers, of blue and red color.

Mountings.—Gold.

Carriage Monthly
July 1889

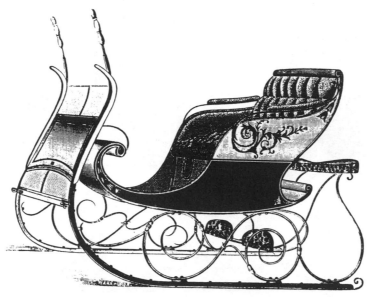

TWO-PASSENGER SLEIGH.

Exhibited by Messrs. Healey & Co., New York.

PLATE NO. 41.—VOL. 25.

Two-Passenger Sleigh.

PLATE NO. 41.

EXHIBITED BY MESSRS. HEALEY & CO., NEW YORK.

This sleigh is partly original ; it has ogee back pillars ; sawed or bent stuff can be used ; bent bottom sides, moldings worked on solid, the back and side panels $\frac{5}{16}$ inch, placed into grooves; carving cut and glued against the panel. The sides can also be made of solid stuff, the moldings and carving worked on solid, which is less labor. Size of runners $1\frac{1}{2}$ inches square, bent in one piece, paneled in front for the dash. Width of body at the front scroll 36 inches ; at the bottom 34 inches. Width of body at its widest part 44 inches, and 39 inches on the back panel near the top scroll. Amount of turn-under each side 5 inches ; height of body from the floor $18\frac{1}{2}$ inches. Saddle 16 by 10 inches, 32 inches from the floor.

Runners $1\frac{1}{2}$ inches square, and shoes $1\frac{1}{2}$ by $\frac{3}{8}$ inch. Side screens $6\frac{1}{2}$ inches wide. Track 39 inches, and on top of dash 34 inches.

Painting.—Upper panels, cream white ; lower panels, bright lake. Moldings a darker shade. Carving on side quarter panels, gold. Runners and stays, bright lake, striped a broad line of gold.

Trimming.—Back, cushion and fall, deep brown plush, with striped lace to match the color. Finish of the back shown on the illustration. Sides plain, with a light roll. Cushions, of which there are two, made up in squares, and driving cushion made up soft, with rolls each side and squares between. Rolls on side rails. Footman's saddle and foot rests covered with tiger-skin. Plumes to match the color of the lower side panels.

Mountings.—Silver.

ANTIQUE SLEIGH.

PLATE No. 29.—VOL. 26.—HALF-INCH SCALE.

Antique Sleigh.

PLATE No. 29.

With this plate we illustrate an entirely new design of an antique pattern. The new antique curricle pattern, only recently made, has plain panels without any recess, which looks exceedingly well on a curricle, and, no doubt, will look as well on a sleigh; but we have made the design with a recess, which gives two different designs to work from; those who prefer the plain sides can use the outlines of the body only. To look well, the body must have a great deal of turn-under, and be convex on top and concave on the bottom.

The Stanhope pillar and front are beaded, and the scrolls on the back end must be well cut. The rumble is of the regular shape, and all the corners, front and back, are rounded; the runners and braces are of the usual shape and finish, with the exception of being heavier.

Painting.—Body: main panels, blue; moldings, Stanhope pillars, bracket-front and rumble, black. Runners: blue, including the front panel, striped yellow or cream color.

Trimming.—Blue cloth; style, squares, very full. Fall, ⅞-inch raisers, otherwise plain. Cushion front plain. Rumble cushion plain finish; edges bound with cloth; fall, ¾-inch raisers, and rails covered. Plumes to match.

Mountings.—Gold.

Carriage Monthly
July 1890

PLATE No. 16.   QUEEN'S BODY SLEIGH WITH RUMBLE.—SCALE, ONE-HALF INCH.

THE most noteworthy features in the accompanying design are the full sweep "queen's" body which, as will be noticed, has very deep quarters, also curved quarter panels and scroll work at the front. Bodies of this design suspended on wheels minus the scroll work, have of late been considered the prevailing style by most of our prominent builders. The carved dragon's heads on top of runners should be of good size to be in harmony with the proportions of the body.

We give a list of the principal dimensions :

Length of body on the belt line from toe-scroll, 44 in.; depth of panels at seat line, 20 in. Height of panels over all, 26 in. Width of body outside at front of the arm-rail, out to out, 47 in.; width on top at rear, 41½ in.; width at tail-bar, 38½ in.: ditto at toe, 38 in.

The runners are 1½ in. square. Shoes, 1½ × ⅝ in. The iron for gear scrolls is 1 × ½ in. oval, fulled and squared at connecting points with runners. The scrolls at the connecting points of attachment to the body require a T at the tail-bar and at the center-bottom. Track, 4 ft.

Painting.—Body panels, dark chocolate. Moulding and ornamentations; black, striped and tipped with gold-leaf. Running part, canary, striped with broad line of black.

Trimming.—Seal plush. Rumble cushion, dark-brown cloth. Mountings

The Hub
June 1891

PLATE No. 16.   QUEEN'S BODY SLEIGH, WITH GROOM'S SADDLE.—Scale, one-half inch.

SCALE, ½ INCH TO THE FOOT.

(See Fashion Plate No. 16.)

FASHION PLATE No. 16 represents a new and pleasing design for a two-passenger sleigh, with a groom's saddle, shaped like a riding saddle. The foot-rests are secured to the back stays, and are fur-lined.

The body is similar to that of a victoria; the sides are comparatively plain, the inside molding being nailed on; the outside moldings are worked on solid, the panels being set in a groove. The bottom-sides can be made of one bent piece, no rocker-plate being required. Runners, 1 x 1¼ in.; shoes, 1⅛ x 1⅝ in.; scroll irons, ¾ in. oval.

Width of body on top, 42 in.; and at bottom, 38 in. Track, measured outside to outside on the ground, 42 in.

Painting.—Large panel, Nile green; panel between moldings, white; mouldings, black. Gearing, yellow, striped black.

Trimming.—Green silk plush. Mountings, gold.

The Hub
June 1893

160

CABRIOLET
or
VICTORIA
SLEIGHS

No. 44. CABRIOLET SLEIGH WITH CANADIAN DASHER.—Scale, one-half inch.

THE body of this design resembles that shown in Plate No 42, but we would call attention to the following distinguishing features. It is somewhat larger, and the driving-seat is more elevated and has an iron seat-rail, with driving-box and lazy-back. The dasher stands perpendicular; it is of wood, and extends the width of the toe-board, and wire snow-screens are added both at the top and sides. The rods for the support of the plumes are inserted in sockets on the front of the dash-board, from which they can readily be removed when not required for use; they soil very easily. Ornamental stays extend from the side screens to the top, and these serve as rein-protectors, to keep them from slipping off. The toe-board and bottom-side of the front are in plain straight lines, and easily constructed. The back seat is built in the usual Cabriolet form, with solid sides. The lower part of the body has a wooden knee-support on the runner, and the other supports are iron stays having graceful curves. Both ascending steps have fenders attached to them. The back scrolls are connected by a cross-stay, as shown, which is essential in all sleighs, in order to prevent the runners from spreading. The back seat has an iron arm-rail, with an arm-rest, stuffed and tufted, secured to it.

Dimensions.—Width of body, across the arm-rail of the hind seat, 40 in., contracted 2 in.; turn-under of side, 2 in. The frame of the dickey-seat is 36 in. long by 16 in. wide. The body stands 16 in. from the ground. Height of rear seat, 15 in. to top of cushion; ditto, front seat, 16 in. Track, 42 in.

Painting.—Body, ultramarine blue, broad-striped with cream-color on the panel, an inch from the molding. Moldings, black, fine-lined with cane color. Dickey-seat, black. Dasher, blue, striped like the body. Running-part, light blue, striped cream-color.

Trimming.—Blue plush. Carpet, blue, figured. Plumes, white horse-hair, with blue tops. Mountings, silver.

The Hub
July 1882

Cabriolet or Victoria Sleighs

The Hub
July 1882

Plate No. 38. CABRIOLET SLEIGH, NEW-YORK PATTERN.—Scale, one-half inch.

(Drawn and Engraved expressly for "The Hub.")

THE outlines of the body of this Sleigh closely resemble those of carriage bodies of the same general type; and all of them, with the single exception of the back edge of the piece forming a pillar at the lower section of the back quarter, are curved according to the latest reigning fashion. The lower line of the rocker forms a continual sweep from the cross-bar to the dash. The appearance of the back quarter is full, according to the present style. A child's-seat can be attached, if desired, as on carriage bodies.

A change at the back quarter could be effected by continuing the portion that forms a pillar at the lower half of the body, up to the arm-rail, thus forming a Stanhope pillar. In this case we would recommend having the panel set in ⅛ in. from the outside of the Stanhope pillar, which should then be worked gradually to ₁⁵⁄₁₆ in. at the corner-pillar, in case solid sides are used. It is evident that, by setting the panel further in at the Stanhope pillar, this pillar will show more distinctly, and will give the back quarter a far better appearance. The lower part of the body is not left open, but a sunken panel is inserted about 1⅛ in. from the outside. This will necessitate closing up the lower part of the back as well. The bottomsides, as usual, are made out of bent wood, 3 in. thickness being sufficient. To get an easy sweep at the bottomsides, it will be necessary to cheat ¾ in. from the outside line of the side-swell, at the point where the horizontal molding intersects with the back corner-pillar. For the rockers, 1⅛ in. ash is of sufficient thickness. It is worthy of note that, as a general rule, there is no need to make the timbers on sleigh bodies as heavy as on carriage bodies.

Great skill is required, on the part of the smith, in ironing this Cabriolet Sleigh, or in fact, any other sleigh where the iron stays of the running-part consist wholly of curved lines, as graceful sweeping of these iron stays is essential to the good appearance of the vehicle. It will prove of great assistance to the smith, if the entire running-part of this sleigh be first drafted on the blackboard, which will not only expedite the work, but insure greater accuracy. There is a wooden trestle in the center of the body, which gives additional strength to the running-part. An iron brace extends from the center of the trestle to the runners, forming a T at the runners.

Dimensions.—Width of body at the arm-rail, in the center, 46 in.; ditto on the back, at the height of the arm-rail, 40 in.; ditto at the height of the horizontal molding, 38 in.; ditto at the termination of the scroll, from out to out, 36 in.; and at the dash, 32 in. Turn-under, 4½ in. Rocker-plates, 2¼ x ⅜ in., fastened with 1½ in. No. 16 screws. Runners, 1⅛ in. deep by ⅞ in. thick. Shoes for the runners, ⅞ x ₁⁵⁄₁₆ in., steel. Stays, 1³⁄₁₆ x ⅜ in., oval. Track, 40 in., from out to out.

Finish.—Painting: Body-panels, English purple lake. Moldings, black, with a fine line of gold. Runners, black, with fine lines of carmine on the top and face of the iron-work. The dash is striped with a broad "panel stripe," and minor fine-lines of carmine. Trimming, purple plush for the back cushion and fall of the back seat, and brown cloth for the driver's-seat. The diamond pattern is recommended for the squab work. The carpet should match the color of the trimming. Plumes, red. Mountings, silver.

Plate No. 27. CABRIOLET SLEIGH, WITH OGEE BACK.—Scale, one-half inch.

The Hub
July 1884
(description next page)

CABRIOLET SLEIGH, WITH OGEE BACK.

(See Fashion Plate No. 27.)

FOR the past ten years the demand for fine sleighs has been rapidly increasing in the larger cities, and improvements in style and finish have kept pace with the demand. New designs have been originated each season ; and while some of these have not proved altogether satisfactory, and therefore have only a short existence, others have been more favorably received, and are now standard patterns. The tide of fashion at present seems to be drifting in the direction of greater display of carved work on sleighs, and work now in progress authorizes us to look for the appearance of specially elaborate turnouts during the coming winter.

On the accompanying Fashion Plate we have adopted the ogee pillar for the back, terminating in a scroll. The rockers on the body can be made of one piece as far as the toe-board bracket. The bracket would become too cross-grained if the rocker were continued to the dash ; and, being light, it would be likely to split when fastening the plate. The rocker terminates at the middle pillar. The bottom sill is made wide enough to be even with the inside of the rocker, and projects over on the outside of the rocker 1½ inch. The middle pillar reaches from the bottom of the sill to the top of the panel, and is framed into the bottomside. The sides of the hind quarter are made of thick whitewood, and are halved on to the middle pillar, thus making the middle pillar even with the inner surface of the sides. The back corner-pillars are made of bent wood, and are framed into the bottomside. The corner-pillars are 1½ in. thick at the open or bottom section of the body. The sill is lightened on the inside from the middle pillar, to the thickness of the corner-pillar at the back end. A cross-bar is framed into the sills. The rocker-plate extends to the cross-bar, and forms an angle long enough for the introduction of three screws. To make a neat job, the plate in the open space is made half round and let into the cross-bar, which is also rounded off on both the inside and outside. The moldings on the back are 1½ in. wide, and rounded over. The moldings on the sides, middle pillar and bottom sill are worked on. The continued molding from the sill to the driver's-seat is glued on. The front seat is made with solid sides and back, but can be changed, if preferred, to a stick seat, or a regular coach seat, having iron rails only.

The wooden runners are fastened to the bottom of the body in front, and a stay extends from the runner to the front of the toe-board, making a nice finish. The dash is made of wood, and is held in position by iron plates bolted to the body. A wooden bench supports the body in the center, which, however, is not absolutely necessary, and can be dispensed with if preferred. In the absence of a wooden bench an iron cross-bar is required, to be bolted under the body, forming a T at the runners, and fastened there by two bolts.

Dimensions.—Width of body at the top of middle pillar, 45 in.; ditto on the back at the arm-rail, 38 in.; ditto at the back cross-bar, 35 in. at the dash, 32 in. Turn-under, 5 in. Rocker-plate, 2 × ⅜ in., fastened with 1½ in. No. 16 screws.

Finish.—Painting of seat panels and center panel of dash, dark green ; and moldings and boot panel, black. The moldings are striped with a fine line of gold. Running-part, green, several shades lighter than the body, and striped with two round lines of gold at a distance, and a medium line of black. Trimming, green cloth throughout. The back on the hind seat has a roll on top. The rest of the back, and the cushion tops, are laid off in large buscuits. Carpet, green, with black figures. Plumes, yellow. Mountings, brass.

Plate No. 40. **CABRIOLET SLEIGH, WITH DOORS.**—Scale, three-quarter inch.

The Hub
August 1884
(description next page)

CABRIOLET SLEIGH, WITH DOORS.

(See Fashion Plate No. 40.)

THE use of light doors in connection with sleigh bodies has been gaining in favor lately, and it will be readily admitted that they not only increase the comfort of passengers, but that the appearance of the sleigh is improved. These doors are light, and can be made of thick whitewood, or frame-work with a thin panel on the outside. In the former case the swell is worked on the outside, and, after completing the outside, the piece is lightened out on the inside. Two ash pillars are glued on the inside, one in front and the other at the back end of the door, for fastening the hinges and lock. Doors made out of a solid plank are in most cases painted on the inside, while doors made of frame-work are trimmed over. The doors are made in the twist, which is necessitated by the considerable turn-under of the front pillar at the hind seat, and the almost straight sides at the boot.

The molding forming a finish at the boot projects over the sides of the body 1 in. at the top of the door, and is worked gradually to $\frac{5}{16}$ in. thick at the bottom, retaining nearly the same thickness to the top. This molding should be made of hard wood. The sides at the hind seat are made of whitewood; and a thickness of 2½ in. will be required, as they will have to be worked winding. This will leave the sides about 1 in. thick when finished at the ends.

The back corner-pillars are lapped into the rockers, but project 1 in. outside of the rocker. The rocker is gauged off on the inside, and shaved off to nothing toward the back face of the corner-pillar; and the sides are then fitted to it, forming a miter joint. The back panel is put into the groove as usual. The moldings are very wide,—or not less than 2 in.

The hind seat is deep, but not of great height, which gives the seat a very light appearance. The depth of the seat, as shown in this drawing, allows the trimmer to put in a very heavy back. A deep seat is a very desirable feature in a sleigh, as heavier clothing is generally worn when riding in a sleigh than in a wheeled vehicle. The boot, as is the rule with sleighs of this class, is of good size, but not out of proportion with the rest.

The runners are fastened to the bottom of the body at the front, in a manner similar to that illustrated in connection with Plate No. 39. One of the step-shanks of the front step is bolted to the runners, and at the same time secures the runners to the body. The front stay on this sleigh, as well as on No. 39, forms a circle with the runner. The remaining stays differ from all others illustrated in this number. They are plain but tasteful, and of sufficient strength to stand all ordinary strain. Three cross-stays and a cross-bar in front add additional strength to the running-part.

Dimensions.—Width of body at the middle-pillar, on top of the arm-rail, 46 in.; ditto at the back on top, 38 in.; ditto at the tail-bar, 36 in.; ditto at the dash, 32 in.; and on top of the boot, 34 in. Turn-under, 5½ in. Rocker-plates, 2 × ½ in., fastened with 1½ in. No. 16 screws. Runners, ⅞ × 1⅛ in. Shoes, ⅞ × $\frac{5}{16}$ in. steel. The side-stays are ⅝ × ¾ in., oval; and the cross-stays, ⅝ × 1⅛ in., oval. Track, 40 in., from out to out.

Finish.—Painting of the hind quarter and door panels, dark green; and moldings and boot panels, black. The moldings are edged with a fine line of carmine. Running-part, carmine, with a narrow stripe and two medium lines of black. Trimming, green cloth throughout. The pipe pattern is used for the back, and the cushion top is laid off in squares at the front and back end, and with an oblong square in the center. The trimming for the driver's-seat is plain. Carpet, dark green, with black figures. Plumes, red. Mountings, silver.

VICTORIA SLEIGH.

(See Fashion Plate No. 28.)

THIS is another elaborate pattern, the carvings being particularly defined at the front of the arm-piece, front of the body, and at the back rail.

Heavy whitewood is used for the sides, about 3½ in. thick, which, after being fitted, is lightened out to ⅞ in. The driver's-seat is of the style used on Victoria carriages, and has an excellent effect. A straight wooden dash is attached to the front, with a wire screen on the top. The rails and also the wirework are plated. As the driver's-seat is liable to be occupied by ladies occasionally, a lazy-back is attached to this, as to all other four-passenger sleighs. The runners are attached to the toe-board bracket, which allows of considerably shortening the running-part. The iron parts are of graceful design, and well proportioned.

Dimensions.—Width of body between the panels, at the height of the seat in front, 39 in.; ditto outside of the rockers at the rear end, 25½ in.; and ditto at front of bracket, 32 in. Turn-under, 6½ in. Runners, 1 × 1¼ in. Shoes, 1 × ½ in., cast-steel. Track, 40 in., from out to out.

Finish.—Painting of the body panels, a medium shade of blue; and moldings, black, striped with a fine line of gold and a hair line of light blue. Runners, carmine, with a medium stripe of gold and a stout line of black. Trimming, blue cloth. The style of the upholstering for the back and cushion is similar to that used for the Shell-body Cutter. The plumes are of the latest pattern, and composed of three sections, each section being of a different color. The colors introduced in the plumes should be made to harmonize with those used in the painting. Mountings, brass.

Plate No. 28.   VICTORIA SLEIGH.—Scale, five-eighths Inch.

The Hub
July 1885

168

Cabriolet or Victoria Sleighs

RUSSIAN CABRIOLET SLEIGH.

(See Fashion Plate No. 27.)

THIS pattern is comparatively plain, as compared with those which follow, both carving and scroll-work being entirely omitted.

The rear quarter is unlike those used on wheeled Cabriolet bodies, being lower and deeper, and while it would not appear to advantage on a carriage, we consider it very satisfactory on runners. Experience has taught sleigh-builders the propriety of introducing deep quarters, as these allow of introducing heavy trimming without encroaching on the seat-room. The use of doors is also a great improvement, as these serve to protect the feet from the cold. The doors are made of whitewood, and the swell is worked on.

The sweep of the lower molding has a pleasing effect. It is worked on. The molded pieces which extend to the front and rear from the door, are made of whitewood. The front extension projects from the boot 1 in., while the rear extension is even with the body.

The sides of the quarters are made of thick whitewood, and the moldings are worked on. A thin panel is used for the back. The moldings on the back are wide, or from 2 in. upward. A wooden dash is used, as on plate No. 28, and the runners are fastened in the same manner as described for the next succeeding design. The style of ironwork generally resembles that shown in plate 28.

Dimensions.—Width of body on top of rear seat in front, 46 in.; ditto back, 38 in.; and ditto at dash, 32 in. Turn-under, 5 in. Rocker-plates, 2 × ½ in., fastened with 1¾ in. No. 16 screws. Runners, 1 × 1⅛ in. Shoes, 1 × ⅜ in., cast-steel. Side stays, ½ × ¾ in., oval. Track, 40 in., from out to out.

Finish.—Painting of the rear quarters, back and door panels, dark green, and moldings and boot panels, black. The moldings are striped with a fine line of light green. The color of the runners is somewhat lighter than the body color, and striped with a round line of black, and a fine line of light green. Trimming, green cloth throughout. The style of the trimming is similar to that described for No. 28. Carpet, dark green, with light green figures. Mountings, silver.

Plate No. 27. RUSSIAN CABRIOLET SLEIGH.—Scale, five-eighths inch.

The Hub
July 1885

CABRIOLET SLEIGH.

PLATE No. 38.—VOL. 24.—HALF-INCH SCALE

This style represents one of the newest of cabriolet sleighs. The main outlines are almost the same as a regular cabriolet body, with the exception of the front scroll. The sides of the body are taken from a solid plank, the shells and moldings worked on solid, and the back of the body has no shells. The boot is made of 1-inch thick board, and a rocker of 1½ inches thickness glued on the inside of the boot, and the sides of body glued against it. This makes the construction of the body very simple, and is also the least labor. Light rocker plates 1½ by ⅜-inch should be put in from the front bracket to part of the body, so as to give sufficient strength to the front bracket and also to the neck, which is only 1⅞ inches wide near the front scroll of the body. The moldings on the boot can be worked on, which is the best for first-class work, but they can also be glued and braded. The stays are of a unique pattern, and are made out of one piece, with the exception of the back stay, which is riveted to the main stay.

Width of body across front, 34 inches ; across bottom, 35 inches ; at center, 45 inches ; across back, 40 inches ; across front of boot, 32 inches ; amount of turn-under, each side, 5 inches ; width and depth of dickey-seat 37 by 16½ inches. Runners : width of track, 41 inches front, and 40⅝ inches back. Thickness and depth of runners, 1⅜ by 1½ inches. Shoes, 1⅜ by ⅜-inch round-edge steel. Width across the runners at front scrolls, 32 inches. Size of stays, ⅞ by ⅝-inch oval iron.

Painting.—Body : main panels deep green ; shells, Indian red ; boot, black. Moldings on main panels, also moldings on boot and shells, striped a fine line of yellow. Runners : Indian red ; dash' outside deep green, and inside black ; runners, striped a ¼-inch line of black ; dash, outside ¼-inch line of Indian red, and two fine lines of the same color on each side, ¼ inch apart ; inside of dash striped the same.

Trimming.—Same as plate No. 34.

Mountings.—Gold.

Carriage Monthly
August 1888

CABRIOLET SLEIGH WITH SHELL BODY.

(See Fashion Plate No. 14.)

SHELL BODY sleighs have been very popular during the past winter, and will retain their popularity for the coming season. The shell is worked out of 4-in. whitewood. A $\frac{5}{16}$-in. panel is used on the sides and back of seat, which are set into a groove. It is necessary to incline the sides in order to get the required turn-under. This method gives a trifle more work to the body-maker, but does away with the opening of joints caused by glueing together thick whitewood. Scrolls might be introduced at the rear end of the arm-rails. A molding might also be nailed around the edges of the boot. The rockers are neither contracted nor inclined, and are made in two pieces, lapped together underneath the boot. To these pieces the boot-standards are framed, as is customary in jobs of this kind, and then paneled. The rear of the boot is paneled down to the scroll. A child's-seat could be used here if desired, in which case, it would be advisable to increase the distance between the boot and rear seat.

Dimensions.—Width of body on top, at front of arm-rail, 48 in.; and at bottom, outside of rockers, 32 in.; ditto at rear, 40 in. Turn-under, 6 in. Rocker-plates, $\frac{3}{8} \times 2$ in., fastened with No. 18, $1\frac{1}{4}$-in. screws. Track, 40 in.

Painting.—Shell-work, ultramarine blue. Seat-panel, dark green. Boot, black. Moldings, black, with fine line of carmine. Scroll-work, carmine.

Trimming—Blue cloth. Mountings, silver.

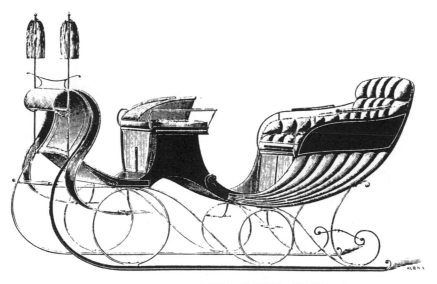

PLATE No. 14. **CABRIOLET SLEIGH WITH SHELL BODY.**—SCALE, ONE-HALF INCH.

The Hub
May 1889

CABRIOLET SLEIGH.

PLATE No. 25.—VOL. 25.

Carriage Monthly
July 1889
(description next page)

Cabriolet Sleigh.

PLATE NO. 25.

The cabriolet style, with its various applications of details, is still very popular, and will be for some time to come. The shape of the body and boot is in imitation of the regular cabriolet body, with a few exceptions. The construction of the boot is the same as that of a cabriolet, which is framed, but for cheaper work, ⅞ or 1-inch boards will do as well for sleigh work, and saves labor. The side panels have moldings ½ inch wide by ⅛ inch full deep, worked into the panel and rounded. The wood is all left in the center and worked down toward the edges, leaving a fullness in the panels, showing the surface varnish to advantage.

The body and seat are made separately, which in this case we believe is an advantage, as it simplifies the construction, and we believe is less labor. The sides of the body are made of solid poplar, and the moldings worked on solid. The side pieces for the seat are of solid poplar, and screwed to a seat frame; the back panel is $\frac{5}{16}$ inch thick, the same as any other panel glued against cross-bars. The finish of the back panel is the same as the sides, and is done by pieces of panels ½ inch thick bent to shape and glued, one piece after the other, over the $\frac{3}{16}$-inch panel. This mode of construction is better by far than by gluing sawed out pieces together, which are liable to split at the joints, and are also heavier and will take more stuff. By the other method, no splitting is possible, as the $\frac{5}{16}$-inch thick panel will hold the shells in their position, and make a strong and very good job. The stays are all curved, and look best for the shape of the body; the scrolls on the ends of stays are forged on solid.

Body: Width across front bracket, 30 inches; width across front of body at scroll, 35 inches; at front scroll of seat, 44 inches, and at back 38 inches; amount of turn-under, 4½ inches. With these measurements as given, with 4½ inches turn-under on each side, the main molding of body should have one straight line on horizontal elevation. Shape of turn-under convex only for both seats and body. Length of dickey-seat, 36 inches. Runners: Width of track, 40 inches over all; thickness of runners, 1⅜ inches thick by 1½ inches deep. Shoes, 1⅜ by ⅜ inch. Size of iron for stays, ⅝ by ⅞ inch.

———

Painting.—Body: lower part of body and boot, black; shell part, blue. Runners and stays: blue, striped two $\frac{3}{16}$-lines of light blue, and a fine yellow line in the center, $\frac{1}{16}$ inch apart, or the entire surface can be painted blue; boot, black. Runners: yellow lake, and dash panel, blue, which is out of the regular run, but looks well.

Trimming.—Blue cloth; carpet, blue with yellow figures.

Finish.—Rails on dickey-seat black, or they can have leather finish. Fenders on sides of dash, patent-leather finish over iron rail. Wire screen, for shape see illustration, gold plated. Plumes mounted on saddle chime sleigh bells; horse hair looks best in this case, but fur plumes will be the latest when the sleighing season is at hand.

Mountings.—Gold.

PLATE NO. 10.   FOUR-PASSENGER SLEIGH.—SCALE, ONE-HALF INCH.

FOUR PASSENGER SLEIGH.

(See Fashion Plate No. 10.)

SCALE, ½ IN. TO THE FOOT.

THE design of cabriolet sleigh shown by Fashion Plate No. 10, was copied from a draft made by one of the most prominent sleigh builders of this state, and is given as one of the styles that will be brought out as a leader for the coming season.   The outlines of the boot are all curved and made to appear light.   The part of the bracket is of ash, and is richly carved.   The body is shaped after a Victoria.   The sides are made of white wood, and have a turned under of 4½ in. on each.   The mouldings are all nailed on; the spaces between the mouldings are slightly rounded.   The back is made to correspond with the sides.

The dash, which is leather covered, has a double sweep, and has a rein rail on top.   Plumes could also be introduced if required.

Dimensions of Woodwork.—Width of body on top at center, 42 in.; and at bottom, 33 in.   Width of body at rear, 36 in.   Width of front seat on top, 36 in.; and at bottom, 34 in.   Runners, 1½ × 1⅝; shoes, 1½ × ½ in.   Iron for running part, ⅞ × 1⅛ in., oval.

Painting.—Boot, black; mouldings, black, striped carmine; body panels, deep lake; scroll work, dark green, edged with light green.   Gearing, carmine, striped with one broad and two fine lines of black.

Trimming.—Blue silk plush; mountings, brass.

The Hub
May 1892

174

VIS-A-VIS
SLEIGHS

A VIS-A-VIS SLEIGH ON PROMENADE

The Hub
July 1883

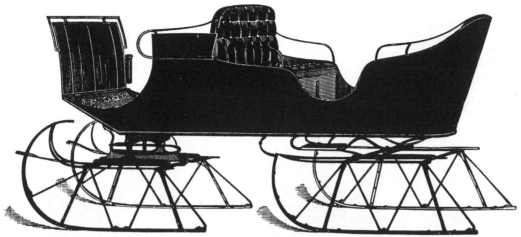

SIX-PASSENGER SLEIGH.

PLATE NO. 62.—HALF-INCH SCALE.

Six-Passenger Sleigh.
PLATE NO. 62.

You will observe in this design for heavy sleigh, something original and different from any previously published. The sides are straight with some flare ; the back and corners rounded off. The sides are cut down to facilitate entrance to the back seat. A photograph of this sleigh was received from R. M. Bingham & Co., Rome, N. Y., together with plate number 58. Though they were the finest photographs of sleighs we ever saw, the scale was not large enough to discern the outlines of all the parts of iron and wood forming the gear.

Painting. — Body : dark green. Runners : lighter green than body, striped with one $1\frac{3}{8}$ inch line of carmine.

Trimming.—Green plush or cloth. Patent-leather cord welts. Falls bound with patent-leather. Plain green carpet.

Mountings.—Silver.

Plate No. 40. SIX-PASSENGER SLEIGH WITH ROCKAWAY BOOT.—Scale, one-half inch.

The Hub
August 1883
(description next page)

SIX-PASSENGER SLEIGH WITH ROCKAWAY BOOT

WE hope and believe that this design will meet with favor on the part of both manufacturers and buyers. By leaving off the middle seat, it can readily be transformed into a four-passenger sleigh; and a coupe-pillar may then be attached to the body, at the usual place, which will add greatly to the appearance of the body. A top similar to a canopy top can also be added, without increasing the cost materially. The top should preferably have eight iron supports, but satisfactory results may be attained with six pillars. Such a top should be provided with leather curtains, which, when lowered, will close in the Sleigh. The iron posts may be secured to the body by the same mode that is followed on Phaeton bodies. The additional expense of adding such a top will only be justified in regions where the sleighing season is of long duration, or where considerable distances are likely to be traveled.

In constructing the body, the rockers require to be inclined and contracted. The contraction is $2\frac{3}{4}$ in. for the hind quarter, while that for the front quarter will be somewhat less, the quarter being shorter. The corner-pillar at the back is lapped to the rocker, and projects over the rocker $\frac{1}{2}$ in. This $\frac{1}{2}$ in. is taken off from the inside, or, rather, the front edge of the pillar, gradually diminishing to nothing at the back edge. The sides are then fitted to it, forming a miter joint. The sides can be made out of one piece, reaching from the top of the arm-rail to the bottom of the body; and 3-inch whitewood will be needed. One piece will answer for the front, reaching from the door to the Stanhope pillar at the driver's-seat; and 3-inch whitewood is required for this piece as well.

The pillar dividing the front from the driver's-seat is straight, and lapped to the rocker, the pillar to project outside of the rocker $\frac{9}{16}$ in.; and this $\frac{9}{16}$ in. is cut off to the top of the arm-rail, forming a shoulder. The sides are $\frac{7}{8}$ in. thick at this place, standing out from the pillar $\frac{9}{16}$ in., which is the thickness of the molding. Thick pieces of whitewood can, if preferred, be taken for the doors instead of panels, but this is not to be recommended, as there is no saving of labor worth mentioning. Two pieces, representing the lock and hinge-pillars, have to be glued on the inside of the whitewood. Furthermore, to work to the required shape the pieces which form the panel, and to work on the moldings, demand considerable time and labor. The greater weight of such a door, as compared with one having a frame and a thin panel glued over, is another important factor to be considered, as it is obvious that a door of less weight will produce less strain on the hinges, and be less liable to get out of order. A common door hinge will be sufficient for the top of the door, while the bottom hinge is similar to those introduced on carriage bodies where concealed hinges are used.

The running-part, with the exception of the runners, is all made of iron, and is very elaborate, requiring special skill and taste on the part of the ironer. A full-size draft of the running-part on a board is recommended, to facilitate the labor of the smith, and to assure greater accuracy. Iron cross-stays are placed in the center of the body at the door, and at the place representing the wheel-house, to give more strength to the running-part.

Dimensions.—Width of body at the lock and hinge-pillars, 46 in.; ditto, back at the arm-rail, $39\frac{1}{2}$ in.; and ditto, across the tail-bar, 39 in. These dimensions will answer for the front quarter also. Width at the dash, 32 in. Turn-under, 3 in. Rocker-plates, $2\frac{1}{2}$ x $\frac{1}{2}$ in., fastened with $1\frac{1}{4}$ in., No. 18 screws. We would add that the above dimensions are suitable for a sleigh of large size, as the accompanying drawing calls for; but they can be reduced in proportion with the reduction of other parts of the body. The runners are $1\frac{1}{8}$ and 1 in. The shoe is 1 x $\frac{3}{8}$ in., steel. The stays are made of oval iron, $\frac{5}{8}$ x $\frac{1}{2}$ in.

Finish.—For the painting, we suggest three different styles, as follow, namely: *First style*—Body panels, Prince's lake. Moldings, black, striped (the same as a carriage body) on the moldings only, with a clean cream-colored fine-line. Runners, vermilion glazed with carmine, striped with double stripes, $\frac{1}{16}$ inch wide each, $\frac{1}{4}$ inch apart. Bolt-heads and nuts, touched with black. *Second Style*—Body panels, medium or deep shade umber brown. Moldings, black, striped with a fine line of pure white. Runners, black, with white stripes, the same as above. *Third Style*—Body panels, bottle green; and moldings black, striped with carmine. Runners, dark green of a different shade, striped with gold bronze.

Trimming.—The color of the trimming material, and of the carpet depends on the color selected for painting the body panels. The backs may be trimmed with a roll on top; this, however, is optional. Wire screens, for protecting the occupants against snow thrown while driving, are placed on the sides and top. Red plumes are recommended. Mountings, silver.

Plate No. 30. SIX-PASSENGER GERMAN SLEIGH.—Scale, three-quarters inch.

The Hub
July 1887
(description next page)

SIX-PASSENGER GERMAN SLEIGH.

(See Fashion Plate No. 30.)

THE design shown in the Fashion Plate makes a very stylish sleigh for family use, being one of the most capacious, convenient and comfortable of its kind. The outlines of the body and ironwork are graceful, and all the parts well proportioned. This is known as the German style of sleigh.

The body shows some novel lines, but, as a rule, follows the prevailing fashion. The sides of the body are concaved gradually toward the top of the pillar, with a carved head at the top of each pillar. Each side has five pillars, as shown in the design, framed to the sill and extending to the top of the body. These pillars are set inside the panel; and, at the top of the panel, they project over the panel the thickness of a $\frac{1}{4}$-in. molding. After the panel has been glued on, glue the molding on top of the panel, directly over the pillar which forms the molding on the sides, and which also forms the pillar on the sides. This way of framing makes a very good job.

The rear corner-pillar is made solid, with the side and back panels grooved into it, and forming the corner molding. The sills are $1\frac{1}{2} \times 4$ in., framed in the flat. There are three cross-bars in the center to form beams, and also one at the front and back ends, to which the runners are stayed. The bracket is framed to the sill, with a cross-bar at the end of the bracket. At this point the runner is secured to the body.

On top of the body, on the line of the seats, a piece is framed across lengthwise; and across the body, on the same line of the seats, a bar is framed for the seats to rest on. At this point there is a heel-board under the front of each of the three seats. This heel-board is hollowed out, so as to afford a convenient place for storing articles without having to raise the cushion and pass them through the seat-lid.

Each stay is made in one section, bolted to the sill of body and to the runner. While in the blacksmith-shop, this body should rest on a wooden bench made for the occasion and strengthened so as to prevent the body from swinging, for considerable care, as well as skill, will be required on ths part of the blacksmith in forming the side-stays, which, if not made properly, will be very apt to spoil the appearance of the sleigh.

The dash is a thin panel, let in flush with the rocker, and extending as shown in the design. At the end of the dash is a light bar connecting the two runners, and finished at the end to match the top of the pillars.

Dimensions.—Width of body at arm-rail, 42 in. ; ditto at back, 38 in. ; and ditto at front, 40 in. Width of body on bottom, 35 in. Runners, $1\frac{1}{4} \times 1$ in. Shoes, $1 \times \frac{1}{2}$-in. steel. The side-stays should be made out of $\frac{7}{8} \times \frac{5}{8}$-in. oval iron. Track, 40 in.

Finish.—Painting of panels, green, and moldings, black, striped with a fine line of vermilion. Runners, vermilion, with black stripe. Trimming, green plush for cushions and back, laid off in diamonds. A plain fall is used. Carpet, green, with red figures. Plumes, red, with silver tops. Mountings, silver.

PLATE No. 18. VIS-A-VIS SLEIGH.—Scale, one-half inch.

This fashion plate represents one of the most recent forms of a Vis-à-vis sleigh. It is pleasing in form, commodious, yet compact and simple in construction, features which cannot fail to commend it.

To the builder of coach bodies there is nothing that would cause any difficulty in putting up the body. The side has a double sweep, the concave beginning a little below the lowest point of the quarter. The side sweep should be about six inches, but a little rounder at the quarter than a coach sweep. The rockers are flat and straight. The arch under the driver's seat may be an offset or an imitation, the line being indicated by the edge of the panel. The side of the arch can be finished in "blind" work.

The body arm rails and corner pillars may be of bent wood, spliced to the drop center at the lower quarter line; the drop center itself should be of whitewood, or fine close-grained ash, worked out. The moldings should be $\frac{7}{8}$ in., tapered to $\frac{5}{8}$ at the upper corner of the quarters. The body should be framed 44 in. on the seat rails. The front end of the rockers are offset against the inside of the back rocker; this will allow the use of a 36 in. driver's seat. The runners should be of the best white ash or white oak, $1 \times 1\frac{1}{2}$ in., tapered at the bracket line to 1 in. square. The track should be 3 ft. 5 in.

The body has a light rocker-plate extending the full length of the rocker, secured by $1\frac{3}{4}$ in. No. 18 screws. The shoes are of steel, $1 \times 1\frac{1}{2}$ in.; the stays are of $1 \times \frac{5}{8}$ in. oval iron.

Painting.—Body, dark green, striped red; running part, red, striped black.

Trimming.—Green cloth. Carpet, green, with red figure.

The Hub
June 1891

SIX-PASSENGER SLEIGH.

PLATE NO. 40.—VOL. 24.—HALF-INCH SCALE.

This style represents one of the many patterns, both American and foreign, manufactured by the well-known sleigh-builders, A. E. and J. H. Christie, of Nyack, N. Y., this firm having a national reputation for fine and original sleigh designs. This sleigh is one of their late styles, and is becoming very popular, and will be extensively used. Other original styles will be designed for the coming season.

Width of boot across front, 33¼ inches. Width of body across front at arm-rail, 40 inches; at front door joint, 44¾ inches; at back door joint, 45 inches; back, at arm-rail, 40½ inches. Amount of turn-under, 2¼ inches. Runners: width of track, 41⅜ inches front, and 41 inches back. Thickness and depth of runners, 1⅛ by 1¼ inches. Shoes, 1⅛ by ⁵⁄₁₆-inch round-edge steel.

Painting.—Body: deep green; boot, black, striped a fine line of cream color around the moldings. Runners: Indian red, dash deep green on the outside, and black on the inside, striped two ³⁄₁₆-inch lines of black; dash on inside striped two ³⁄₁₆-inch lines of cream color.

Trimming.—Green cloth.

Mountings.—Silver.

PLATE No. 21. SIX-PASSENGER VIS-A-VIS SLEIGH ON BOB RUNNERS. SCALE, ONE-HALF INCH.

The Hub
June 1890
(description next page)

Vis-à-Vis Sleighs

SIX-PASSENGER VIS-A-VIS SLEIGH ON BOB RUNNERS.

THE accompanying Fashion Plate represents one of the latest designs of vis-à-vis sleighs, for which we are indebted to Mr. Eugene Ford, of Rockford, Ill., a pupil of the Corresponding Class of the Technical School for Carriage Draftsmen and Mechanics, New-York City.

Fig. 1.

In this design some very pleasing features will be noticed, especially the graceful lines in the boot. The dash is quite high. The dash posts are made of bent elm, and are secured to the body by iron stays which continue up some distance on the posts. The dash fenders can be made of bent wood with the grain running vertically and fastened with irons. The body is swelled one inch in its length to the point of the boot. The shell is made of 1½ in. whitewood, and tapers to ¾ in. at the bottom ; this shell is glued and nailed to the outer surface of the body. The rear seat-frame projects one inch beyond the body on each side. The seat-sides are convex, and are contracted to suit the swell of the body.

The circle in front bob is of ½ × 1½ in. iron. Instead of a top circle, balls are used, 1¾ in. in diameter, and bolted between two projecting ears of a plate which is fastened to the cross-bar under the boot, revolving when required (see Fig. 2). The kingbolt is placed in the center of the iron plate on the top of the bolster-plate as illustrated in Fig. 1. The back bob is secured to the cross-bar with the same irons used for the kingbolt. (See Fig. 1 for kingbolt, and Fig. 2 for circle balls, which are drawn to the scale of 3 in. to the foot). The body at the bottom be-

Fig. 2.

tween the seats is 36 in. wide, and on top, under seats, 38 in.; the boot is 32 in. wide. The seats are 44 in. wide on top, outside.

Dimensions of Bobs.—Runners, 1⅛ × 1 in. Shoes, 1 × ½ in. Beams, 1 × 1¾ in. deep. Knees, 1¾ in. wide at the beam, 1 in. at the runners and ⅞ in. thick. They should be made of second-growth hickory. The circle is 20 in. diameter. Track, 40 in.

Painting.—Body, dark green throughout. Moldings, black, striped with fine line of carmine. Bobs, green, a shade lighter than body, striped carmine.

Trimming.—Green cloth. Mountings, silver.

Plate No. 31. SIX-PASSENGER VIS-A-VIS SLEIGH.—Scale, one-half inch.

THE six-passenger Vis-à-vis Sleigh, although not so popular as many of the four-passenger sleighs, will always occupy a prominent place both in the repository and on the drives. The cost is greatly enhanced, as compared with that of the latter, and limits the number of customers, at least in this latitude, for so expensive a vehicle intended for a sport of such short duration; but the Vis-à-vis must be counted among the most imposing vehicles of its class, and the accompanying drawing of a recent New-York pattern deserves being studied by all sleigh-makers.

The outlines are graceful, curved lines being employed exclusively, except on the bottom between the seats and the toe-board. The front and back quarters are well proportioned, and look light, yet afford ample seat-room. If desirable, a door could be introduced, which would perhaps be preferred by many customers. The sides of the body have considerable swell, and the rockers will have to be inclined and contracted similar to those of the Four-passenger Cabriolet Sleigh, Plate 30. The center piece should be made from 2½ in. ash. All the rest can be made 1⅜ in. thick. On the boot rocker, ½ in. must be glued on the outside for fitting to the rocker on the front seat. The two short rockers, connecting the center with the seat rocker, have a flare of 2½ in. If solid sides are used, 2½ in. whitewood will be necessary. A piece will then have to be glued to the outside of the front and back seat rockers, 1¼ in. thick at the front end of the seats, and worked off to nothing at the back panels. A wooden trestle or bench is put up in the middle, under the center rocker, similar to that on the Cabriolet Sleigh, Plate 30. An extra iron cross-stay is fastened to the inside of the runners, forming a T. A bar is framed into the rockers to allow the stay to be bolted to it; this cross-stay is secured to the side-stays by a clip, and can be made either straight or slightly curved.

Dimensions.—Width of body in the center, 46 in.; ditto on the front and back, at the height of the arm-rail, 39 in.; ditto at the dash, 32 in. Turn-under, 5 in. The runners are 1⅜ x 1¼ in. The stays ought to be somewhat heavier than on a four-passenger sleigh. The shoes are 1¼ x ₁⁷₆ in. Track, 40 in., from out to out.

Finish.—Painting: the panels on the body are dark blue; moldings and panels on the driver's-seat, black. The moldings are edged with a fine line of gold. The runners are painted blue, of a somewhat lighter shade than the body color, striped with a medium stripe and two fine lines of gold. Trimming, either blue cloth or plush. The backs and cushions are made up in the diamond pattern. The falls receive a raiser, 1 in. wide, about 1½ in. from the edge. Cushions, and fall for driver's-seat, blue cloth. Plumes, blue. Mountings, brass.

186

CLOSED-BODY
SLEIGHS

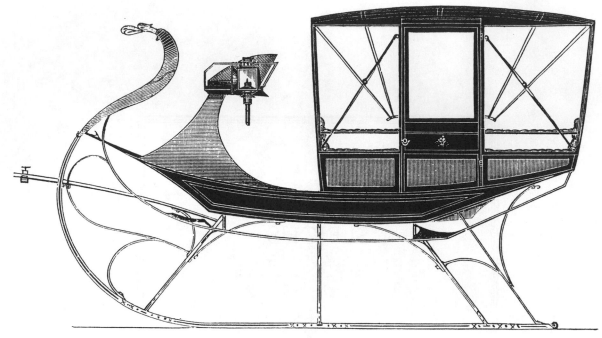

LANDAU SLEIGH.

PLATE NO. XXXIX.—HALF-INCH SCALE.

Carriage Monthly
November 1874
(description next page)

LANDAU SLEIGH

There has been within the last few years considerable attention paid to getting up new designs of sleighs, and which necessarily produced some very good designs, and differing from the Albany and Portland styles to a marked extent. The most noticeable change is in the front, substituting the toe board or bracket front for the curved front, and also making the front or driver's seat on the family six-seat sleighs separate from the other seats.

The designs of sleighs which we present in this number are from the pencil of Mr. D. Ford, Milwaukee, Wis., acknowledged to be one of the best sleigh designers in the West, to whom we return our thanks for the interest he takes in the welfare of the MONTHLY. The design of landau sleigh, Mr. Ford states, was taken from one which he had just finished, and which was greatly admired by all who saw it. The lines of the sleigh are original and unique, making a very raking and light appearance, yet giving all the room requisite for comfort. The landau top, in combination with a sleigh, has met with great favor in the Northern cities. They are made the same as for a carriage, some being made close, others with curtains as in this design. The door is made different than for a carriage, as the glass frame cannot drop in the doors, being made to take off when the top is lowered by hanging them with slip hinges, and when removed they are placed in the boot, in which a suitable place is made to keep them from rubbing against each other.

The side curtains are knobbed to the valance, and when not in use are placed in the boot. The shaded panels on the body are boxed in, or they can be put in grooves as best suits the builder. The main panel is swelled same as upon an Albany sleigh, grooved into the frame. A molding is put on the panel as shown.

In constructing this sleigh Mr. Ford gives the following: The bottom rave (bottom side) is made $\frac{7}{8}$ inch deep by 3 inches wide. The top rave is swept to give a full swell, and is $1\frac{1}{4}$ inches deep by $1\frac{5}{8}$ inches wide, and projects over the panel 1 inch, which gives a fine finish to the panel. The piece that forms the bracket is got out of 4 inch thick, to get the proper swell. The toe piece is glued and screwed to the top of the bottom rave. The boot is made of 4-inch white wood, and rounded. The dash panel extends to the point of bracket. The wings made of iron covered with leather.

Dimensions.—Width of the body at center of the door outside: 51 inches; at the back: 36 inches; on the bottom outside: 33 inches. Runners: $1\frac{1}{8}$ by $1\frac{1}{2}$ inches deep. Knees: $1\frac{1}{4}$ by 2 inches at the beam, $1\frac{1}{8}$ by $1\frac{1}{4}$ inches at the runner. Beams: $1\frac{1}{4}$ by 2 inches. Fenders: $\frac{7}{8}$ inch square.

Painting.—Body: panels, ultramarine blue. Box panels: dark lake. Molding frame and boot: black. Gold stripe on the belts and moldings. Runners: dark lake, striped with gold broad line, edged with black.

Trimming.—Brown broadcloth, with broad seaming and pasting lace.

Mountings.—Gold.

LANDAU SLEIGH.

FASHION PLATE NO. 13.—VOL. 30.—HALF-INCH SCALE.

PLATE NO 13.
LANDAU SLEIGH.
This new and attractive design of landau sleigh is made by Willoughby, of Rome, N. Y. The construction of the boot and top is similar to a landau, while the body is very appropriate for a sleigh design, as the shells under the side quarter molding are very neat and attractive. The side quarters are constructed of poplar planks, and the shells are worked on the solid stuff, also all of the moldings. The doors are framed the same as regular coach doors, and the glass frames are held up with flappers. The runners are as usually constructed by other houses, with the exception of the movable coupling, which is original with Mr. Willoughby. It moves in a socket, with flanges on upper part, and is secured with a bolt through the flanges, and consequently cannot be twisted out of the sockets in case of accident. These couplings are patented by Mr. Willoughby.

Painting.—Body: panels, green; moldings, black; shells, coach painters' red, shaded with carmine; gear, carmine, striped gold.

Trimming.—Claret Wülfing broadcloth, with broad lace to match; style, blocks and diamonds. Dickey seat and fall, hand buffed enameled leather.

Finish.—Landau leather for top; silver plated nuts, and top joint, silver plated 3½ inches from each side of nuts. Silver screen wings on dash; silver line rail and plumes. Gear well ironed and braced, steel shoes, with rounded edges.

Carriage Monthly
May 1894

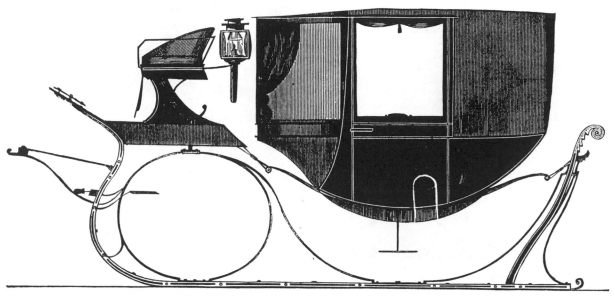

No. 79. SMITH'S BOOBY SLEIGH.—Exhibited by J. T. Smith & Co., of Boston, Mass.

SMITH'S BOOBY SLEIGH.

EXHIBITED BY J. T. SMITH & CO., OF BOSTON, MASS.

The " Booby," or " Booby-Hut," is one of the finest and costliest of sleighs for private use, which has its home in Boston and a few other cities in the East. So far as we know, this style of sleigh has never been made or used in New York City.

Messrs. J. T. Smith & Co., of Boston, Mass., deserve much credit for having sent so fine a specimen of this style of winter turnout to the Exhibition, which we now for the first time illustrate in The Hub. The body is the regular full-size Clarence style, with circular front, and the lines of the dickey-seat and iron-work connecting it with the runners appear to us quite original and very tasteful ; they certainly show a great improvement over the patterns familiar to us, and of which our predecessor, " The New-York Coach-Makers' Magazine," was the first to publish an illustration—see its issue of September, 1865, in which appears an article from which we quote the following : " The body is not—as some might suppose—an extemporized affair from some family carriage, but it is generally made expressly for the purpose, much cheaper than the ordinary coach-body," etc. It has given us peculiar pleasure that this Boston house should exhibit a specimen of this typical American style, the more so as it combines elegance with superior workmanship.

The principal dimensions of the Booby exhibited are as follow :

Width of body over all, 50 inches. Width of back, 43 inches. Width of dickey-seat, 30½ inches. Width of toe-board, 35½ inches. Track, 55 inches, out to out.

Painting of body and carriage-part, brown, with fine line of carmine. Trimmed with crimson silk, and in an admirable manner. .

The Hub
October 1876

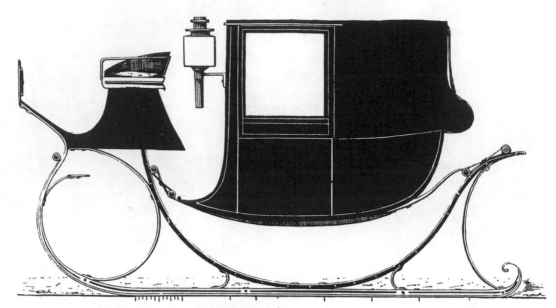

No. 45. BOSTON BOOBY, OR BOOBY-HUT.—DRAWN FOR "THE HUB" BY CHAUNCEY THOMAS, OF BOSTON, MASS.

SCALE, ONE-HALF INCH.

A BOSTON BOOBY, OR BOOBY-HUT.

(See Plate No. 45.)

103 CHESTNUT-ST., BOSTON, MASS., May, 1882.

EDITOR OF THE HUB—DEAR SIR : I read with interest your article in the February *Hub* on "Bob Runners and How they are made." The illustrations presented give a very correct idea of one device which we make use of in Boston for converting wheeled vehicles into sleighs ; but we call these "Hub Runners," and apply the term "Bob Runners," or "Traverse Runners," to a pair of somewhat similar runners, but minus hubs, when connected together by a framework into the form of a sled, to which the body of the vehicle is directly attached by means of swivel joints on the rear sled and by the usual king-bolt and circle in front, instead of leaving the axles on, and passing these into the hubs. These "Bob Runners" are now very little used for carriages, but are confined to express wagons, pungs, etc.

You may be interested to know that such a set of "Hub Runners," ironed and painted, and provided with straps by which to bind the forward part to the lower part of the body, command from $50 to $75, in

The Hub
July 1882
(continued on next page)

Boston ; while a similar set of " bobs," for private carriages, cost from $100 to $125.

We have in Boston several other similar devices, which deserve special mention. We have, for instance, what are called the " Booby Runners," which consist of a single pair of runners, with four sloping posts and iron braces, from which the body is suspended by thoroughbraces, without springs, the driver's-seat forming a part of the same structure, being built upon the runners and framework. With these runners a peculiar style of body is usually employed in Boston, known as the Booby proper, which resembles the old Chariot body. The most useful runners, by which carriages of all descriptions are converted into sleighs, and those most in favor at the present time, are what we call " Long Runners." Our own method of hanging a Coupé or Brougham on "Long Runners" is to curve the front of the runners up and backwards in the form of a C-spring, from which, by a shackle, hangs a short thoroughbrace. The looped ends of this brace carry a bar, to which a bottom circle and an eye for the king-bolt of the carriage is hung down. This front is very simply connected. From the rear end of the runners rises a sloping and gracefully curved post, which carries a cross-bar placed at the right point to receive a thoroughbrace. This brace passes around an iron bar, which bar is attached to the back hangers by the spring-bolts. We have made these for many years. It is a very perfect arrangement and very pretty.

The Booby Hut, or, as it is commonly called, the Booby, is a very old Boston institution. Old English C-spring Chariot bodies have always been in demand for conversion into Boobies, and at the present time there is quite a rage for these old family keepsakes in Boston and vicinity, many of which are upwards of a century old. How and where so many of these old bodies have been preserved is a wonder. See illustration accompanying (Plate No. 45). At the back of the body will be seen the "sword-case," which is the projecting end of a box, accessible from the inside of the body, in which they used to carry arms in the old highway robbery times.

The full sweep C-spring Coach body also makes a very nice Booby, and this form and an elongated Chariot have generally been adhered to for many years past. Latterly, however, the circular-front or Clarence form, and the Coupé, have been largely used.

The running-parts of Boobies in the olden time were ugly enough, having straight turned posts and stiff straight braces, a huge dasher, and a simple board on which the driver sat. Many changes have been made in later years, but the newest Booby and the one most copied is our own style, which is illustrated in the accompanying drawing (See Plate No. 45.) In this plan, in place of the four posts, a bent piece is substituted, plated on the inside. The runners are turned down to form a foot-board, and a box, of good shape, is used in place of the old shelf. This construction is very light, strong and elastic, can be made very graceful, and is especially adapted to the light Coupé style.

(continued from previous page)

THE CONSTRUCTION OF SLEIGHS:

IRONING

Ironing

SOME HINTS ON IRONING HEAVY SLEIGH BOTTOMS.

In response to requests, we herewith illustrate and describe the ironwork of the scroll or skeleton bottom of a heavy sleigh. To those who are not accustomed to sleigh work, the term bottom may appear out of place, but the technical or shop term among sleigh builders for the under part is "bottom," and for the body, or upper part, "top."

As a starting point we begin the center form as per Fig. 1. When this is completed work on the other sections can begin.

Before cutting or forging an iron have a complete and thorough working drawing of all the ironwork of the side placed

or projection, from the same, about 1½ in. wide, which extends under the bottom and is drilled for two ⅝ in. holes. All bolts used for securing the stays to the top ought to be ⅜ in.; those for securing the stays to the runners, because of the clips, hereafter explained, will be sufficiently strong if 1/16 in. C shows one side of the lug B, which clasps the runner at that point and materially helps to prevent the splitting of the runners at the bolt holes when subjected to severe twisting strains. The same form of clips is used at other points on the runners, as they materially lessen the strain on the bolts securing the shoes and stays to the runners. The branch stays, extending front and back from the center piece, are shown by K K. These are joined to A A by welding, as illustrated by Fig. 4, and which will be explained later. L, L, represent sections of connecting stays on each side of A A, being joined at G, as illustrated by Fig. 3. X X X X indicate the bolts used for securing the joints and the stays and shoes to the runners. H H show the indispensable clip at those points to assist in preserving the joint of the stays as well as preventing the splitting of the runners.

For a sleigh calculated to carry four or five persons, two on front seat and three on back, make the stays of oval 1¼ in. x ¾ in. iron at normal point and taper to 1½ in. x ⅞ in. where the connections are made with the runners or top. The bearings on the runners ought not to be less than 5 in. long, those on the body 1 in. longer, in order to give the necessary harmony

to the structures. If the sleigh is larger or smaller than as above described, reduce or increase the size of the stays, accordingly in breadth and thickness. Do not have the stays too thick or flat an oval, as such stays appear round, and materially detract from the fine lines and beauty of construction aimed at.

Fig. 2 illustrates the bottom or lower section of Fig. 1; M, the bearing on the runner; N, the lug; OO, sections of AA, Fig. 1. Fig. 8 illustrates how to get out the center piece or top bearing of Fig. 1. Take Norway iron of sufficient size, fuller in at YY, and draw down A, as per dotted line C, which forms E, Fig. 1. The foregoing operation converts C, Fig. 8 or E, Fig. 1, into a

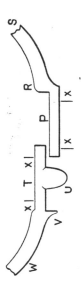

FIG. 3.

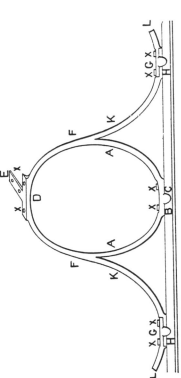

FIG. 1.

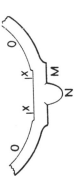

FIG. 2.

on a piece of sheet iron sufficiently wide and long to get on the the whole of the running part. No. 8 iron is about the thickness of the running part. No. 8 iron is about the thickness required, as the plate must be sufficiently heavy that it will not bend. Place it on a bench or on planks laid on strong trestles. We recommend an iron plate because it will not burn, split, break or warp when the hot iron comes in contact with the drawing, which it has to frequently before the proper form is secured and the stays ready to be attached to the runners and top.

Fig. 1 is the center piece, A A forming an oval or round, as may be desired; B the lower flat section, where it is secured to

the runner by the bolts X X; D is the upper flat section, by which it is secured to the top, or body, with bolts at X X; E is a lug,

June 1895
(first of three pages)

195

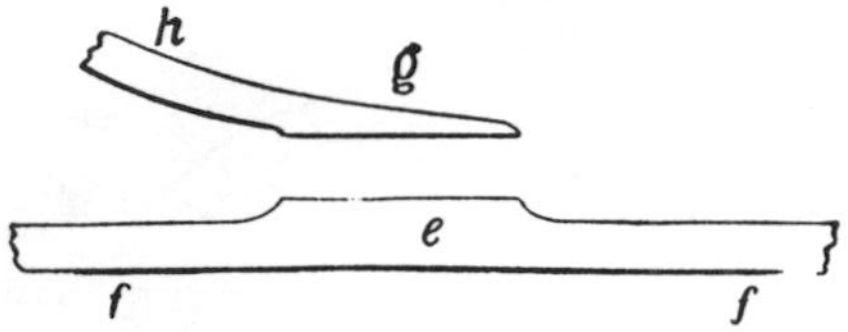

suitable condition for further manipulation. Split at *d*, and while at welding heat turn off ZZ, as per dotted line *bb*, which forms the upper section of AA, Fig. 1. After getting the top bearing complete, prepare the sections of AA, as far as the sections KK, Fig. 1, are welded to them as at FF, which as shown in Fig. 5, which are the sections of AA, as above referred to, *ff* being the oval portions, R a swell at the center, flat on one surface and rounded at the other. To the flat surface is to be welded *h*, Fig. 4, section of oval K, in Fig. 1—G, the point to be welded to *e*, Fig. 5, forming the connection as at FF, Fig. 1.

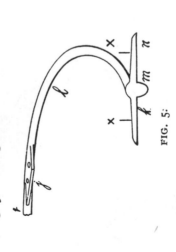

FIG. 4.

FIG. 5.

FIG. 6.

It will be noticed that G, Fig. 4, tapers on the round surface, the object of which is to show no joint, but a continued sweep or swell through the whole structure. So far as we have gone we have about completed Fig. 1, and will next call attention to Figs. 4 and 8, and proceed to weld on Fig. 2 on one side to the center; then form, as per drawing, and weld on the other side, which is as far as we can go until KK are completed and are ready for welding on to the center.

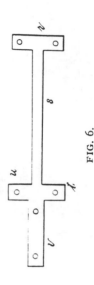

We must first secure Fig. 1 to the runner and top, and therefore must so make our calculations and forgings as to permit of adding the other sections without straining or unnecessary manipulation; consequently make KK, Fig. 1, so that it can be secured to the runner, and LL so as to fit over them, as shown by Fig. 3. Fig. 3 is a section of K, Fig. 1. P shows the flat and upper section, with raised portion R, so as to make the joint perfect and not perceptible when the two pieces are together. T the upper section fitting on to P. V shows the raised portion opposite to RW, the oval section, and U the lug as per H, Fig. 1, which clasps the two parts together at the joint and extends below enough to protect the runner, as heretofore explained. Fit the two together closely, drill the upper section first, then mark on P and give sufficient draw to keep the joint close and use drift pins in all until the parts are adjusted and secured; by such action there will be no open or loose joint.

Fig. 7 shows a section of the hind end of the shoe, with scroll finish. The usual size of metal for a sleigh which we are describing is 1½ x ½ in., square edge, either Bessemer or crucible mild steel. About four or six inches from the back or hind end, prepare a piece of Norway iron, as per Fig. 7, C; O, wearing section; Q, scrolled section, oval. P shows a slightly beveled shoulder to allow of close fitting to the runner without the probable splitting up of the immediate back end; when all complete and adjusted to the runner, weld to the shoe proper, after the shoe has been completed throughout, the other portion, and leave about ⅛ in. to allow of close fitting when finally applied to the runner.

A very important agent in the strengthening of sleighs is what is termed the cross stay, the duty of which is to prevent the spreading of the runners at the back end. Because of its shape and its functions, it requires to be made of a goodly sized metal, which necessarily brings quite a strain on the bolt which secures the front section of the stay to the shoe. After we have done with explaining the stay proper, of which we show a section in Fig. 5, we shall explain a novelty—and a very wholesome one, original with the writer—which will lend additional strength to the bar, and relieve it of the central strain and weight as heretofore imposed on it.

Fig. 5: L shows the side or section of the cross stay; K, the front section of the foot as secured to the runner; N, the hinder section; M, the lug. It has always been the custom to extend this stay from runner to runner, at a height of from 12 to 14 in. above the ground, without any center support. When we take into consideration the weight of a piece of

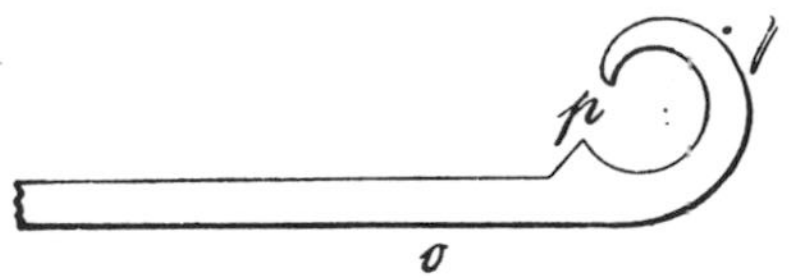

FIG. 7.

iron extending to the width of forty-two or more inches, 1 in. in diameter, or 1½ by ⅞ in. oval, we can readily wonder how it performs the service required of it, and do all this without breaking, and cease to wonder at the frequent breaking of the front foot bolt, and occasionally of both bolts securing the foot to the runner.

The continuation of the cross stay, J, is a flange or lug at the mean center of the cross stay, furnished with two holes. I is a section of the other side of the stay. The object of this leg is to relieve the cross stay by securing to the same a stay which extends to and under the bottom of the body, as explained by Fig. 6. Z is a T securing to flange J, Fig. 5; S,

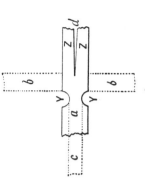

FIG. 8.

neck or oval section between lug and tail bar of body; I and U show the lug or cross T to secure to tail bar, by means of bolts passing through bolt holes shown in the same; V, an end extending beyond the tail bar to permit of securing to the bottom of the body by means of bolts, thereby lending additional support and security.

Make all iron and iron and wood connections or joints more perfect, when all done, by a sufficient application to the same of good mixed white lead.

"And Bob-runners would hurt the sleigh trade," complains another.

That proposition is debatable, and their more general use would certainly promote the business of carriage-building, which forms a part of nearly every sleigh-builder's occupation.

We have lately received a number of inquiries from foreign correspondents (including the one printed above), in reference to the construction of Bob-runners and their use in this country; and Mr. Adolphus Muller has filled several orders for sketches and working drawings of the same. We are thereby led to present the accompanying engravings, representing three views of a well-built model, and showing in detail the method employed by leading builders for producing a durable and first-class job.

The proportions of these runners and size of the iron plates of course vary widely, according to the relative size and weight of the vehicle, and our description is therefore confined to the principles of construction, which remain the same whether the runners be light or heavy; but our illustrations have been drawn carefully to the scale of one inch to the foot, and the principal dimensions of the model illustrated can therefore be learned, by means of a pocket-rule, by our Jersey correspondent or any others who desire to ascertain them.

Fig. 1 represents the face of the runner, and it will be observed that the shoes are continued over the top spoke, encircling the hub, extending down the hind spoke, and ending at the rear end of the runner. Thus the whole frame is firmly inclosed. In addition, three of the spokes have inside plates, as shown by Fig. 2, which represents the inside of the runner. The manner in which these plates are bolted to the hub is shown by Fig. 3, which is a cross-

---

BOB-RUNNERS, AND HOW THEY ARE MADE.

35 and 49 LaMotte-st., Jersey, C. I., Eng., Dec., 1881.

To the Manager of The Hub—Sir: With pleasure we received our November number of *The Hub*, containing copy of letter, amusing sketch of sleigh, and answers to our questions. The difficulty here lies in the bending and adjusting of the runners. We have scores of bodies suitable, and a large staff of carriage-builders, but they are to a certain extent inexperienced in that class of work. We think your final remarks most suitable to our requirements, and would be glad of a little more explanation as to price, etc.; and, if not too much trouble, a rough sketch of the articles you designate as "Bobs."

We are, sir, yours respectfully,

W. Gregory & Sons.

Bob-runners are largely employed in all our Northern States, though it is questionable whether their utility is even yet fully appreciated in America; and in many European cities, particularly St. Petersburg and Moscow, they are generally looked upon as necessary adjuncts to all fine carriages, as by their aid the coachman can, at short notice, convert the family Coach into a comfortable and easy-riding Sleigh. A Vienna correspondent writes: "We use runners more and more, and build less sleighs; but in this country, the Bob-runners, as I believe you call them, are not yet used as extensively as in Russian cities, where the climate makes them indeed indispensable."

If considered "indispensable" in a cold climate like Central Russia, where sleighing is the rule and not the exception, it must be evident why Bob-runners should prove useful in a climate like that of New-York, or even Boston, where the grand Six-passenger Albany may or may not find a half-dozen opportunities to air itself during the season; or in such cities as London and Paris, where opportunities for sleighing are so infrequent as to dispense with the trade of sleigh-making.

"But a sleigh can be bought so cheap!" exclaims one.

This is true so far as America is concerned; but the Bob-runners may be bought still cheaper; and the carriage already in your stable, bought and (we trust) paid for, is much more comfortable than a cheap sleigh. In most European cities, however, it is not true.

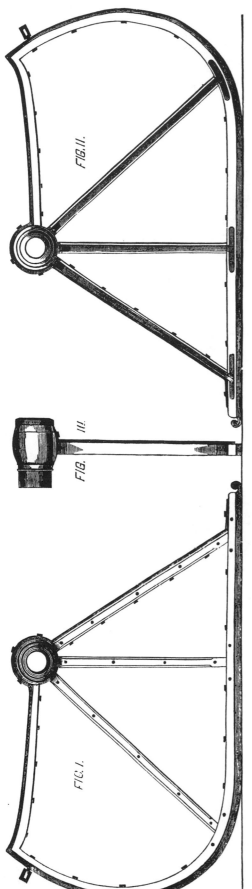

BOB RUNNERS FOR ADAPTING CARRIAGES TO WINTER SERVICE.

SCALE, ONE INCH TO THE FOOT, OR ONE-TWELFTH FULL SIZE.—DRAWN BY ADOLPHUS MULLER.

(See description accompanying.)

section. The number and position of the bolts are plainly shown.

Their application to vehicles is clearly indicated in the additional wood-cut, Plate 137, where a Landau is shown as supplied with them preparatory to the sleighing season. Various patented forms of Bob-runners have from time to time been introduced by those making a specialty in this line; and this Landau is provided with the Abbott Buggy Co.'s "patent runner attachments," which possess known advantages, and have been widely adopted. The address of these well-known

(continued from previous page)

The Construction of Sleighs

HINTS ON SLEIGH-IRONING.

"ANXIOUS," of Minnesota, asks the following questions about sleigh-making : "Ought the sleigh-runner to be straight, rounded or hollow on the bottom? I mean when the shoe is on. Ought there to be any difference in the width of the track between the front and rear ends? Which is the proper place to square the runners? Does it make any difference where the draft-eyes are placed? if so, please give a good rule for locating the same."

It is proper to have the runner flat. If rounded, a rocking motion will ensue when the sleigh is in notion. If hollow or concaved the wear will be at each end of the runner, which will then cut the snow instead of gliding over it.

The disposition of all sleigh runners is to become wider at the rear end ; consequently, it is wise to have or make the rear end of the sleigh runners a trifle narrower, say from one-fourth to three-eighths of an inch, according to the construction of the sleigh and the weight of the material used.

There is but one safe way to try the equal of the runners, which is to measure from the beam at the corner on one side, diagonally, to the opposite side runner, and *vice versa*. The beam-stays ought not to be bored on or fitted until the runners are equal as per squaring-line and held securely in position. Begin at the front and work back. The treads of the shoes ought to be strictly horizontal, laying a straight-edge across the same or from one runner to the other.

It makes very material difference where the draft-eyes are placed. If too high, the sleigh will "nose" or draw by the head: if too low, it will "heel" or drag on the rear ends, both of which are very disagreeable features and would soon put the builder "under the ban."

The center of gravity is the driving point. To ascertain this, draw a line from the rear end of the runner at the ground to a point where the shafts would rest in the tugs of a fourteen or fifteen-hand horse. Then measure from the ground to the line at the point in front of the front beam where you place the draft-eyes, and you arrive at the right height to place the same. Very high or very low horses sometimes necessitate a change, but the above rule is a safe one.

The Hub
June 1889

HINTS ABOUT SLEIGH IRONING.

OWING to repeated inquiries regarding sleigh ironing, we have prepared the following chapter, in which are embodied answers to numerous questions from members of the trade.

The shoe-bolts which secure the stay to the runner ought to be stronger than those which serve only to hold the shoe on, because of being called upon to perform more labor. It is customary to make the stay-bolt ⅛ in. larger.

A shoe of crucible cast steel will wear longer and with less friction than one of Bessemer steel in parts where the snow does not pack close or freeze hard, as in the Middle States and southern tier of Western States. In the Canadas and northern tier sections, where frost is almost continuous during the whole winter, we would prefer Bessemer steel to crucible steel for shoes.

While it is proper to rivet the T plates to the runners and posts, we would not advise riveting the stays to the runners or beams. In the event of the breaking of a stay, too much trouble is entailed in cutting out rivets, and there is that amount of bruising and tearing of the wood to warrant the use of bolts over clips. The distance between the rivets of the nose plates ought not to be less than three inches for cutters. A greater distance allows of the springing of the neck-plate from the wood, causing sufficient vibration to break the plate at the rivet hole, or to break the burr on the rivet.

No matter of what kind of iron the rivets or bolts are made that enter into the bottom of the sleigh, heat them to a red heat; put them into an iron vessel filled with hardwood sawdust; set the vessel on the forge hearth, and let it remain until the whole has become cold enough to handle. This simple method of annealing practically places the bolts and rivets beyond the possibility of breaking.

For plain work, ¾ x ¼ in. band iron, slightly champered on the outer edge, looks quite as well, and to all intents and purposes is equally as good as half-oval plates.

For cutter shafts, do not put on iron heads. Let the shaft end be sufficiently thick to turn the iron around the end, and thus allow the draft or jack-bolt to pass through the wood; or, if it please you better, bore the hole large enough and insert a piece of rubber tubing, which will prevent rattling and may be removed when worn.

It has long been the custom to secure sleigh shoes with what is termed a sleigh-shoe bolt—a bolt with a long countersunk or taper head, requiring a deep countersinking of the shoe, which materially weakens the shoe and makes fracture at the bolt hole. It is better to use an ordinary tire bolt, and as the shoe wears down and the head wears out, re-countersink the shoe and insert new bolts, and thus lessen the chances of fracture and lend strength to the shoe.

The great feature in sleigh ironing is to have the sleigh bottom strong, and yet competent to yield to all the imperfections in the roadway, or to conform to the same without breaking any of the parts. To make the bottom strong and yet yielding requires good judgment, chiefly in the construction of the inside stays from post to beam. While the connection at beam and post requires to be strong, the central part may be much lighter. The same rule also applies, to a certain extent, to the side stays. The body must not be too strongly fastened to the bottom; if it is, the panels will be split by the wrenching which is sure to occur.

Soft or mild steel makes better stay centers than either iron or crucible steel. Norway iron only ought to be used for stay heels and ends and Ts, and is exceedingly useful in fitting and securing all irons.

While it makes a much cleaner finish to secure the nose-plates with countersunk rivets, the T head is better, as it wraps around the wood and prevents the splitting of the wood, and at the same time it entails much less labor in the construction.

To round the bottom of a sleigh shoe is a mistaken idea; better to leave the shoe flat on the bottom. It costs less.

IRONING SLEIGHS.

(See Illustrations Accompanying.)

It has often occurred to us that in the ironing of the heavier grade of sleighs of the period, where the whole under or intermediate structure is of iron or steel, forming a net work of scrolls, that there is not sufficient security in the attaching of the ironwork, to either the body or the runners. The whole security is based on a few bolts, without any auxiliary support. That accidents have been so infrequent is very remarkable, and savors more of a chance result than an ordinary every day affair.

We have seen a number during the past few years, that, after a squeezing in ruts, street railroad tracks and switches, have come out second best in the general fight for the survival of the fittest.

As stated above, no proper provisions have been made for ample security.

Fig. 1 shows a combination outline section of shoe runner and stay, as bolted to the runner and shoe. A, the shoe; B, the run-

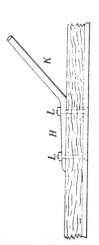

FIG. 1.

ner; C, section of the stay which bolts to the runner and shoe; DD, the securing bolts. By this sketch it will be seen that there is nothing to depend on but the two bolts at this point. The bolts are usually $\frac{5}{8}$ in., seldom as large as $\frac{3}{4}$ in. diameter. There is nothing to prevent the splitting of the runner, should the runner become entangled in a surface railroad switch or deep track, or in turning out of a well frozen rut.

Fig. 2 shows how to prevent splitting of the runner, and at the same time makes the stay more secure, by lending very material aid to the two other bolts, as described. E is the inter-

section of a stay where the same is secured to the runner; F is a lug or lip formed on each side of the center section of the stay, and made wide enough to prevent crushing of the wood, and extending down the runner far enough to admit of the insertion of a bolt or rivet at about the center of the runner between the stay and the shoe.

Fig. 3 presents a section of that part of the back or cross stay which is secured to the runner. The importance of this stay is great. Its province is to prevent the spreading of the back

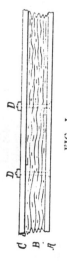

FIG. 3.

section of the runners, and to sustain the weight when the sleigh is freighted. It has also to sustain all the pressure in turning out of ruts and in turning corners. It is usually made as per Fig. 3. H, the section resting on the runner; K, section of the intersection between the two ends resting on the runners; L L represent the two securing bolts.

By this sketch it can be readily seen that there is a great lack of support and security; the bolt may be broken and the runners split readily.

Fig. 4 shows a proper and secure method for making the ends for the cross stay; M, stay, and resting on runners; N, section of intersection between the two ends; P P, the bolts; O, the lug or lip extending down on the runner on each side, and furnished with bolt holes to secure to runner, the same as in Fig. 2. This

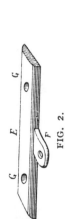

FIG. 2.

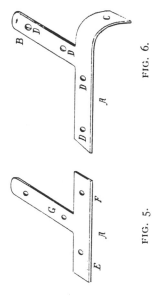

FIG. 5.

FIG. 6.

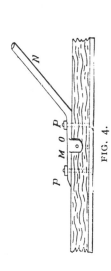

FIG. 4.

method alike insures security and prevents a possibility of splitting the back end of the runner, and thus letting down the hind section of the sleigh.

The usual manner of securing the upper section of the stays to the body is by two bolts only, which allows of a wringing strain on the bolts, causing them to break, draw down in the rocker, and in due time producing splits therein. The back upper stay ends are usually secured by but two bolts, which are also subject to and receive the same strain as the center section.

Fig. 5 illustrates a safe and desirable method of construction—one which does not entail much additional cost, and, when compared with the security gained, more than pays for such moderate increase of cost. A, the section of the stay which is bolted to the rocker; B, a lug formed on the inner side of the stay and extending under the bottom of the sleigh; E, F and G are the securing bolts. It is wise, where the lug, B, is secured

to the bottom, to make that section of stiff ash, about six inches wide.

Fig. 6 shows the improved method of making the upper section of the back stay where it is secured to the body. A, the part that is attached to the rocker; B, the angle secured to the under part of the tail bar; C, section of the end extending down to the runner. By making the end in this manner the great strain on the rocker and the bolts by reason of the angle, B, and the four bolts, D, is relieved, the liability to fracture of the bolts and splitting of the rocker is reduced to a minimum, and the whole structure is strengthened.

The Construction of Sleighs

Sleigh Shafts.

WATERLOO, PROV. QUEBEC, Sept., 1873.

MR. EDITOR:—If worthy of notice an answer to the following question through your valuable MONTHLY would be of benefit to many of its readers. Is there a rule or method to lay out or hang sleigh shafts, so that the sleigh will track our country roads; that is, the side draft.

Respectfully yours, L. P.

ANSWER.—To hang the shafts, a bar is fitted to the back of the runner, and fastened by clips or bolts; the former is the best. The bar projects to one side to have the shafts (when fastened to it) that the center of the bar or whiffletree will be opposite the runner. Another method is to have two bars to the shaft, the one on the back end having an extension half the width of the runners in front, extending on off side to take the stay from the shaft. This stay has a shaft eye on the end to fit into the jacks at the runner. The shafts being set to one side allows the horse to travel in the same track with the sleigh, and give the driver a full view of the road. Where jacks are forged to the stay, between the runner and front bench, the bar has two heads or eye bolts fastened to it to fit in the jacks; the bar resting upon the heads of the jacks which prevents its working.

Carriage Monthly
October 1873

Sleigh Shafts.

PIKE, N. Y., Oct., 1873.

MR. EDITOR:—Noticing the inquiry of "L. P." in the October number of the MONTHLY how to hang shafts to track in our country roads, I will give my rule, which may hit the point he wishes to know. The outside of nigh runner on bottom should range about 5½ inches inside of nigh shaft, measuring at the front part of shafts where they come nearest together, or one-quarter the spread at this point.

Yours, truly, S. N.

Carriage Monthly
November 1873

HOW TO PLACE SHAFT-IRONS ON A SLEIGH.

One subscriber asks us to tell why all the cutters he builds wear on the hind end of the runners. Right on the heels of this comes another, wishing to learn why his cutters all wear on the fronts of the runners; and still another wishing to know just how a cutter should run, whether on the nose, by the tail or level.

The one which drags on the heel has the shaft-iron set too low. The one which ploughs on the front has the irons set too high. The sleigh shoe ought to rest (the whole length) on the snow. To arrive at the right position to set the shaft-irons, place a medium-sized horse in front of the sleigh at a proper distance from the front. Then draw a line from the shaft-tugs on bearers at the horse to the extreme back end of the runner. Then take distance from the ground to where the shaft-heels or heads strike on the line. This will give the center of gravity, and consequently the place to set your jacks. Increase a little for a higher horse or lower for a lower horse, and your sleigh will always run easy provided there is snow enough.—*Coach, Harness and Saddlery.*

The Hub
December 1886

HOW TO FIND THE POINT OF DRAFT ON A SLEIGH.

(See Illustration accompanying.)

A SHOWS the sleigh, and B, the line of draft. To ascertain the proper point at which to place the shaft-jack on this sleigh, first attach a line to

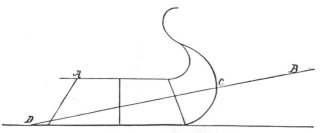

the runner at D, and extend it to the end and height of the shaft when in use; and, where the line crosses the runner, as shown by C, place the jack.

F. J. F.

The Hub
June 1887

POINT OF CONNECTION BETWEEN SLEIGH AND SHAFTS.

(See Illustration Accompanying.)

EDITOR OF THE HUB.

Dear Sir—Is there any rule for placing the connection between the shafts and the sleigh? If so, please illustrate as plainly and briefly as possible. Yours respectfully,

L. R.

[Answer.]

The accompanying outline sketch plainly illustrates the answer to the above question. To determine the line of draft or traction, we must first find the center of gravity between the point of traction and extreme resistance. These are shown in the drawing. D is the point of traction; B, extreme resistance; A, base line and bottom of runner; C, front of runner; E, top of sleigh bottom.

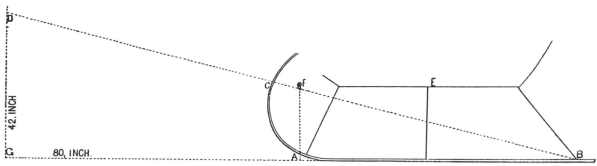

POINT OF CONNECTION BETWEEN SLEIGH AND SHAFTS.

From the earth to the bottom of the tug-strap bearing, or bottom of shaft at that point resting in the tug-strap, for the average horse, is about forty-two inches, or ranges from forty inches to forty-four inches. We take forty-two inches as the mean average, which is at D. The tug-strap on the average horse, in a majority of cases, is about eighty inches from the point of connection with the vehicle. Having located these two distances, draw a line from D to B, and obtain the line of connection C.

For economical purposes, the connection is usually, in this and most countries, made in front of the front posts, as at F—that is, for light sleighs or cutters. With the heavy and larger grades it is customary to put the jacks or connection on the nose-plates.

In Russia and Asiatic countries it is customary to make the connection with the runners only, using a long round pole for the purpose. The same custom prevailed in this country, with the freight sleighs and heavy sleighs, until about 1838.

The Hub

June 1893

SPREADING OF SLEIGH BOTTOMS AT RUNNERS AND WEARING OF SHOES.

(See Illustrations Accompanying.)

MANY questions have been asked in relation to the spreading of sleighs at the runners, also in relation to the wearing of the shoes on the same and how it can be overcome, to which we give the following answer:

Much or nearly all of the spreading of the sleigh is due to improper construction, a weakening of those parts which ought

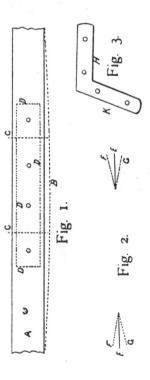

Fig. 1.

Fig. 2.

Fig. 3.

to be strengthened. The beams are made of the same dimensions from post to post, or do not have swell enough on the under side to prevent deflection, or what is usually termed sagging between the connection of the posts with the beam. Fig. I—A shows the usual method of making the sleigh beam; C C indicate two bolts which secure the stays to post; beam, which also tends to weaken the beam at the center, and as soon as the sleigh is loaded the beam sags at the center and the runners spread, which brings the wear chiefly on the inner side of the shoes.

To overcome this unmechanical feature the beam must be made heaviest on the under side, by a gradual swell from the posts to the center, as per dotted line B, Fig. I. The strain of the stays on the beam at the bearings or securing bolts C C is also to be overcome, and may be by means of a thin band iron plate, as per dotted lines D D D D, which overcomes the weakening of the beam, caused by the passage of the bolts through it, the plate being riveted to the beam.

Another weak spot is where the post frames or tenons in the beam are, and is easily overcome by means of a thin angle plate, as per Fig. 3. H to be riveted to the beam, and K riveted to the post. This virtually prevents the working of the tenon in the mortise, and consequently avoids any spreading at that point.

With the cutter the greater part of the weight is carried over the hind end of the runners. The back post has a greater amount of bevel than the front post, all of which expresses as plainly as can be that due precaution ought to be taken to strengthen it at that point; consequently the back beam and back post ought to be proportionately stronger than the other ones.

The inside back stays and the back side stays must also be made of stronger metal than the center or front stays. The bolts securing the inside back stays ought to also be stronger. In fact, it would be much better to secure this stay to the beam with two bolts.

The round portion of the stay next to the stay heel, at the beam, can also be much stouter than at the central portion.

The position of the flat or the tread of the runner must be horizontal when the weight is in the sleigh. In order to accomplish this (see Fig. 2), set the runners by means of the inside stays so as to assume a position similar to F F, dotted lines; then when sleigh is freighted we get the horizontal line, as per E E. If, however, they are set the same as at E E, when the freight is in the sleight gets the result as shown by dotted lines G G.

TO PREVENT SLEIGH-RUNNERS FROM SPLITTING.

(See four Illustrations accompanying.)

A CORRESPONDENT asks: "How shall I prevent the splitting of the shoes at the back end, and at the same time the shifting of the shoes and the breaking of the back-stay and shoe-bolts? I have kept on increasing the back bolts in size until I am afraid to add any more to their caliber. If you can suggest or illustrate a good method of overcoming that of which I complain, you will greatly relieve others who are in the same trouble as myself." "C. C."

ANSWER.—"C. C." and others who meet with the same back-sets in sleigh-building, will find the following methods fully explained.

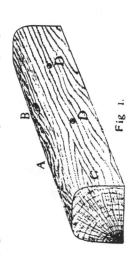

Fig 1.

The splitting of the runner may be overcome as set forth in Fig. 1, which represents a section of a runner: A, upper side; C, side of runner; B, hole through which the bolt passes, which secures runner, back-stays, heel and shoe. D, D, represent holes for rivets, sufficiently removed from the bolt-hole to in nowise interfere with the bolt. Countersink the outer side of the runner and use countersunk rivets 1/8-in. in diameter, and fair size riveting burs on the inside. When well riveted, finish the rivet heads flush with the wood. This will prove a very effectual method to prevent the splitting of the runner, but affords no relief to either the bolt, shoe or back-stay.

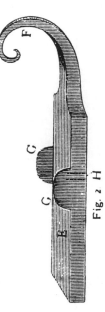

Fig. 2 H

Fig. 2 illustrates the back section of the shoe: E, upper surface; F, turn up or scroll, to prevent fouling when backing. The line H shows the direction in which the shoe and stay-bolt passes. G, G, are clips or ears, turned up on each side of the shoe, forming a recess into which the runner fits or rests securely.

Weld the clips on the shoe—using best iron—before forming the back end and fitting the shoe to the nose. Lay on the shoe a piece of iron just the width of the shoe, and bend the clips or ears while hot. This yoke will alike prevent the runner from splitting, the shoe from shifting, and the bolt from breaking. Do not round the scroll; thin down and

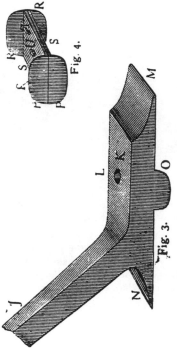

Fig. 3.

Fig. 4.

narrow a little, then scroll. This looks better and is much more efficient than rounding.

Fig. 3 shows back-stay, heel and section of back-stay: K, upper surface of heel; J, section of stay; M, back, or extreme end of stay; N, a spur on front end of heel to prevent sinking in wood; L, the hole for the bolt which secures shoe, runner and stay-heel together. O, is one of the two lugs which turn down from the stay-heel and encloses the sides of the runner as illustrated and described in Fig. 2. While the heel may be made of good ordinary iron, and the lugs welded on, it is much cheaper to make the whole of Norway iron, as the ears may then

The Construction of Sleighs

STAY FOR SLEIGH-RUNNER.

(See four Illustrations accompanying.)

"SLEIGH-MAKER" asks, in a recent letter, as follows: "Can you devise or illustrate a stay-heel for cutters on which the runners are beveled or sharpened up the same on an inverted V or V turned bottom-side up —a heel which will rest solidly on the runner, prevent its splitting, and leave a base for the nut to rest on securely?

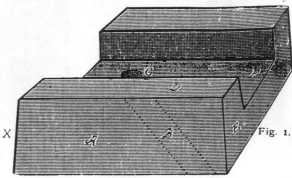

Fig. 1.

By Fig. 2, we illustrate the stay-heel and section of stay, as asked for. G is the crane side of the heel, H shows the top with the hole K for the passage of the shoe-bolt, M a section of the stay, L where the stay connects with the heel; N shows the V shape of the under side of the heel, which rests upon the upper surface of the so-shaped runner.

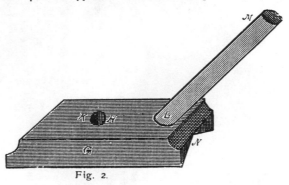

Fig. 2.

In order to make such a stay-heel, we must first make two tools, as per Figs. 1 and 3. Fig. 1 is the head of a tool similar to a bolt tool, the handle section projecting from the end marked X. A is one side of the tool, E the outer end, D D the top sections or walls which form the recess F, C is the hole into which the end M is inserted when forming the heel; the dotted lines B show the course of the hole.

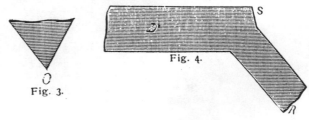

Fig. 3.

Fig. 4.

We first form the heel in the rough, as per Fig. 4. R is rounded to fit the hole in the tool, D is left or made narrower than the recess F, turn off R at the same angle as the hole in the tool. Raise a good heat on the whole and insert in the tool and set home well. Then, with a fuller, as per Fig. 3 (O the working point, and made smaller than the runner, after first forcing down S to fill out the end), form the groove on the underside of the heel. About two heats will be required in order to make the heel perfect. Fit the heel to the runner by filing, before welding on the balance of the stay. In making the tool, Fig. 1, be sure that the hole C is much larger on the under side, to prevent the stay end becoming fast in the hole. Also, have the recess F slightly wider at the top to prevent the sticking of the heel.

The Hub
October 1888

Ironing

USEFUL HINTS ABOUT IRONING SLEIGHS.

We doubt if there is any other mechanical trade demanding as much guess-work as that of carriage, wagon and sleigh-building. You have not only to study carrying capacity, strength, durability and style, but to guess at the condition of the roads, state of the weather, rate of propulsion, and distribution of the load, so that the vehicle, whether on wheels or runners, will under all conditions glide along without friction and almost noiselessly.

The builder who makes sleighs a specialty is by no means free from the same irritating conditions, for the average sleigh-rider nearly always looks for impossibilities, demanding that the sleigh be as light as gossamer, and carry two persons at a rattling pace, and meet with an occasional collision, and run on bare ground, and suit a thirteen-hand horse to-day and a sixteen-hand horse to-morrow,—and do all this without breaking down, or wearing out or losing shape. Under these trying circumstances, he is naturally often put to the extent of his resources to overcome them. Now we know that, the nearer the motive power is brought to the body to be moved, the less the exertion required to move the same. For this reason the shafts are brought well back, and have high back ends so as to clear the limbs of the horse when in action. For the same reason, we place the front inner stay-heels as close to the front post as possible, and still preserve its usefulness. Having placed four front stays in the position above mentioned, it becomes necessary to make up the loss of strength at that point in the disposition of the central and back stays, by allowing them to extend nearly to the center of the beam. Experience teaches us that iron stays will not stand the pressure without bending, unless we use iron parts so large as to destroy the general outline, while cast-steel is too brittle to carry us through safely; and we consequently have to resort to a mild steel that is tenacious and also has resisting power.

Sleighs receive rough usage at both ends, and these two places consequently require the most support. It may be necessary to use $\frac{7}{16}$ in. round steel for the front and back side-stays, while a steel $\frac{3}{8}$ or $\frac{5}{16}$ in. may answer for the two central stays.

In making the T's which unite the runner and post, we advise using a solid T, or one formed by splitting and turning off, which will prove more secure at all times. Avoid, as far as possible, placing any securing bolt, rivet or screw where the joint occurs, but place such quite near the joint, and thus prevent breaking of the wood and iron.

The tendency of sleigh runners is to grow wider at the back after the sleigh has been in use a while, but this may be overcome by drawing in the runners a trifle by means of the back stays.

The so-called "drawing by the nose or heel" is due to the improper position in which the shaft-irons are placed. If too high, the friction will all be at the nose; and if too low the friction will be at the heel. It is not difficult to ascertain the proper point for locating the shaft-bolt. Presuming that the average horse is 14½ hands high, this would place the shaft-tug at about 48 in. from the ground. Place the points of the shafts at that distance from the floor, and draw a line from the heel of the sleigh to the point of the shaft; and we thereby learn the center of gravity and the point at which to hook on the motive power. N. Y. S.

IMPROVEMENT IN SLEIGH IRONS.

(See seven Illustrations accompanying.)

WE are indebted to Mr. P. S., of Hattey, P. Q., for the following interesting hints on the ironing of sleighs. He says:

MR. EDITOR OF THE HUB: We live in a sort of out-of-the-way place, but we manage to get our *Hub* every month, just the same as those who do business in the larger towns, and we perhaps read it more carefully.

Up here in Canada almost every one who does wagon-work knows also how to do nearly every thing about sleighs as well. I learned my trade here, and have learned both blacksmithing and wheelwrighting. I know that I cannot make a fine coach, and trim and paint it the same as they can in the large shops in Montreal and Quebec, and in the large shops in the States; but I manage to do a pretty good job in my line of wagon and sleigh work, which satisfies our farmers and lumbermen, and I make a tolerably good living. When times are really good, I have a wheelwright, who can also do trimming, and a boy to help me on ironwork and painting. My wife and daughter sometimes help me in the trimming and painting; and, when I am short of help, they even help me in the blacksmith-shop and wheelwright-shop.

I have seen a good many good things in *The Hub* about sleighs, but I have never seen any sleigh ironwork of the same kind that I use. I therefore send you some drawings of such ironwork made after my fashion. If you can make them out, and if they are of any use to you, they are at your service.

Yours truly,
P. S.

NOTES.—We have touched up the sketches and description of our correspondent a little, and now take pleasure in presenting them, believing that they offer points of interest to all sleigh-builders. Clips will prevent any possibility of the splitting of the woodwork.

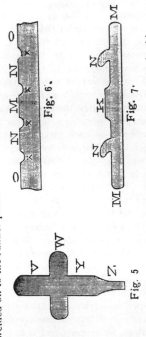

Fig. 1 shows the stay complete, including *a*, the plate under the beam; *e*, a clip on the back side of the beam; *b*, the stay; *c*, the standard plate; *g g*, clips on the same; *d*, the runner-plate; and *h h*, clips on top of the runner, through which the shoe-bolt passes.

Fig. 2 shows the method of smithing used. Take iron of the right size, and fuller it in at E E E E. The parts B B form the clips *g g*, Fig. 1, and C makes *c* of Fig. 1. The part D is the end to which the runner-plate is welded; and A makes the stay *b*, the same as is shown in Fig. 3 by S, P, T, R, U.

Fig. 4 shows how *a*, *c* and *b*, of Fig. 1, are made, which is further explained in Fig. 5.

Fuller in at L L. The part G gives V, Fig. 5; H gives W; and K gives Y and Z.

Fig. 6 shows how to smith *d* and *h h*, Fig. 1, which is further explained in Fig. 7. Fuller in at *x x x x*. The parts O O give M M, Fig. 7; N N give N N; and M gives K, the place where the standard is welded on to the runner-plate.

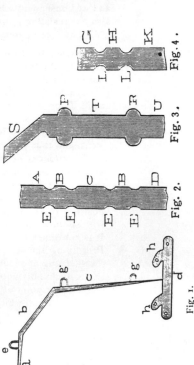

Our correspondent tells us that he irons all his sleighs in this manner, and that he has never had a split beam, standard or runner. He adds that some of his sleighs are quite heavy, being used in lumbering, wooding and sugaring, and for such other purposes as the people of his section use them on the rough and hilly roads.

FOOT SCRAPERS FOR SLEIGHS.

(See Illustrations Accompanying.)

THE unpleasant feature of sleigh riding is cold feet. Notwithstanding this is a fact of many centuries' standing, but very few persons, either riders or sleigh builders, take any precaution to prevent this disagreeable feature.

On leaving the house, office, or road-house, the feet are warm, and impart much of their warmth to the footwear, which same, as soon as it comes in contact with the snow, causes it to melt just enough to cling to the shoes. The matter of removing the snow from the shoe never enters the mind, or, if it does, there is nothing by which the snow may be removed.

But few builders of the present day think of such a thing as a snow or foot scraper. He who does ought to be awarded a golden medal inscribed, "Intelligent and humane sleigh builder," on the obverse side, with his name; on the reverse side, "Presented by the Humane Society of the World."

The sleigh builder of half a century agone would not have thought of turning out a sleigh without foot scrapers, any more than he would of sending out a wheel without a tire. Every comfort was looked after, no matter if some few minute details

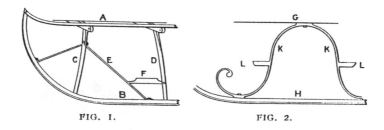

FIG. 1.   FIG. 2.

of style were suspended to make room for such necessary comforts.

A foot scraper is inexpensive, and does not detract from the harmony of any line which may be drawn. To the contrary, the same may be made ornamental, as well as useful, in its application. We illustrate two very simple methods. Fig. 1. A, body rocker; B, runner; C, front post; D, center post; E, back stay of front post; F, foot scraper welded to stay E, and so made as to rivet to the center post with two rivets. The scraper should be about 3½ or 4 in. long, 3¼ in. wide, less than ⅛ in. thick at top or upper side or edges, and ³⁄₁₆ in. at under edge. The position is such as to permit of scraping the right foot prior to stepping into the sleigh, also the left foot, before bringing that up and into the sleigh.

Fig. 2. G, the rocker; H, the runner; K K, sections of one of the stays, to which are welded the foot scrapers L L. We place it this way from the fact that this stay usually centers under the front seat of a two-seat sleigh, and therefore admits of the one scraper being placed with advantage on each section of the stay. With the heavier grade of sleighs, the scraper should be made sufficiently heavy to correspond with the other surroundings.

The Hub
August 1894

Ironing a Berlin Cutter.

BELVIDERE, N. J., November, 1885.

MR. EDITOR:—Having noticed that the iron-work of sleighs has not received the attention it should in the trade journals, I will illustrate and describe that of the Berlin cutter published in the August number of the MONTHLY, plate No. 29. The greatest trouble among mechanics with work of this class is to know where to begin. As a rule, the smith-shop is seldom supplied with a draft-board of any description, and a smith, to be successful in ironing a sleigh of this description, must first make a draft of it, side and end elevations of which being all that is necessary.

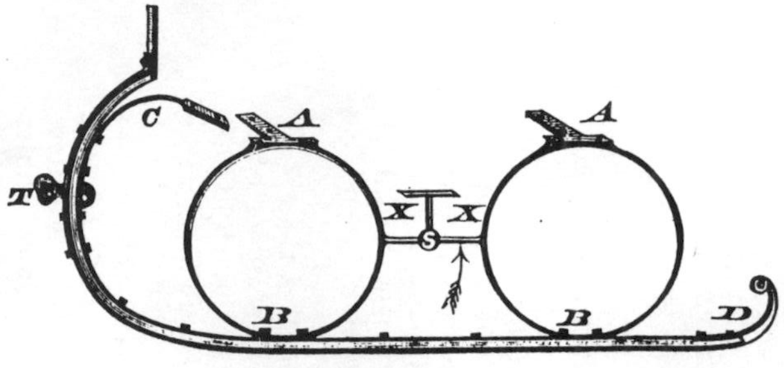

Fig. 1.

Side elevation, *Fig. 1*, will be a guide for the smith to work by; from this he can get all the lengths and shapes of the irons, and it will give him the proper place for the holes and bolts. *A, A, Fig. 1*, is a welded forging. The **T** of this forging is welded in the tool, *Fig. 13*. *Fig. 4* shows the shape of this iron before it is pieced out.

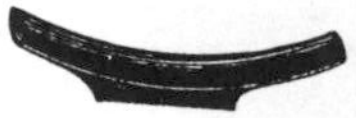
Fig. 2.

Fig. 3.

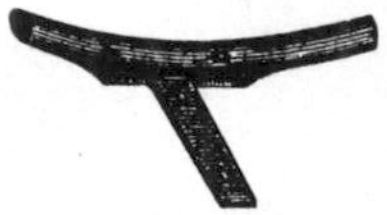
Fig. 4.

B, B, Fig. 1, is also a forging, which is also shown in *Fig. 3*. *X, X, Fig. 1*, are solid forgings, of which *Fig. 5* is the forging. The eye *S, Fig. 1*, is forged as in *Fig. 8*; to this is welded the step-pad, *Fig. 9*. *D, Fig. 1*, is shown in *Fig. 12*; this is welded to the sleigh-shoe. Brace *C, Fig. 1*, is fully illustrated in *Fig. 6*. The eye in this brace is for the front cross-rod; this cross-rod is made the same as the middle cross-rod, which is fastened in the eye of the step-shank at *S, Fig. 1*. *Fig. 10* shows how these cross-rods are made; they are of $\frac{5}{8}$ by $\frac{3}{8}$-inch oval iron, with a collar on each end; on the round end of the collar is cut a $\frac{3}{8}$-inch thread for an octagon nut.

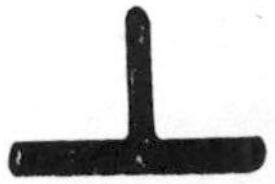
Fig. 5.

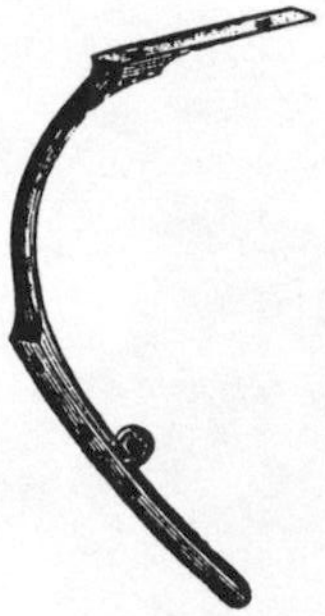
Fig. 6.

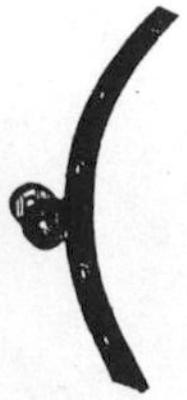
Fig. 7.

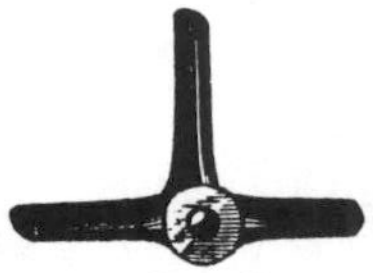
Fig. 8.

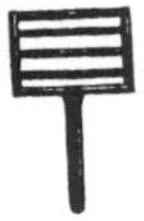
Fig. 9.

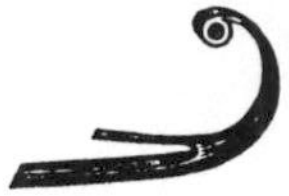
Fig. 12.

Fig. 7 shows how the coupling for the shaft is made; this coupling is shown at *T, Fig. 1*. *Fig. 11* is the back cross-bar; this bar has a collar in the center, and tapers from $\frac{3}{4}$ by $\frac{1}{2}$ inch to $\frac{5}{8}$ by $\frac{3}{8}$ inch oval, it being largest in the middle; on the ends it has collars and threads the same as *Fig. 10*. Compare the forging of *Fig. 3* with that of *Fig. 2*, and you will see that *Fig. 2* is curved, while *Fig. 3* is straight. It is very important in forgings *Figs. 2* and *4* to forge the sweep as shown, for if made as in *Fig. 3*, it will make a bad job in the curve, which it will be almost impossible to get true. The circle-stays are made of $\frac{5}{8}$ by $\frac{3}{8}$-inch oval iron; the connecting brace between the circles is $\frac{5}{8}$ by $\frac{1}{2}$ inch oval. Size of the eye in *Fig. 8*, outside measurement, $1\frac{1}{4}$ inches; size of step-shank, $\frac{5}{8}$ inch wide, tapered from $\frac{5}{8}$ to $\frac{1}{2}$ inch oval. It is very important to make the top forgings *A, A, Fig. 1*, with the **T**, as this helps much toward stiffening and holding the side stays in place. The side stays are made in one piece, and the last weld is taken at the arrow-point.

Fig. 10.

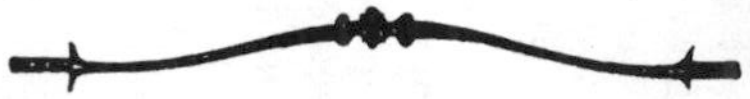
Fig. 11.

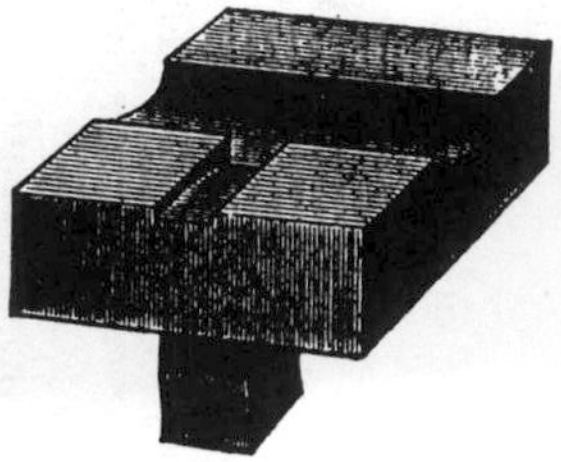
Fig. 13.

The brace *C, Fig. 1*, is made of $\frac{5}{8}$ by $\frac{3}{8}$-inch oval iron; this brace is bolted to the bracket-front of the body with two bolts, and on the inside of the runner with four bolts, as shown.

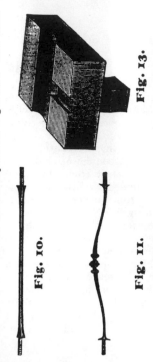

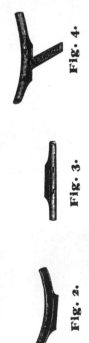

Bob Sleds.

SCRANTON, PA., August, 1889.

MR. EDITOR:—The accompanying drawings of bob sleds are new and original. They are suitable for four or six-passenger surries. *Fig. 1* is the front bob. By looking at the cut you will notice only one wood knee and bench. The cross pieces *A, B,* are framed to the side rail, and should be put together so that no end wood shows. These cross pieces are stiffened by corner braces and light plates as

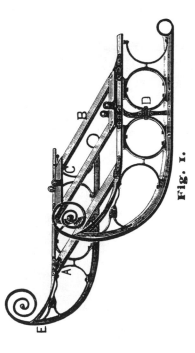

Fig. 1.

shown in *Fig. 3* at *X, X, X, X.* The corner braces are bolted to the cross pieces *A,* the full length as shown.

Fig. 2 shows how the knee, bench and side rail are made and braced. Brace *G, Fig. 6,* are braces *B, B, Fig. 2.* Brace *F, Fig. 6,* are braces *A, A, Fig. 2;* braces *E* and *D, Fig. 6,* are bolted to brace *A, Fig. 2,* as shown in *Fig. 1* at *D.* The braces *D, E, Fig. 6,* are forged out for the runner bearings; the **T** is welded; the offsets are solid forgings. Piece *C* is for the pole or shaft coupling. *B* is a corner iron; this is fastened to the under side of side rail, and inside on

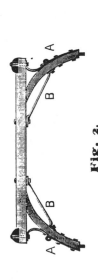

Fig. 2.

top of runner at *E, Fig. 1.* This corner iron is fastened to the circle with the first bolt as shown at *E. A, Fig. 6,* is shown at *C, Fig. 1,* and at *A, Fig. 3;* in this coupling brace is fastened the spring *Fig. 5.*

On these springs is clipped the circle and frame as shown. These springs are arched about 1½ inches, and hang on loose hangers. The bent bar *A,* is wood, to which are clipped and bolted the irons

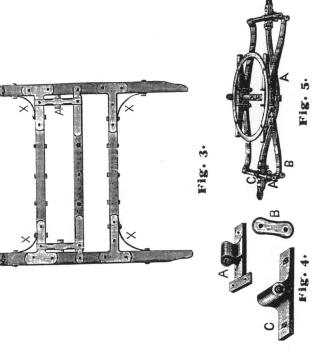

Fig. 3.

Fig. 4.

Fig. 5.

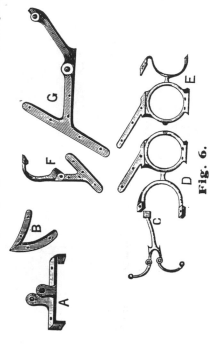

Fig. 6.

shown in *Fig. 4. C* is *C, Fig. 5; A* also *A, Fig. 5. B* is one of the spring hangers. I show the front bob only. The back bob is made the same as the front, excepting it has no circle but one wide spring

bar on the springs. The height of the sled is from the floor to top of side rail, 13 inches. Track, 3 feet, 6 inches.

Yours, truly,

H. R. H.

THE CONSTRUCTION OF SLEIGHS:

BODY DESIGN

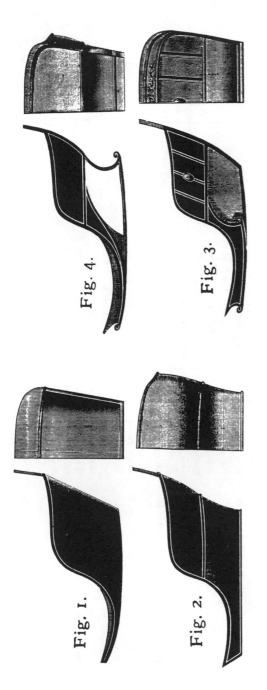

SIX DESIGNS OF SLEIGH BODIES.—SCALE, ONE-HALF INCH TO THE FOOT.

(See description accompanying.)

HINTS FOR BODY-MAKERS AND DRAFTSMEN.

XV. SIX DESIGNS OF SLEIGH BODIES.

THIS number of *The Hub* being devoted largely to the presentation of sleigh designs, we give below six patterns of sleigh bodies, including four two-passenger sleighs, or cutters, and two four-passenger sleighs. These bodies are all plain, although there seems to be a tendency at present toward greater elaborateness, of which we have given expression in the fashion plates appearing in this number.

Fig. I represents a plain cutter. The sides are inclined, as shown on the back view. The sides lengthwise can either be left straight, or be swelled about ½ in. The latter method will produce a better effect when painted. We would also advise swelling the sides slightly from top to bottom, when cleaning off the body. The body shown in our drawing has round corners, but these can be left square if preferred. The molding is put on as shown, and is made light. It is either rounded off slightly on the outer surface, or left square. Where extreme plainness is desired, moldings can be omitted altogether. The width of the body is indicated on the half-back view. Track, 37 in., from out to out.

Fig. 2 will make a handsome body. The back, as shown on the drawing, is of the ogee pattern. This involves more work, but the result will repay for the trouble. The rear bottom corner is square, but, from that point, the corner is rounded gradually toward the top, where considerable curve is given. The sides are swelled, and have a concave-convex curve is given. Sleighs of this pattern are generally painted in showy colors,—for instance, with the upper part of the body light blue, the lower section black, and the moldings striped with a fine line of gold. Kunners, carmine, striped with black and gold. Track, 37 in., out to out.

Fig. 3 shows a body having swelled sides and back. The back is swelled about 1 in. The panels are glued to the rear corner-pillars. There is no absolute need for mitering the side and rear panels, as the joint formed at either the side or back will be covered by the moldings, which are mitered. The distinction between the top and bottom sections is indicated by moldings, which are glued and nailed to the body. The sticks have the thickness of the moldings, and are V-shaped. To make the contrast between the top and bottom section more apparent, the top part should be painted, as on No. 2, with a different color from that on the lower section, which is always black. Track, the same as for Fig. 2.

Fig. 4 shows a body having an ogee pillar similar to that on Fig. 2, excepting that the outline is more defined. Bent wood should be used for the corner-pillars, which are framed into the bottom sills. The bottom sills are also made of bent wood, about 1 in. thick, lightened on the outside to the thickness of the molding, which is ¾ in. wide. Near the front of the seat an upright is framed into the sill, and connected with the corner-pillar by a horizontal bar. To this bar, and the corner-pillar, the sides are glued, which are made of thick whitewood. A panel is glued to the upright, extending to the front, as shown on the drawing, and grooved into the bottom sill. The molded piece commences at the bottom of the seat, and is made of whitewood, and finished off in a concave-convex shape. The moldings are worked on. Track, 38 in., from out to out.

Technicalities of Carriage Drafting.

PART I.—LIGHT WORK.

(Continued from page 86.)

CUTTERS AND SLEIGHS.

In continuing our series on carriage drafting, we have thought it advisable to devote this number to the discussion of cutters and sleighs, and with that object in view have prepared several diagrams of which we propose to write, in connection with styles more modern and more agreeable with the present demand for fashionable cutters and sleighs as shown in our fashion plates.

In our diagrams will be recognized the old time swell-side cutter and sleigh; the Portland, an innovation that met with such an unexpected welcome, that in many sections of the country it has entirely superseded the swell-side cutter; and later still, styles similar to diagram 6, which are warring successfully upon the style represented in diagram 5, and the introduction of which has paved the way for an entirely new departure in cutter and sleigh building. This ignoring old-time styles with which many veteran carriage-builders have been familiar from boyhood, is a step that will be duly appreciated by the fashionable driving portion of the carriage-builder's patrons; and although some important features have been sacrificed in order to produce this change in styles, they perhaps will not be considered as real objections, because just claims can be advanced for improvement in other arguments than that of style. While other points would be more objectionable in same localities than in others. These several features we propose to point out and discuss in a general manner before giving dimensions.

Two important rules have always governed the designer in drawing a sleigh or cutter aside from those of comfort and lightness, though we must confess that comfort—ease of position—when riding has not always been one of the first considerations. Any one will attest to this who has ridden ten consecutive miles in one of the handsome swell-side cutters, many of them having possessed decidedly uncomfortable, "back-breaking" qualities. Of the two gov-

erning reasons or rules claiming our attention, viz: (1) that of guarding against the cold, and (2) obstructions, we find in the old style of swell-side cutters, diagram 3, that this is provided for in the depth from the rave A, to the sill B, and the same (letters A, and B) in diagram 5, while the front of the latter though lacking in depth still possesses considerable protection. This allows the garments about the extremities, especially in female apparel, to be kept in position in connection with the robe, as a protector against the cold and winds, while in diagram 4 and 6, as well as in our later styles, no such provisions are made. As an offset to this, we have greater convenience in getting in and out the cutter or sleigh. This is certainly an advantage, but whether of sufficient importance to counterbalance the other is a matter of opinion. The protection in by-gone years might have been considered more important than at present. When we consider that in olden times, ere the various modes of quick transit had been so greatly perfected as at present, travelers were required to ride long distances, while now the sleigh or cutter is used more as a pleasure vehicle, we are induced to more readily accept this opinion. Certain it is, that for use in the cities, the convenience of getting in and out by far counterbalances the other advantage.

As to guarding against obstructions, there is a wide difference between the old and new styles. In the past as well as in the present, in some portions of the rural districts, the depth of the snow both on the level and in drifts made it necessary that sleighs and cutters should be made with the body high up from the ground. The roads had not then reached their present state of perfection, while adjacent fields through which, in consequence of drifts, travelers were obliged to drive, had not become as now free from stumps, rocks and other obstructions. These impediments necessitated the elevation of the body, and in connection with the lightness and depth of the fall of snow, through which the runners readily cut when beating a fresh track, one other argument is advanced for the use of long knees, namely, that of necessity. In some sections of the country these arguments still hold good, but in the majority of places, a demand is created for styles similar to those

given in our fashion plates.

It may be suggested that in the old Russian sleighs the bodies are placed close to the ground, while their snow-fall by far exceeds that of any portion of the states. In making this suggestion it would be well to bear in mind that while the Russian winter, with its larger fall of snow is a certainty, ours is decidedly uncertain. The former is long, cold and severe, causing the snow to become solid and often encrusted over so as to bear both horse and sleigh on its surface, while our winters are comparatively warm, with falls of snow so light and fleecy that the runners cut through to the ground. Even in Central New York, where the winters are long and severe, the ground-work or bottom for good sleighing is frequently of no account before the last of the winter. So common is this that the oft recurring expression of "six weeks sleighing in March," is frequently heard, from the fact that the whole winter's work—hauling sawlogs, lumber, &c.—is deferred until snow falls, and then is crowded into that one month.

The depth of the lower panel as a safe-guard against the wind is of no consideration in the cities and greater portions of the country where runners are used as a mode of transit. Then again as an argument in favor of short knees, the closer to the ground the passenger can be placed the less liability there is of his being overturned, at the same time he is not so much exposed to the wind. These are the two principal reasons, that in the later styles, conflict seriously with those of the past, while the other changes should be considered more as improvements in ease, comfort and style than as detrimental to the general make-up.

In designing cutters similar to diagrams 3 and 4, having first drawn the base line K, measure up the distance the body is to be from the ground, at the lowest point, as shown by the dotted line C, C, diagram 3. This height frequently varies, according to the old style being from 18 to 20 inches; 18 inches is sufficiently high to clear obstructions, and on later styles the distance is less, making it no more than 15 inches and as little as 13 inches. The latter is sufficiently high in most cases and especially for city use. In cases of a heavy fall of snow or drifts it would make additional work for the horse. Of late years a fall of snow rarely occurs, in the majority of sections, of suffic ent depth to preclude placing the body 15 inches from the ground even for country use. It therefore follows that either of the figures given may be used at the option of the designer. The height of seat, 12 inches from the dotted line, can then be measured as shown at D. Make the seat-room from 16 to 20 inches (D, to E,) dropping ¾ of an inch from a horizontal line at E. Give the back from E, to F, a good height, from 20 to 24 inches in the center. In diagram 4 this measurement is but 14 inches, which is decidedly too little for making an easy and comfortable back, while in diagram 3 the distance is 20 inches. This allows of a spring back and a luxurious cushion.

The foot room in a sleigh or cutter should always be as roomy as possible, for we have not only to make extra room for the robes, but it is equally necessary to guard against the limbs being obliged to occupy cramped positions. The limbs must be easy and comfortable in order to maintain a free circulation of the blood, thereby preventing the occupant from feeling the cold so intensely. When the body and limbs are left free to change positions, the cold can be endured to a greater degree and for a much longer period. The shape of diagram 4 is much better for the attainment of this object than that of diagram 3, owing to the peculiar style of the former. In this (diagram 4) the distance is 30 inches from the front of seat at D, to H, while in the swell-side it is but 26 inches, and owing to the shape of the sill more inconvenient for shifting positions.

The object of the dasher is to prevent the particles of ice and snow from flying from the horse's hoofs into the rider's face. It should therefore be of sufficient height for the attainment of this object, otherwise it may be regulated as desired by the designer. A good rule is to carry it up, when without a leather dash, from two to three inches above the line of the back. When with a leather dash, the top should reach the same height.

An existing fault in many designs is the crook of the runners, they being bent with too much fullness at I. The object should be to get a good graceful curve, striving at the same time to keep the horse as near as possible to the load. This object is attained to a greater extent in diagram 4 than in 3. We do not know that any rule is necessary for placing the knees. The designer should exercise his judgment in regard to this, being governed by the shape of the body.

The usual width of cutter bodies is from 34 to 36 inches at the arm K. From 29 to 30 inches outside on the bottom of sill, carrying out the same width on a swell-back, along up the back and front of body. Width of track 39 and 40 inches.

In the construction of a sleigh the same rules will apply as given for the cutter, so far as the seat, height of the knees, height and width of the seat, height of back and dasher are concerned. The foot-room for the back seat in diagram 5, will be increased by the space under the front seat, while in a style similar to diagram 6, it must stop at L, the measurement being 29 inches. For the front seat the foot-room of necessity is cramped, it being in the swell-side 21 inches, a very inconvenient space when used for long driving. This may be improved upon by raising the seat though it is not policy to show too much difference between the two. In diagram 6 the foot-space is more roomy, the seat having been placed higher up in order to gain space for the child's seat N, O. The child's seat is 10 inches from the bottom of the body. This can be lowered to 8¼ or 8 inches but should be made no higher. The frame for the front seat can vary in measurement, being made all the way from 12 to 18 inches from M, to P. When narrow in width, no back should be put on it, while the extreme width—18 inches —should not be used unless to harmonize with other parts. 15 to 16 inches will make a good roomy seat. The width across back seat on top at K, 39 or 40 inches; the width under front seat frame M, P, should be 6 inches narrower. Width outside of the sill 31 or 32 inches. Track, 42 inches.

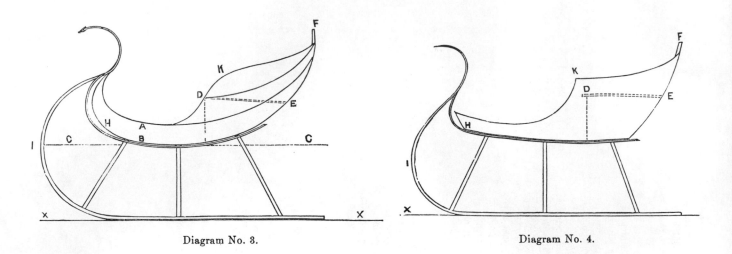

Diagram No. 3.

Diagram No. 4.

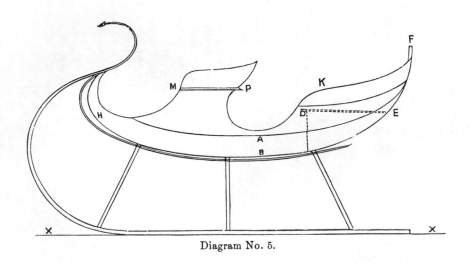

Diagram No. 5.

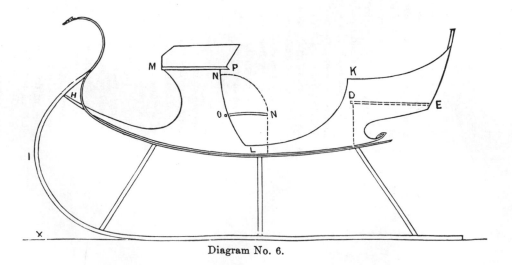

Diagram No. 6.

How to Make Patterns for Sleigh Wings.

To those who first set out in sleigh building, the matter of making wings for the dasher is no easy task, and many times we have seen our young friends of the smith shop exhaust their patience at trying to arrive at desired results. To those who know how, the matter is not difficult. The method of procedure is as

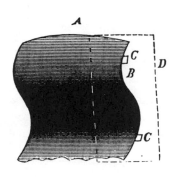

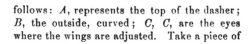

follows: A, represents the top of the dasher; B, the outside, curved; C, C, are the eyes where the wings are adjusted. Take a piece of

heavy manilla paper, and attach to the back side of the dasher, as per dotted line D, and mark with a pencil the line B, also the eyes C, C. Cut out with shears, and you have the inside line, as per F, and where eyes come, E, E, lay your paper on a board, and mark the inside line, the outer line, A, to be made to

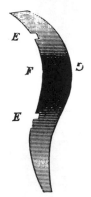

suit any desired form which you may fancy. The marks E, E, Fig. 2, show where to fasten the pins for securing the wings.

Carriage Monthly
December 1878

Cottonwood for Sleigh Bodies.

EDITOR CARRIAGE MONTHLY: In the communication published in the April number of the CARRIAGE MONTHLY I did not mean to condemn cottonwood for all classes of work. We have used it for many years in all kinds of sleigh bodies, and think it just as good as any timber for that work, as sleighs are used only in cold and dry weather, which has little or no effect on any timber, but our experience with it for panels in carriages, which are exposed to all kinds of weather, leads us to condemn it for the latter use. We have also found that it makes very poor bottoms for bodies. There may be differences in the qualities of cottonwood according to the locality in which it is cut. The timber I refer to grew in our vicinity.

Leipsic, Ohio, May 16, 1894.   J. H. FISHER.

Carriage Monthly
May 1894

Styles and Finish of Sleighs.

¼-INCH SCALE.

In addition to the sleigh styles in the April number, we here give some shapes and varieties of finish which are new, particularly the finish, in their application to sleigh bodies. We illustrate the side elevation and full back view in connection with the description for each sleigh.

The rear panel has four moldings between the main moldings. Its shape must be as illustrated, and its size must be the same as on the side surfaces. The front surface of the panel is generally plain, but moldings can be put on to correspond with the main moldings, excepting those that run up and down.

With Figs. 3 and 4 we illustrate a different style and finish from any shown last month. The rear panel is a regular convex, and the side surfaces are the same, but they can be made convex on the upper and concave on the lower part of the body the same as for victorias and cabriolets. The main molding is made of two pieces, ⅛ inch thick, glued and bradded on. The molding that forms the cabriolet side quarters is the same size as on cabriolets, with the exception of the thickness, which is ⅜ inch, to correspond with that of the other moldings.

To give an extra finish to the main molding the edges can be beaded on both sides, which gives a better finish, and when painted in different colors and striped on center of beads, is very attractive. The rear moldings are similar to cabriolets with the exception that they are set in from the edges. The upper edge of the back panel has a roll running across, which is best shown on the back view.

With Figs. 5 and 6 we illustrate a style similar in shape to several of those illustrated, but its finish is decidedly different. The main

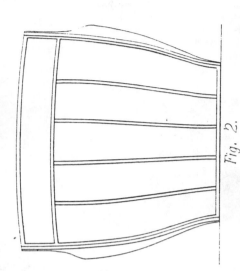

Fig. 2.

molding is on the cabriolet order, but with a scroll front and the edges are beaded. The lower edge and back corner pillar moldings, instead of being set in as explained in the other designs, are directly at the edge, and the rest of the surfaces on the back and sides are finished with turned spindles.

These spindles are flattened one side, which is in contact with the panel, and the other side is flattened also, with the exception of center

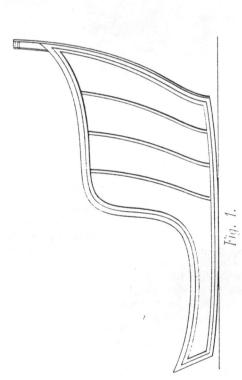

Fig. 1.

With Fig. 1 we illustrate a design similar in shape to one of the April number styles, with the exception of the moldings. The main moldings are ¾ inch wide and ⅛ inch thick, and the corners are rounded a trifle, just enough to give the sharp corners a half round finish. The moldings up and down are ⅝ inch wide and a full ⅛ inch thick, and finished the same as the main moldings. The finish of the back moldings corresponds with the side surfaces of the body. The moldings around the edges are set in from the edges of the body on the side and rear elevation with the exception of the top and ... tom of rear panel, but those two moldings can also be set below ... l above the edges the same as the rest.

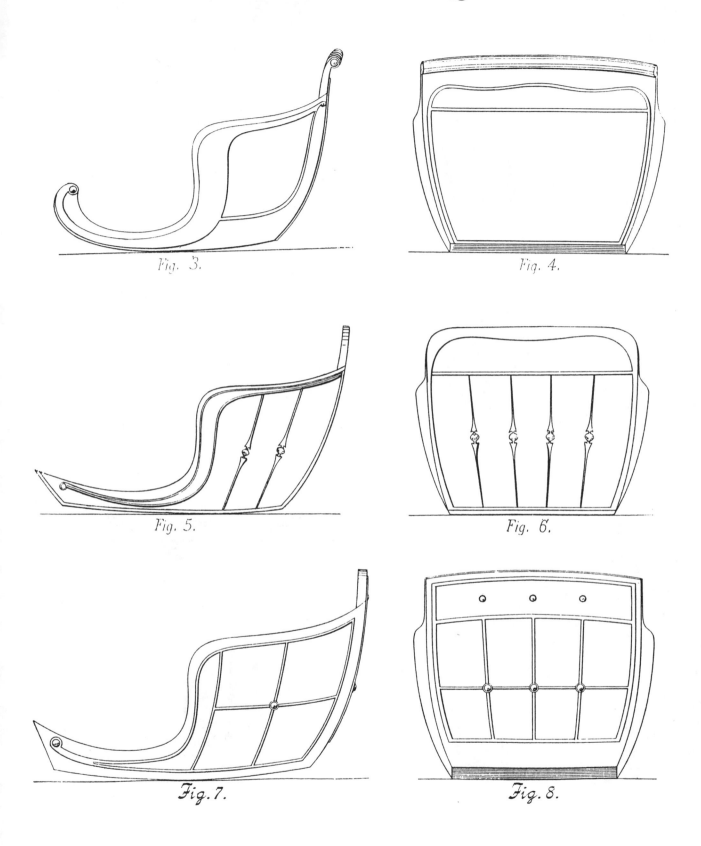

Fig. 3.

Fig. 4.

Fig. 5.

Fig. 6.

Fig. 7.

Fig. 8.

Carriage Monthly
May 1894
(second of four pages)

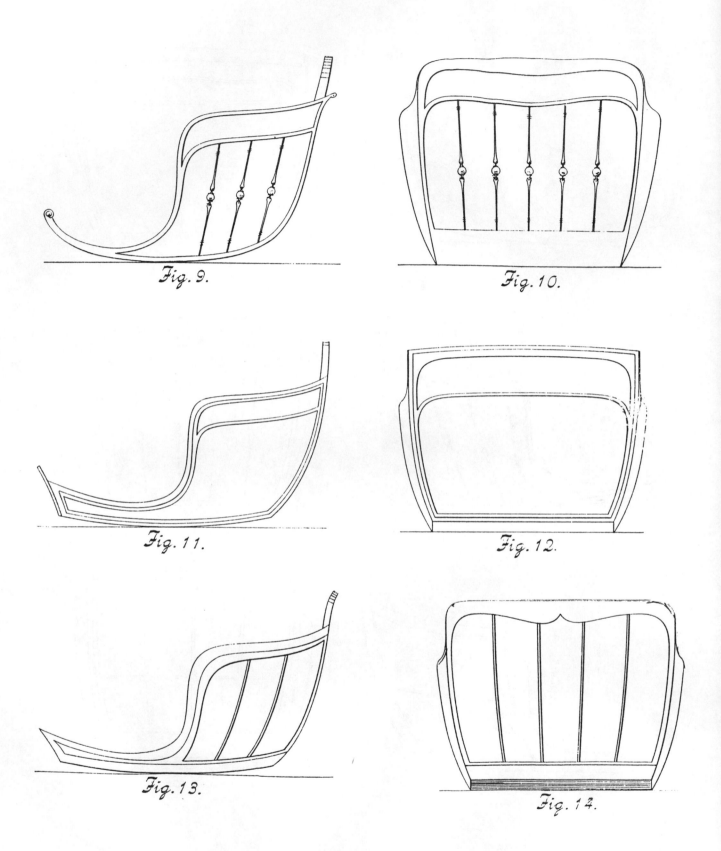

Fig. 9.

Fig. 10.

Fig. 11.

Fig. 12.

Fig. 13.

Fig. 14.

Carriage Monthly
May 1894
(third of four pages)

beaded on both sides, and give the same finish as on victorias. The shape of the molding on the back panel is the same as on Fig. 14, except that it is set in all around from the edges, and corresponds with the side surfaces.

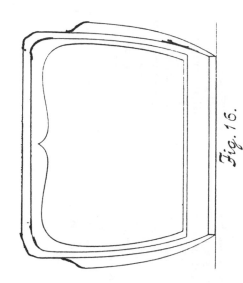

Fig. 15.

Fig. 16.

part, which is left round. The object of lessening the thickness is to make the spindles pliable, so that they may be bent over the panels. To increase their pliability it is best to make them of basswool or poplar. The side surfaces have two spindles each; the back surface has four spindles, and the moldings are edged to correspond with the side surfaces.

With Figs. 7 and 8 we illustrate a decidedly novel finish for side and rear panel. The surfaces are first finished and the moldings are cut and finished to shape and glued and bradded to the panels. The moldings are $\frac{3}{8}$ inch wide by $\frac{7}{16}$ inch thick, and finished to suit the builders. The square finish, with the sharp edges taken off with sand paper, is the cheapest. The rosettes are turned and moldings are jointed against them horizontally and vertically. All moldings are the same thickness, but the main moldings can be made heavier than those between. The upper space of the back panel is finished with three rosettes somewhat smaller than the lower ones.

With Figs. 9 and 10 the style is different from those illustrated, and so is the finish. The side panels are high, with a belt on top of $4\frac{1}{2}$ inches intermediate moldings, and this same belt is carried out on the rear panel. This space, to make it attractive, should be finished with imitation cane, and the same should be done on the back panel. If the cane is not wanted the space can be finished with a pretty design of carving. The moldings are $\frac{1}{4}$ inch thick, $\frac{3}{4}$ inch wide, and beaded with a square bead (similar to those on victoria and cabriolet bodies), and are put level with the edges and glued and bradded on. To avoid the joints of the moldings they can be beaded all around the body, which gives a very good finish.

With Figs. 11 and 12 the shapes of the moldings are similar to those on Figs. 9 and 10, except that they are set in from the edges on the back and side surfaces, and the lower back edge has a corner similar to the back edge of the body. The space on the belt can be finished with imitation cane, imitation basket wood, or left plain and painted with a different color from the rest of the body.

Figs. 13 and 14 give a decidedly good idea for placing the moldings. The back corner molding is level with the edge, while the rest is set in, a trifle more at the bottom than at the top. The upper edge of the main molding can be beaded, and the lower one also, if desired; but in this case the inside edges of the rear and bottom moldings must be beaded also, while the rest is left square.

Figs. 15 and 16 show a different style; that is, the application of the moldings is different from the others on side elevation, and is similar to the wing pillars of victorias and cabriolets. They can be

Framing Back Panels.

MILWAUKEE, WIS., Feb. 19, 1888.

Mr. EDITOR:—I witnessed an argument between our body-makers in regard to shaping lower back panels, so that they will be finished and smoothed all around their ends and entire surface, and also finished to go in the groove before bending. Only one body-maker understood this, and he says it is very difficult, and can only be learnt with great difficulty. I have only worked three years at the trade, and principally make light bodies, but have helped to finish heavy work. Since this argument I have made a study of this subject, have also questioned the body-maker who appeared to know all about it, as he said the ogee pillar back panels are the most difficult to prepare without fitting, and I believe this to be true. I have been looking over my three volumes of the MONTHLY, but could find no explanation in regard to fitting back panels, and notice you invite all apprentices to ask questions. I suppose you are able to explain this in such a manner that an apprentice could understand it from the book, and I would be pleased if you will illustrate the style of body so that I can see what kind it is and how it should be shaped.

APPRENTICE.

In answer to the above, we will explain and illustrate this subject so as to be comprehensible to all, so that even apprentices can understand and apply the method on all bodies, no matter how they are shaped or constructed.

In *Fig. 1* we illustrate the back part of the side elevation of a plain body with no moldings, and consequently if there is a $1\frac{5}{8}$-inch thick panel, it is generally mitred to the side quarters. To obtain the length of the back panel in all cases, there are three different methods. The first, and which is generally used in practice, is to bend the panel to the required shape, lay it against the frame, fasten with thumb-screws, and mark with a peculiar tool specially made for that purpose. The second method differs entirely from the first one; the panel is shaped in length and width and finished entirely on the bench, and bent after it is finished; its manner of proceeding we will explain further on. The third is to take the shape of the back panel entirely from the draft without the aid of the body, but it is very seldom practiced, as the greatest accuracy is required to be successful.

The first method is to set the body up, put in all the cross-bars, regulate the body cross-wise, as shown by *A, B, Fig. 2*, bend the panel to the required shape, and mark the length with a scratch-awl. This operation is so simple and correct that no other method is wanted nor necessary, but the conditions of the body are not always the same, and consequently other methods must be employed to obtain the required results. Suppose we could not mark the panel as we have explained on *Fig. 2*, then we divide *Fig. 1*, from *A* to *B*, in two equal parts, and make line *C*. As *Fig. 2* represents the skeleton body, line *C* is not made on the side elevation of body, but at the back end ; that is line *C, Fig. 2*. Now take the panel as represented in *Fig. 3*, face the bottom edge, and make center line *A* ; give some margin below *B*, and start your measurements from *B*. Take space from *A* to *C, Fig. 1*, and put it from *B* to *C, Fig. 3*, and as the space from *C* to *B, Fig. 3*, is equal, then we take the same space and put from *C* to *D*. This gives us the width of the panel. Now we must have the length. On all pieces running cross-ways of the body, the body-maker always has the center line marked on the cross-piece. Take the width from center line to *D, D, Fig. 2*, and place it on *D, D,* from center line *A, Fig. 3*. Do the same with bottom edge *E, Fig. 2*, and place it on *B, Fig. 3*. Then make a pattern fitting exactly against lines *F, F, Fig. 2*, and mark the edges *F, F,* of *Fig. 3*.

This operation will give the exact shape and length of the panel if taken accurately. Now you can plane and smooth the panel, put on the mitre, and then bend it into the required shape. This explanation and illustration is the method in its simplest form that our correspondent desires to know, but does not contain all the details that should be known for such proceedings, which we will further explain in *Figs. 4, 5* and *6*. Divide the back view of the body, *Fig. 5*, into five, six; seven or

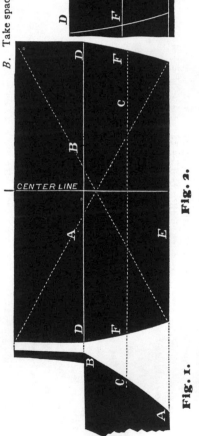

Fig. 1.

Fig. 2.

Fig. 3.

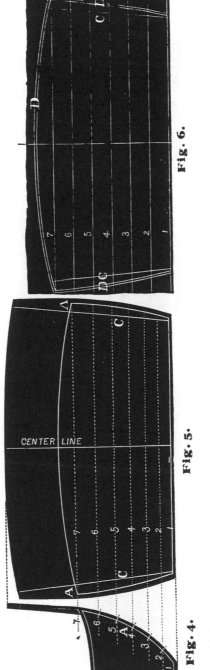

Fig. 4.

Fig. 5.

Fig. 6.

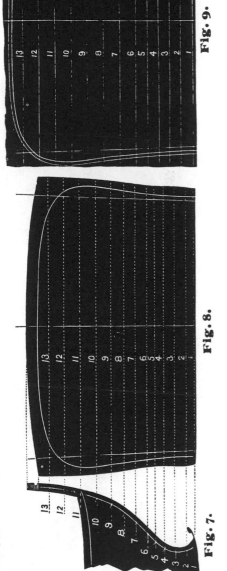

Fig. 7.

Fig. 8.

Fig. 9.

more divisions, as the shape of the back pillar may require, because the more curved the back pillars are the closer the divisions must be. The latter must be made on the back pillar, on line A, *Fig. 4*, and special care should be taken not to make the divisions on the outside surface of corner pillar, but on the surface where the panel is in close contact. To simplify it, make all the spaces alike from the bottom edge to the top line seven, level with the joint of the cross-piece; see, A. A. *Fig. 5*.

Take a panel wide and long enough, as illustrated in *Fig. 6*, straighten the bottom edge, and square up the center line; take the exact space of the divisions from *Fig. 4*, and space them off accurately, as illustrated on *Fig. 6*. Lines C, C, *Fig. 5*, are the inside surfaces of back pillars, which will aid us here considerably. Produce same lines as shown on C, C, *Fig. 6*, and from C, C, from one to seven, we take the length of the panel, without the space which goes in the groove; the length of the groove is put on afterwards, as shown by lines D, D, D, *Fig. 6*. The upper curve on *Fig. 6* is either marked with the cross-piece, which is the most proper way in practice, or, with the pattern the sweep of the cross-

piece was marked. Finish the panel by cutting the edges all around; fit the thickness of the groove, level it the best that can be done, and then bend it to the required shape; put it into the grooves, and see if it fits before gluing.

In *Figs. 7, 8* and *9*, we give the most difficult panels to fit accurately into the body. In this case the body-maker is obliged to use the method as explained in *Figs. 4, 5* and *6*, if he wants to produce first-class work, because a panel of this kind should be finished before it is bent, as this cannot be well done after it is put on the body. The proceedings are exactly the same as explained in *Figs. 4, 5* and *6*, with the exception of lines *1, 2, 3, 4, 5* and *6*, *Figs. 7, 8* and *9*, are closer, because the curve is so short that in all such cases it is necessary to obtain the exact width. Our correspondent will see, after he has studied this article and examined the illustrations, that it is very easy, after all, to fit back panels by this way, and not so much a secret as many believe.

Working-Draft of a Modern Sleigh Body.

ONE-INCH SCALE.

This sleigh body represents one of the modern styles, and its peculiar construction necessitates a correct working-draft to obtain the curves, and all the thicknesses of the pieces, which the body contains. The peculiar construction consists in its side surfaces being perfectly straight at the bottom line, and having the usual swell and contraction on the upper part of the body. The difficulty in obtaining the correct size and side surfaces for the back corner pillars, is evident from its peculiar construction, being straight at the bottom line and curved on top of the body, producing a wind on the corner pillar, which cannot be otherwise done, except by planing it until the correct side surfaces are obtained. The best method is to construct a correct working-draft, laying out the side surfaces on the horizontal plane, and regulating it by longitudinal lines, which are best adapted to regulate the side surfaces in all such cases.

The side quarters at A, Fig. 1, are paneled over, and two strainers, B, B, are mortised in to keep the panel in the required shape. The back corner pillars C are to be bent, but can be sawed out of planks. The arm-rail is lapped against the back pillar, and fastened with two screws; at the front end D, it is framed together to pillar E, with a regular tenon. At F the pillar is framed into the bottom-sides, as shown at F, Fig. 2. G, Fig. 1, is framed to the bottom-sides, as shown by dotted lines.

The bottom-sides are dressed square, but it is an advantage to the body-maker to bevel it after line A, Fig. 2; if this is done, the back corner pillars, being level with the inside, can be gauged from the inside surface of the bottom-sides. This is also the case with the horns G, at the front end; it is better if they are inclined a trifle, as they have the appearance of being narrower on top.

The back pillars C, horns G, and the bottom-sides, are dressed after inclination A, Fig. 2; pillar E after inclination B, Fig. 2, and the arm-rail is dressed square, vertically, but is contracted after line A, Fig. 3. Dressing pillar E, Fig. 1, after inclination B, Fig. 2, requires a secondary pattern; the one that is used for drawing the side elevation will not do, and a pattern must be made in shape, as shown on dotted lines H, Fig. 1, which shows that if we used the original pattern it would be 7/8 inch too short. This lengthening is obtained in Fig. 1. Line B, Fig. 4, is the same inclination we have in B, Fig. 2, and A, Fig. 4, the same turn-under line as C, Fig. 2. Make verticle line C intersect with B and base-line; carry over lines 1, 2, 3 and 4 parallel with base-line, as shown on 1, 2, 3 and 4, Fig. 1. Set dividers on D, Fig. 4, and strike curves from line C and 1, 2, 3 and 4, and carry them over to Fig. 1, which will give the right length of the pillar at each point. These pillars E, Fig. 1, need not be as heavy as shown in the draft, in fact, this thickness of 4 inches is required when finished, but a piece can be glued against the pillar, saving labor and time, as illustrated in Fig. 1. E, Fig. 1, is the thickness of pillar on that place, and 4⅛ inches at 2; all the wood on G is removel, leaving a wedge at 2; if this piece is glued on, the pillar can be made out of 2-inch stuff, which is much less labor.

ESTABLISHING THE SIDE SURFACES ON HORIZONTAL PLANE.

Establishing the required lines for obtaining the correct side surfaces on the horizontal plane, varies from those we have given before, because the cross widths of the body differ from the regular mode of construction; the bottom-side being straight in its entire length necessitates using other means to obtain the desired results.

The body has 6¼ inches turn-under at D, Fig. 3, and its shape is convex-concave. The body on the back is contracted 3⅜ inches each side; that is the body is 41¾ inches wide at K, Fig. 1, and 37 inches on L, Fig. 1. Line B, Fig. 3, represents the side swell, and C, Fig. 3, the outside bottom edge of body, which is straight and not contracted. Draw oblique line M, Fig. 1, square down Q, from intersections of M and N to O, extend line B, Fig. 3, to Q; extend line C to B, Fig. 3, as shown on D, and draw line E, from intersection of E, Q, and P, D, Fig. 3. From this line E we commence operations by squaring down all dotted horizontal lines, 1, 2, 3 and 4, to E; take also all the spaces between C and E, on 1, 2, 3 and 4, Fig. 2, and carry them over to F, Fig. 3. Now you draw lines 1, 2, 3 and 4 on Fig. 3, as we have drawn them, and you will obtain all the thicknesses on the back corner pillar, as shown on Fig. 2. The recess on K, Fig. 1, is paneled up, and the panel is level with G, Fig. 2.

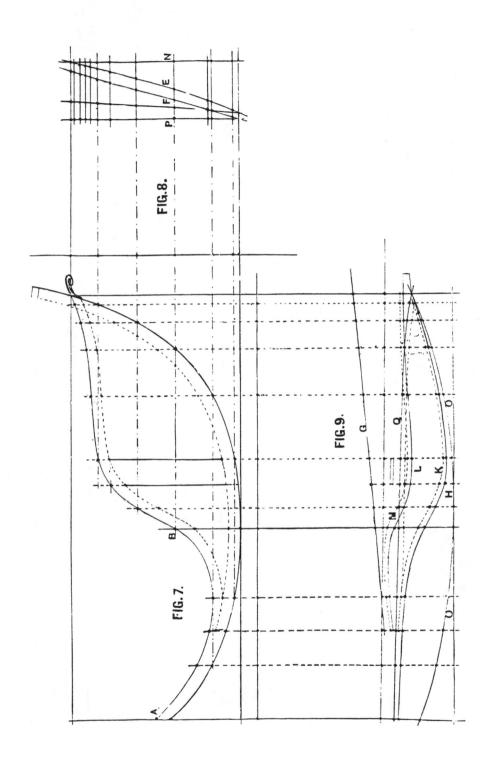

Carriage Monthly
July 1888
(second of three pages)

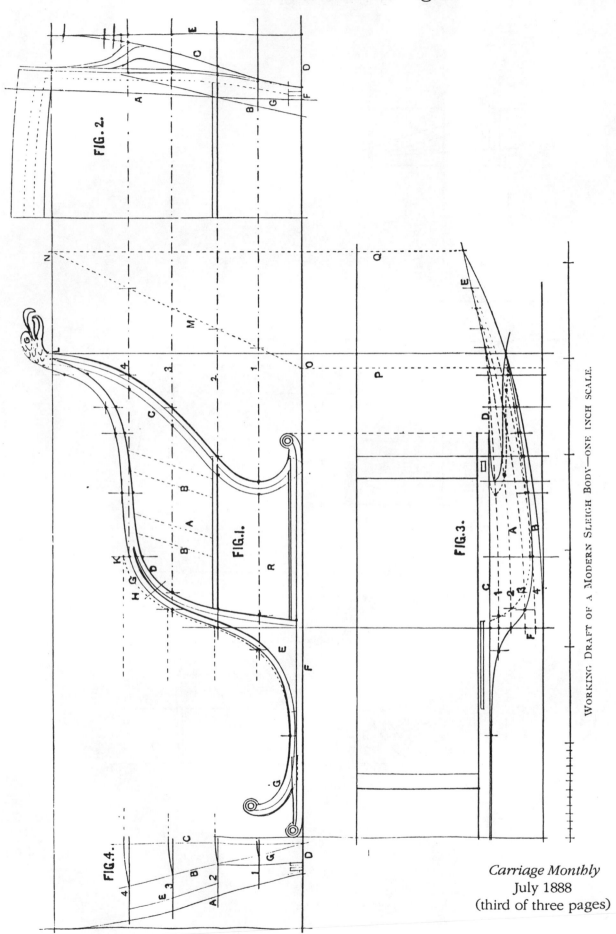

FIG. 2.

FIG. 1.

FIG. 3.

FIG. 4.

WORKING DRAFT OF A MODERN SLEIGH BODY—ONE INCH SCALE.

Carriage Monthly
July 1888
(third of three pages)

Wire Fenders for Sleighs.

We have learned of a less costly way to apply or make wire fenders for sleighs than the customary plaited fender, although not as beautiful; it is especially adapted to old sleighs which one does not feel justified in spending much money upon; the illustration suggests one of the styles of sleighs to which it was applied. The method was the same as the method of covering with leather, that is, the frame, or iron work, was done the same, but the bars through the center were left out as much as possi-

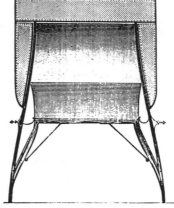

ble. The wire used was No. 20 brass wire, which is fine; it should be bent around the frame and sewed at short distances with wire; the edges then should be covered with harness or oil leather, and if the bars or iron work is not made unnecessarily heavy, a very neat job may be expected, as by turning the wire around the bars, a narrow binding may be effected; the edges get but one row of stitching.

The first of these fenders were made without turning the wire, but simply cutting the wire even with the inside edge of frame-work. This was not so durable and not so neat, because of the wide hold necessary to hold the wire.

Carriage Monthly
February 1885

THE CONSTRUCTION OF SLEIGHS:

PAINTING

CORNER-PIECES FOR PORTLAND SLEIGH.

(See three Illustrations accompanying.)

DESIGN No. 1 will have a very neat appearance on sleigh work. Decoration and stripe should be done in gold, and, if a subdued appearance

is desired, the gold can be glazed with a glaze made of one part burnt sienna and two parts asphaltum, mixed with gold-size, japan and rubbing varnish. This should be put on evenly (so that it will not look darker in one place than another) with a camel's-hair pencil, and glaze as you

would glaze a vermilion stripe with carmine. The best and safest way is to try the glaze on a leaf of gold, previously gilded on something, merely to be used as a test so as not to spoil the gold with too dark a glaze. If a high yellow metallic cast is desired, glaze with yellow lake mixed with japan size and rubbing varnish. The margin on the outside of the stripes could be filled in or chamfered as follows: If black body, chamfer with deep blue; if green body, chamfer with a glaze of verdigris; if deep red body, have tuscan margin; if a fine line is desired, it can be done the same as the Portland sleigh decoration described in the November (1889) number of *The Hub*.

G. B.

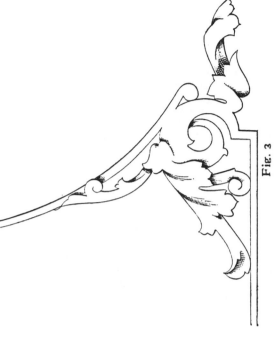

Fig. 1

TOP CORNER.

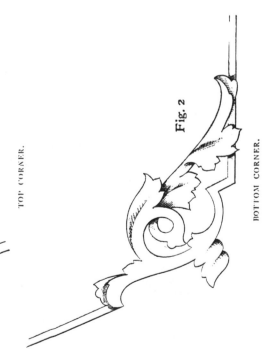

Fig. 2

BOTTOM CORNER.

Fig. 3

SIDE OF BODY.

CORNER-PIECE FOR WAGON OR SLEIGH WORK.

CORNER-PIECE Fig. 1 can be used on a light top wagon with good effect, and if a heavy appearance is desired, an intermediate color can be used. For instance; if corner-piece and stripe are gold, and ground color dark, (tuscan or green) the fine line can be black, and the color between the stripes a few shades lighter than the ground color. But if a heavy appearance is desired, the reverse order should be followed, namely : a few shades darker.

Fig. 2 is suitable for heavy work such as omnibuses, street cars, vans or trucks. X is to represent the chamfer or edge stripe to form a panel ¾ in. stripe. Y is to represent the broad line and Z the fine line. If

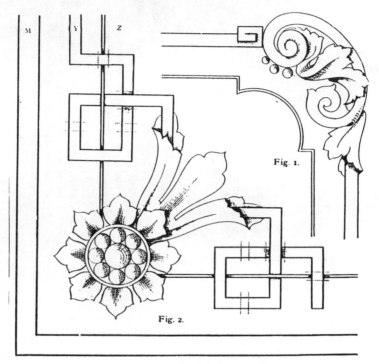

Fig. 1.

Fig. 2.

desired, the decoration and Grecian corner can be stenciled ; dotted lines show where to make the "bond," or in other words, where not to cut, so as to hold stencil together ; after stenciling, such places can be touched up so as not to show the "breaks." If vermilion ground, chamfer color can be tuscan red, ¾ in. wide, and broad line ⅜ in. wide ; and between the two glaze with sienna. This line can be Prussian blue or black, broad line would look well gold or gold color. On account of decoration being so isolated, it would look well to have it the same color as broad line. Glazing or shading will depend on what color is selected for same.   G. B.

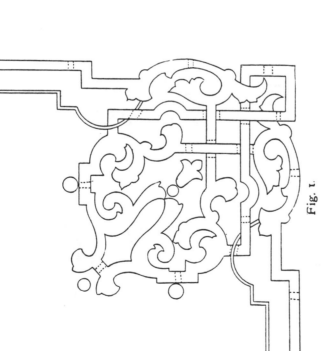

Fig. 3.

Fig. 2.

Fig. 1.

CORNER-PIECES FOR WAGONS OR SLEIGHS.

(See three Illustrations accompanying.)

Fig. 1 is an example of the Arabesque style of decoration, and is suitable for corner-pieces for wagon or sleigh work. It is easy to execute, and can be done by an ordinary workman with the striping pencil.

Whatever color the striping is, the corner can be done in the same. This style of work can be executed with a stencil, if desired, and at places designated by the dotted lines can be left uncut so as to hold it together—breaks can be touched up afterwards. It will be found that an old 1 in. or 1½-in. bear's-hair varnish brush, cut off at about half the length of the hair, will make a very fine stencil brush. Sandpaper the end off so that it will not be harsh or uneven. This style of work will not require edging unless it is done in gold-leaf.

Figs. 2 and 3 : Renaissance corner pieces. These are more suitable for fine work. The broad line would look well if done in gold, and leaf done in same, only, glaze the decoration or leaf part with equal parts of sienna and asphaltum ; that is, where a too showy appearance is not desired. If otherwise, leave it in clear gold, edged with black or Prussian blue, if on a dark ground. On a medium or light color ground, edge with umber or sienna. The reason of the above is to prevent too

much contrast between edging and ground color. If a heavy corner is desired, I would suggest placing an intermediate color between the stripes 1 and 2. To better illustrate this : if the ground color is vermilion, either glaze with carmine or stripe with a color a few shades darker, an addition of about one tuscan to six vermilion. If a light appearance is desired, use orange or sienna, assuming the broad stripes to be gold and the fine lines black or some dark color. If done with stencil, it will require edging so as to sharpen up the edges and give a clean appearance.

B.

FOUR CORNERS FOR BUSINESS-WAGONS OR SLEIGHS.

(See four Illustrations accompanying.)

FIG. 1 is a simple striping-pencil pattern for coarse and fine lines, and requires no particular directions. As will be noticed, the coarse-line part of the corner must be of the same color as the stripe, of which it is a continuation. First put on that part, then the fine-line, and then with a short pencil put on the center ornament, making it the same color as the fine-line.

Fig. 3 is a simple flat-scroll design and can be of the same color as the stripe, or of an entirely different color, as preferred. The corner itself can be of more than one color if desired, for it is composed of three disconnected parts.

Fig. 4 is an oddity: but there are all sorts of people in the world, and

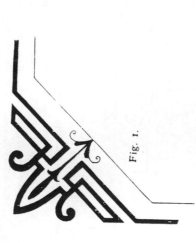

Fig. 1.

Fig. 2 is a design well adapted to a top where there is no stripe, or it can be used with a stripe in the usual way. It will be noticed that it is a double design that is composed of two distinct parts, and if something particularly striking is wanted, make the two parts of different colors.

Fig. 2.

Fig. 4.

it takes all sorts of designs to hit the various tastes. This is designed to be put on in gold, edged both sides with some sharply contrasting color. As will be noticed, a continuation of the edging makes the fine-line parts of the design. The stripe can terminate as in the design, or with a square end as usual.

A. F. MANCHESTER.

I do not recommend bright contrasts, excepting in special cases. Put on with a light and a dark shade of the same color, it would look well.

THREE CORNER-PIECES FOR WAGONS OR SLEIGHS.

By A. F. Manchester.

(See three illustrations accompanying.)

Fig. 1 will give the painter a chance to show his color taste, as more than one color can be used, and, if harmoniously combined, very pretty effects can be produced. If the stripe is of gold, make the whole design of the same, and then get the different colors by glazing. The painter's natural taste is a better guide than any description other than what has been given heretofore in *The Hub*.

A fine line can be used with this design, ending at but not touching the end of the leaf forms.

Fig. 3 can be done in gold or colors. If in gold, shade either with asphaltum or verdigris green, high-lighting with Naples yellow if the asphaltum shade is used, and with white if it is verdigris. The touches in the openings and dots can properly be of some bright color, red for instance. This design is intended for a fine-line only.

' Fig. 1.

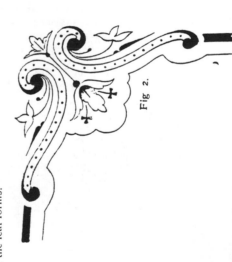

Fig. 2.

Fig. 2 will look well done in gold and touched up with asphaltum and carmine, the dots and little touches being carmine.

PLAIDING SLEIGH PANELS.

JEWETT CITY, CONN.

EDITOR OF THE HUB—DEAR SIR ; I have seen sleigh bodies and other jobs painted green plaid. The groundwork was a very light green, and the plaid was formed by broad stripes of different shades of green, running diagonally across the panel, and crossed at right angles by other green stripes, equally broad. The stripes were fully 2½ in. wide, and every fourth or fifth stripe had a bluish cast.

Of course, this work looked somewhat ridgy where the stripes crossed each other, but the color effect was grand. These broad stripes were all transparent, and I suppose they were made of verdigris ; and, every place where one stripe crossed another, a diamond was formed of a still darker shade.

I wish to be enlightened in regard to this branch of the painters' art, if you will kindly write me a letter of instruction. Please answer, and oblige,

Yours truly,   F. G.

ANSWER.—The best way to produce such work is to first procure a sample of the plaid you wish to paint, from some of the decalcomanie supply houses, such as Palm & Fechteler, of this city. Having this before you, then proceed to copy it in colors.

The ground is a matter of choice, but it should be laid with reference to the color of the plaid you desire to produce. For instance, if it is to be a tartan, then your groundwork must be of the same order, that is, of light or neutral green, etc.

Your colors must be transparent, and they will then show a dark shade every time you cross one over the other.

A very fine effect may be produced where a sleigh panel is plaided in the following manner. When your stripes are about set or on the tack, run around the edge of each a margin of ½ inch, with a stripe of raw linseed oil, which will soften up the colors ; and, when washed off next day with a little soap and water, they will show a clean edge all around, which may be edged with a heavy or full fine line of black or any other color. If left plain, they will also look well,—very much better than to have the stripes run up flush with the moldings or edges of the panel.

The colors you mention are suitable ; but if you get a suitable pattern, that will give you the correct colors.   L.

HOW TO PAINT A BAKERS' SLEIGH.

———

MILWAUKEE, WIS.

EDITOR OF THE HUB—DEAR SIR: Can you tell me any way to make paint stay on a bakers' sleigh, so that the steam from the hot bread will not cause it to come off ? The body in question has had to be painted from the start every year, because the steam has caused the paint to peel off. We think of applying Valentine & Co.'s P. W. F. *hot*. Do you know of anything better ?

Kindly reply as soon as you can, and much oblige,

Yours,   F.

ANSWER.—Either a wagon or sleigh, to be used by bakers for carrying hot bread, is subject to the trouble our correspondent describes, owing to the dampness produced by the steam arising from the bread, which is absorbed by the panels, necessarily straining them and the paint coats lying upon them.

It is impossible to wholly remedy this trouble, for paint cannot be expected to hold its place securely upon damp wood. The object of the painter must of course be directed toward preventing, as far as possible, the entrance of dampness into the wood. To keep out the steam entirely is impossible, for nothing is more penetrating ; but it can be partially excluded by the use of P. W. F., as mentioned by our correspondent, applied hot as a priming coat, to both the inside and outside surfaces of all the panels.

On the outside, wipe off the P. W. F. after fifteen minutes or so, and allow this coat as much time for drying as you conveniently can,—say four to six days or more. Then proceed as usual with subsequent coats, but use rather less oil than commonly, so as to give the paint an opportunity to dry quite hard.

The inside can be painted or not, as may be desired, but painting is preferable, so long as colors are used that have but a medium gloss, and that are allowed to dry quite hard.

In re-painting such a vehicle, it is best to burn off the old paint thoroughly, as this will help to dry the wood, and thus give a more secure foundation for subsequent coats. Then prime with hot P. W. F., the same as if the job were a new one, and proceed as above described.

The Construction of Sleighs

BORDERS FOR SLEIGHS.

THE recent sleigh season has brought in several inquiries for ornamental borders suitable for this class of work, and suggestions made public now may prove of advantage during next summer and fall.

The Hub has already covered the subject pretty fully in previous volumes, and considerable attention is given to it in my "Studies in Scrolling," which I recommend to the attention of all sleigh painters. In that book appear numerous designs adapted for the purpose, most of which are simple and easily applied.

In order to give something new at this time, I select more complicated designs than those heretofore presented, merely adding that they can be modified and simplified to any extent.

Figs. 1 and 2 show a scroll leaf pattern, which many of our readers should be able to put on without difficulty, particularly if they have followed the directions given in "Studies in Scrolling." One section should first be drawn on tissue paper, and then pricked and pounced along the belt. In regard to the colors to be employed, I will speak further on.

Fig. 3 is a neat design of a ribbon and vine twisted together. The colors for this border should be more distinctive than any of the others. All the others should be painted in relief, or in different shades of the same color; while this should have two colors. If painted on a black ground, the vine may be put in green, and the ribbon in shades of vermilion and dark red. Particular attention should be given to the shading of the ribbon, and the blending of the shades should be as nearly perfect as possible. Upon this will depend much of its effect.

Figs. 4 and 5 are similar, both being composed of scroll leafing, and the description given of Figs. 1 and 2 applies as well to these.

Fig. 6 represents a ribbon scroll twined around a stem. It is not so easy to make a small pattern of this, and pounce it along, and we doubt whether it will prove of value except as a suggestion.

Fig. 7 shows an ivy entwined around a limb. The leaf may be drawn, and repeatedly pounced along the panel, to save time and labor. It may also be simplified to advantage.

The colors to be used for the above designs, with the exception of Fig. 3, depend upon the ground. If the ground is black, gold or imitation gold will look well, with appropriate shading. On a dark blue ground I would use lighter shades of blue; on a lake ground shades of vermilion; and on a green ground lighter shades of green. Patterns of this kind look best in subdued colors, or tints of the ground color. F. B. GARDNER.

The Hub
March 1881
(Illustration next page)

FIG. 1.   FIG. 2.   FIG. 3.   FIG. 4.   FIG. 5.   FIG. 6.   FIG. 7.

The Hub
March 1881
(continued from previous page)

HOW TO PAINT GRECIAN BORDERS ON SLEIGHS.

THE term "Grecian border" is applied to a meandering stripe composed entirely of lines which are horizontal and vertical, or approximately so, which is frequently used in striping sleighs and body belts.

To paint such a border in a quick and easy manner proceed as follows: First draw three, six or eight parallel stripes or fine lines, according as you wish to make the border more or less elaborate. Now, space off equal distances, and draw the cross lines at right angles, as in Fig. 1. You need take no particular pains to form square corners,

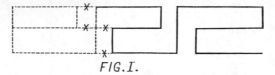

FIG. I.

as these can all be made right by clipping out with dead color. The parts in dotted line show the laying out, and the crossed lines are those to be covered or cut out with dead color. The solid lines show the finished pattern of a single or simple form of this border.

Fig. 2 shows how to lay out a curved border of the same description. For curved borders it is better to draw the cross lines perpendicular, rather than to have them radiate from the center.

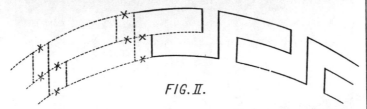

FIG. II.

For a running border on some light glazed ground, first draw a broad black stripe, a little wider than the border is to be; allow this to dry, and then put on the border as above. The object of this is to overcome the difficulty of cutting out the lines on a delicate ground.

The Hub
July 1882

SLEIGH BORDERS.

THE present number of *The Hub* containing our fashion plates of sleighs, we have decided to furnish to painters at the same time four original designs for borders. There are many patterns of sleighs on which a border is almost indispensable; at any rate it never fails to produce that enlivening effect which is more or less a requisite in the painting of a sleigh. We would

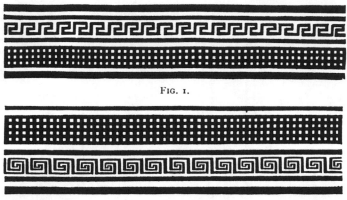

FIG. 1.

FIG. 2.

show borders more frequently on our cuts but for the reason that their scale is too small to design them plainly and with effect.

Our illustrations Nos. 1 and 2 are so-called compound meander patterns; a checker-board belt is added to the narrow meander,

FIG. 3.

FIG. 4.

either at the bottom, as in No. 1, or at the top, as in No. 2. This belt on deep panels may be made both at the upper and lower edge of the meander, as in No. 3. The latter design is also in the Grecian style, and looks light and neat.

No. 4 is a style from Vienna, and will please those who are in favor of curved lines.

The Construction of Sleighs

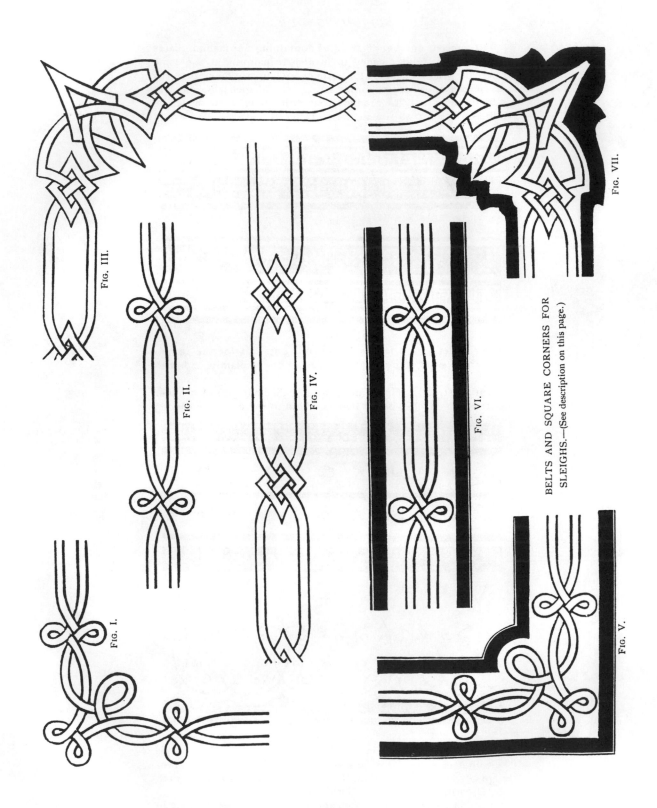

Fig. III.

Fig. VII.

Fig. II.

Fig. IV.

Fig. VI.

Fig. I.

BELTS AND SQUARE CORNERS FOR SLEIGHS.—(See description on this page.)

Fig. V.

Painting

ADVANCED STUDIES IN SCROLLING.

BELTS AND SQUARE CORNERS FOR SLEIGHS.

WE present below several patterns of belts and corners particularly suitable for sleigh bodies, and also adapted for some classes of wagons and light carriages.

Figs. 1 and 2 represent the "rope border," it being a twisted continuation of two strands of rope. This may be put on as two stripes of different colors, or with four fine lines as shown in the engraving. When two stripes are used, the laps should be shaded to show where one part runs under the other part.

Figs. 3 and 4 represent the "chain border," which makes a beautiful stripe on sleighs or buggy bodies. It should be accurately copied and pricked; then stripe on the job with a short striping pencil. A gold stripe on a black ground will look well.

Figs. 5 and 6 are similar in design to 1 and 2, but, as will be seen, the "chain" is put upon a broad stripe, outside of which is a distanced fine line; for example, on a black ground draw the broad stripe; then distance fine line with dark blue, green or lake; then lay the "chain border" over the broad stripe with gold, or light cream color.

Fig. 7 shows a corner, having Fig. 3 inclosed by a stripe of another color. F. B. GARDNER.

The Hub
August 1879
(continued from previous page)

RUNNING BORDERS FOR SLEIGHS.

THIS being the season when many of our subscribers are painting sleighs, we have prepared for them a variety of samples of running borders, which we hope will be found timely and valuable.

All of the five patterns shown in the accompanying cuts belong to the class known as the "meander pattern," so called from the intricacy of their windings. Fig. I is a very simple pattern, and they increase gradually in elaborateness as numbered, Fig. V being one that will require considerable work.

The parts of a sleigh where such borders may be introduced to advantage are around the arm-pieces, the back, and the inside of the dash. The method of putting them on is briefly as follows :

First, transfer carefully to a sheet of tissue paper the outlines shown in wood-cut ; lay this over a piece of writing paper, and perforate the outlines with a pin or needle, thus forming a pricked pattern to work from. Lay this pattern upon the painted panel, and pounce it, thus leaving the outlines plainly indicated in whiting upon the work.

There are now two methods of painting the design. The first and best way is to begin by covering the ground inside of the outlines with "dead" color, the same shade as the ground color of the panel. By drying "dead" (*i.e.*, without gloss), the pattern may be readily distinguished. Then proceed to fine-line the edges in any desired color. The object of proceeding in this way is to prevent destroying the pounced lines, which would be likely to occur if the painter attempted to use the second, and apparently simplest method, *i.e.*, putting on the fine lines at first. Providing the inside of the border is to be painted in a different color than the ground, the required color should of course be substituted for the "dead" coat already mentioned.

Here is a suggestion which the painter may find of value when putting on borders of this kind, where many angular corners are introduced. It is very difficult to make square corners with the striping pencil, even when the red-sable pencil is small and the striping color sufficiently limpid. It is therefore the custom with many of the best sleigh painters, to cross the lines slightly at the corners; and then, when the striping color is quite dry, to cut off the lines sharply at the corners with a striping pencil filled with the ground color.   F. B. GARDNER.

The Hub
September 1877
(continued next page)

FIG. V.

FIG. I.

FIG. II.

FIG. III.

FIG. IV.

RUNNING BORDERS FOR SLEIGHS (THE MEANDER PATTERN).—See description.

The Hub
September 1877
(continued from previous page)

Repainting and Varnishing Cutters and Sleighs.

Cutters and sleighs for repainting, revarnishing and brightening up generally, should be got into the paint shop as soon as possible after the carriage work declines in the late Fall. This enables the painter to avoid the rush which is sure to be upon him with the first "run of sleighing." It also enables him to do more satisfactory work in several ways. The work taken in early has a measure of time given it while being carried through the several processes not accorded that received late in the season. Varnish coats given proper time to dry, not only surface up better, but wear and retain their brilliancy longer, and do not fire crack when run out in the cold. Upon the average class of cutters and sleighs, a less expensive varnish, as compared to that used upon first-class carriages, will serve all necessary purposes. Expensive finishing varnishes are not needed. Cutters and sleighs are not exposed to the severe and destructive forms of service that wheeled vehicles are, consequently, they do not require highly elastic finishing varnishes to furnish the needed durability. They are in service for only a comparatively small part of the year, and mud spotting and troubles of that order do not intrude themselves. Save in the case of the highest-class sleigh work, a first-class gear finishing varnish will furnish satisfactory results for finishing cutter and sleigh bodies. A heavy gear varnish will answer perfectly for the running parts. But in this selection of varnishes, choice should always fall upon those of first-class quality. Whatever the grade, get the best in quality of that grade. First-class paint and varnish stock is more handily worked, and will cover more surface than inferior stock, and judged from any point of view one may elect, it is the most economical material to buy.

When a cutter or sleigh comes in for a thorough repainting, examine the vehicle closely, and if the body can be removed without too large an expenditure of labor, removal should be insisted upon. There is usually considerable dirt under the edges of a cutter body that cannot be cleaned out except the body be taken off. And a little of this dirt caught up in the paint or varnish brush worketh evil to the whole job. Moreover, the brushes brought in contact with such accumulations of dirt are unfitted to produce pleasing results in the immediate future. The touch-up-and-varnish sleigh job is, in the main, a troublesome affair, especially the running parts. The merry and pretty colors which chiefly obtain on sleigh running parts painted in former years, are not so easily matched as the colors used upon the bodies. In point of fact, it doesn't pay to devote much time in trying for a match. Instead, mix a color to about the shade of the old color, and go over the running parts entire. Then restripe and finish, and in the great majority of cases money will be saved thereby. In rubbing cutter or sleigh work furnished with heavy varnish moldings out of varnish, use, for surfacing such moldings, any varnish brush of a small pattern worn to a stub. Cutting through on the edges of the moldings is nicely avoided in this way. For the large panels on sleigh work a 3-inch finishing brush will serve as the best tool. It carries a greater quantity of varnish, and enables the finisher to coat the surface quicker than he could do with the smaller brush. In finishing, the quick and adroit placing of the varnish is an item of chief importance.

During the sleigh season there usually drifts into the jobbing paint shop a lot of not very particular work. As for example, heavy work, sleighs, bobs, etc. Upon such work there may be used the accumulated odds and ends of colors of various shades, lines and tints left over from doing sleigh work of a better class and from carriage work. Some very neat combinations may be effected by the judicious employment of these left-over bits of color, and it helps to slick up and put into profitable use certain materials which otherwise might eventually find their way into that quagmire of the paint shop—the slush keg. Briefly stated, cutter and sleigh painting opens the way for the employment of considerable material which cannot be termed strictly "available" in the other branches of painting; it comes at a time when the painter is better able to appreciate a lean loaf than a fat icicle, and, if conducted according to business-like and workman-like practices, it will supply a handsome source of profits.

Practical Carriage and Wagon Painting.

Painting

HOW TO PAINT A WAGON, HEARSE OR SLEIGH IN PURE WHITE.

I NOTICE that correspondents often apply to *The Hub* for directions how to paint wagons or sleighs, and particularly children's hearses, in pure white, and I beg to contribute a few suggestions on this subject. In my own experience, I find that a great many carriage-painters, even when thoroughly posted on all the other kinks of the business, do not know how to proceed when a job comes in to be painted white. This is probably owing to the fact that such jobs are exceedingly rare, and many painters never have occasion to do such work, and have, as a consequence, never given the matter any thought; but it still remains a fact that a sleigh or hearse or business wagon is liable to come into the shop at any time, and every painter should learn how to take hold of such a job and carry it through to the finish without any fussing or experimenting. It's the unexpected that always happens, and the reader who carelessly tosses his *Hub* to one side, saying: "O, pshaw! There won't be a white job to do in this town this week!" may be in the depths of despair and humiliation next week, with a white elephant on his hands that he doesn't know what to do with.

Most of the painters that I have interviewed prepare the surface for a white job just the same as for any other color, and then put on a coat of clear white-lead. My experience has taught me that this is not the best way to do. A coating of white-lead mixed thin enough for color cannot be applied over a dark ground without leaving it a mass of dark streaks; and all painters will admit that it is a more difficult operation to cover a ground that is streaked than it is to cover one that is solid, no matter what the shade may be. In fact, you are further from the desired result after putting on a coating of this kind than before you started at all. It is almost impossible to cover a variegated ground with any reasonable number of coats.

A much better plan, according to my idea, is not to try to go from dark to light with one jump, but to go by easy stages. Instead of using clear white for the first coat, tint it with some opaque color, such as black or blue. Make it dark enough to cover solid, and, if it is a large flat surface, tint the next coat also,—only, of course, make that very much lighter; and then put on the clear white. In this way I get a solid white job with less coats and bother than by any other plan I have tried or seen tried. I then mix the last white coats with some nice finishing varnish, and use sugar-of-lead for a drier.

Don't try to get the same surface on a white job as you do on a dark one. In the first place it isn't necessary, and, moreover, you can't do it if you try. There are many painters who go to the same pains and expense to get the same kind of a surface for all colors; but, in the case of a light color, this is mainly labor lost, for, the lighter the color, the less imperfections will show. This is a paint-shop axiom. On the other hand, the darker the color, the more perfect must be the surface. A surface that would look wretched in black, will look all right in white or any of the light colors.

Smoothe each flat coat with fine sandpaper, and all the varnish coats excepting the last one with fine pumice. Be careful also to use only clean water, sponges and shammies.

If, on account of ornamenting or striping, varnishing is necessary, go over the stripes and ornaments with clear finishing varnish thinned with turpentine. By being very careful you can go over the whole job and not stain it much, but I cannot recommend this plan, for, no matter how nicely it looks when you get through with it, it will turn yellow in a short time, especially if kept in a dark place; and a great many stables and carriage-houses are dark. If there is no ornamenting, as in the case of a hearse, then finish with the color-and-varnish.

Don't try to work white-lead with a camel's-hair brush, especially a single thick one. A good, double-thick one will do sometimes; but a nice chiseled bristle brush is better, or a good fitch tool,—that is, something with considerable life.

Painting a white gear is not nearly so difficult an operation as a great many painters suppose. As a matter of fact, such work can be done more easily than a good dark-colored job. For example, take a new wagon gear. Instead of surfacing with lead, giving three or four coats of lead and as many of color-and-varnish, proceed as follows: Prime the woodwork as usual, before the smith takes it; and, when it returns to the paint-shop, sandpaper it clean and smooth and give a coat of lead-color, as light as it can be and still cover well. When this is dry, putty with lead-colored putty. When the putty is dry, smoothe with fine sandpaper, taking pains not to cut through, especially on the iron parts, and give a coat of clear flat white. Smoothe this a little with dead sandpaper and flow on a nice coat of white-lead and finishing varnish (or flake-white, if you have it), using sugar-of-lead for a drier, and thinning with turpentine to a nice working consistency. Rub this with pumice-stone, and the job is ready to stripe. After striping, give a coat of finishing varnish, thinned with turpentine. If preferred, you can varnish it with dammar varnish, which will stain less, but it is not very durable. Or give it two coats of the color-and-varnish, making the last one mostly varnish, and do the striping with oil-gloss colors. Or stripe with ordinary colors and varnish the stripes only.

It will be seen by the foregoing that, even if one more coat is given than I have named, the process of painting in white is cheaper than painting with dark colors, for the lead and color are one in white painting. The only requisite is to be very particular throughout. But, then, we should be particular in all things.

A. F. MANCHESTER.

Painting the Factory Cutter.

The fact, as announced in a former issue of the MONTHLY, that the factory cutter output bids fair to be unusually large this year, invests the subject of factory cutter painting with a very considerable interest. A large number of painters hold cutter painting in the factory shop as a thankless task, ill paid, laborious, and barren of satisfactory inducements of any sort. But to the factory painter, cutter season, when it means cutters in plenty to paint, comes clothed in the alluring garb of prosperity, and fills his mind with a serene and tranquil hope which makes life seem another thing. It means employment during a dull and, usually, a gloomy season of the year; a season when your average painter, whether of the custom shop or the factory, is glad to greet and wild to welcome a stroke of business of a fairly remunerative kind. The cutter painting season, then, despite its detractors, is one to be welcomed by all painters, regardless of their classification or the particular type of shop to which they belong. As a rule, contractors do not realize the profits from cutter painting that they do from carriage painting, nor does the day workman get as much per hour for working on cutters as he does on carriages. This, however, does not deter the workman or the contractor from welcoming the advent of the cutter because, as before stated, it comes during a season of inactivity when the metallic ring of a dollar carries to its possessor the exhilarating knowledge of suddenly acquired wealth. As in carriage painting, specialists flourish in all the different grades of work connected with cutter painting. One party, for example, takes the contract of putting the bodies into roughstuff and into shape for coloring. There are always two kinds of cutters going through; one kind receiving roughstuff and the other kind being surfaced down without it. The contractor puts the one grade into roughstuff, ready for rubbing, and the other grade he puts into a condition fit for coloring. Another party does the rubbing of roughstuff. A third party puts the bodies into color, and gives them a coat of rubbing varnish. The fourth contractor sees to rubbing out such jobs as are rubbed, mossing off the cheaper ones and finishing all the output, bodies and gears. In this way the forces of labor are distributed throughout the entire process from priming to finishing. The painter performing a certain duty, whether it be rubbing roughstuff, striping or finishing or coloring, is a specialist.

The best grade of cutters, when they arrive in the paint shop, are given a coat of priming throughout, body and gear. This priming is made light in body, and dries so as to admit of puttying forty-eight hours after it is put on. Usually two workmen labor together in priming, and of the ordinary Portland style cutters, a dozen are primed in an hour. To do this number in an hour, the priming mixture has got to work about as free as the linseed oil alone. The next process is the puttying. A quick, hard drying putty is used, and the morning after a cutter is puttied, it is put into the first coat of roughstuff. Before the second coat is put on, the surface is inspected and all places overlooked or not completely filled up during the first puttying, are treated to a slicking over with the plastic pigment. The following day two coats of roughstuff go on, and the third day the fourth and final coat is applied, followed in the afternoon by the guide coat of yellow ochre. If the bodies are removed from the gears, the removal occurs before the roughstuffing begins, and the gears are worked along to suit the demands of the foreman. If they are not removed, which is usually the case, the gear is sanded off and given a coat of flat lead, before the job is rubbed out of roughstuff. After being rubbed out of roughstuff the cutters go into the hands of the contractor, who colors them and puts them into the clear rubbing varnish. On the very best jobs the gears are color varnished, and on all the others the striping and finishing are done on the dead color. But one coat of rubbing varnish is given the cutters. Then the party who has the contract of rubbing the varnish, and putting on the finishing coat, rubs the job out and turns them over to the contractor who does the striping. Then they go to the varnish room to be cleaned, touched up and finished.

The cheaper grades, including Portlands and swell bodies, are primed, and then either given a coat of deaf lead or the anti-kalsomine treatment. The cutter that sells on the streets of your city for $16 cannot, at best, receive a very expensive process of painting. Having worked in the factory which puts out a cutter (a Portland, too), which sells for that price, and which one season sold as low as an even $12, the writer is in a position to know the supreme importance of keeping down the cost of painting such work; and that cost, of course, depends very greatly upon the painting process employed. The dead lead method requires a "dead game" painter to follow it in order to be in a constantly fit condition to eat well and look well. The sand papering of this dead lead on the surface of a cutter body, raises a cloud of powdered lead, well calculated to make healthy men grieve. When it is used, the puttying is done on the priming coat, sanded down smoothly, and a single coat of the dead lead applied. When surfaced down with sand paper, the jobs are turned over to the color room, colored, given one coat of varnish, mossed off, striped and finished. Provided the anti-kalsomine is used, the cutters are primed and puttied, and the anti-kalsomine is put on hot over this. Three coats of the kalsomine, all applied in a day, are generally used. Then a thorough sand papering is given, followed by the application of a liquid mixture of oil, japan and turpentine, the proportions being about ⅝ oil to ⅜ japan and turpentine. This mixture penetrates the kalsomine fabric, and acts in the capacity of a binder. In ten hours six workmen will apply three coats of kalsomine to fifty cutters, sand paper the surface on the same, and apply the oil, japan and turpentine mixture. As an example showing what is considered a day's work in cutter painting, in addition to what has already been given, it may be said that in rubbing varnish, the workman is expected to rub and wash up clean, fourteen cutters of the old Comfort pattern in ten hours. Two stripers working together, one striping the dash and gear, and the other the body proper, stripe from sixty to seventy-five jobs a day, the number depending somewhat on the style of cutter. In finishing, four workmen, two varnishing gears and two working on bodies, finish from 100 to 150, and sometimes as high as 175 cutters every ten hours. On the best grade work, from eighty to ninety jobs are done. The washing up and touching up of the work preparatory to finishing, requires from three to four workmen in order to keep the finishers busy.

M. C. H.

The Construction of Sleighs

Ornaments, and Ornamental Belt Striping for Sleighs.

We give herewith four original designs drawn expressly for sleighs. The first two are for panel spaces, the last two for either belt or margin spaces. By margin spaces, we refer to the outer edge of the body of a sleigh, which is sometimes defined by moldings, while on cheap work it is represented by a color different from the panel. In the absence of moldings—especially on the "Portland"—the side panels are made to appear much lighter by laying off an imitation belt and coloring it different from the main part of the panel. On this imitation of a defined margin or belt, the last two patterns given will be found of service.

ORNAMENTS Nos. 1 and 2 were drawn to correspond in outline with the triangular shaped panels, to be seen on fashion plates Nos. 33 and 34, in this issue. The first one is composed of interlaced bands, terminating in plain scrolls, and may be put on with but little expenditure of time. Having marked the pattern to its place on the panel, take a short striping pencil of a proper size and run

on the interlaced portion. After which, with the same pencil, stripe in the main curves, paying no attention to the leafing. Next, with an ornamenting pencil, finish the ends of stripes by putting in the leafing. A narrow lining pencil will give the line at the base, which may afterward be clasped as shown. This pattern will admit of being painted in one color, without relief by lighting and shading, and if desired, may be wrought into a very showy ornament. The coloring we leave to the taste of the painter. Broad stripes, either edged or with distant fine lines, should inclose the ornament.

ORNAMENT No. 2.—This is much more elaborate than No. 1, and will require, therefore, considerable more skill on the part of the ornamenter. But to one accustomed to painting similar pieces, but very little extra time need be consumed in its reproduction. We have in this an attempted representation of a polar bear, lying in his ice cave, which will answer to represent cold. A sleigh robe, and a horse girth with bells, to suggest the

pleasures of sleighing, plain scrolls to add variety, the whole surmounted by "shinty" or "shinny clubs," with a ball, which are suggestive of another very delightful winter pastime, namely: skating. The whole forming an ornament appropriate to the season, and the work on which it is to be placed. To those unskilled in painting this class of ornament, we give the following hints: First, secure a correct outline, after which decide on what colors shall be used on the several parts. The polar bear: white. Ice cakes: greenish white. Mantle: outside, brown; inside, dull red. Girth: blue and white. Scrolls: gold. Clubs and ball: brown. Size in and lay the gold. Next, paint the bear with two or three tints of gray, being careful to put the shades in their exact position, and from these to graduate the lighted parts. The ice cakes may be laid in with the same color, to be afterward glazed with asphaltum and verdigris. Now, color the robe a dull red; this will form a dark background, and clear up and give distinct outlines to all the objects resting on the robe. The girth: blue and white. Bells: gold color. Having thus coated every part, when it is all dry, touch up the bear with white, tinted with raw umber; the highest lights, clear white. Deepen the shadows with a wash of asphaltum, and while you have this glaze in hand, wash in all the shades and shadows. High light with straw color. The striping shown above this ornament may be placed at a greater distance if desired.

Carriage Monthly
October 1873
(continued next page)

No. 3, BELT OR MARGIN ORNAMENT.—
This may be used as shown, or the fret work
may be placed on each side of the ornament. *One* ornament placed where it will
most readily catch the eye, with striping on
either side of it, and continuing around the
margin, would accord with our taste in the
matter. The coloring must be selected according to the tone of the ground color. On
a claret or carmine space, olive, lighted with
white and shaded brown, looks extremely
clean and neat. The ornament is composed
of a horse's head and shoulders, showing

very plainly that the animal is in rapid motion, and alive to the sights and sounds
about him. The border represents a string
of bells. The combination being appropriate to sleigh work.

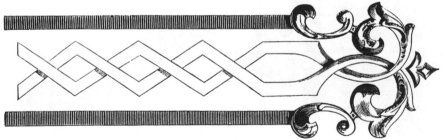

No. 4, is likewise a pattern for belt space,
and one that will repay the labor required to
paint it.

Coloring scrolls and cross-barred striping,
gold ; outer stripes, green.

STRIPING PATTERNS FOR SLEIGHS, &c.

CORNER PIECE AND BROAD STRIPE.—This will

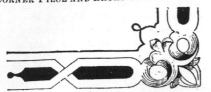

make a very neat and attractive corner piece, and broad stripe for sleighs, or other work where showy striping is required. The corner piece should be painted the same color as the broad line, shaded with dark tint of the same color, so that all will harmonize.

The dark color or broad line near the scroll, should be painted with the darkest tint used in shading the scroll, and put on the stripe when it is dry. It is not continued throughout the length of the stripe, as may be seen by the pattern. The fine line should be of a different color from any of those used on the broad line.

ORNAMENTED BROAD LINE.— Another design for sleighs. This is intended to be placed in the centre of the stripes on the dash. On a dark ground, the centre and stripes will look best done in gold; on a drab, or other light-colored ground, the centre may be laid in gold, and the striping of a suitable darker color than the ground color, so as to bring out the full brilliancy of the gold.

CORNER PIECE.—Corner piece to connect with

stripes. Paint it according to your own taste. The instructions given for similar patterns may assist the student in some particulars, but we would advise him to not rest satisfied with the few colors named in *our* explanations but experiment with others, and select from among them those which are most pleasing to the eye.

Painting Cutters and Sleighs.

MR. EDITOR:—As this is the season of the year we commence to paint sleighs, perhaps a few lines on the subject would not be out of place. Many think that a sleigh can be painted almost any way, just so that it shines a little, and it will stand and look well for years, for the reason that it is used but very little. I do not exactly agree to this, for to have the paint stand, keep its lustre and be in good shape for repainting, it must have some solid foundation, and a few turpentine coats will not do this.

To do a first-class job I should proceed almost the same as with a wagon, only with not quite so many coats and not quite so elastic. Prime the body with oil lead, in which a little turpentine will do no harm. In three or four days putty with hard drying putty; in five or six days sand off with 1½ sandpaper, not too close, saving the corners. Sand-paper moldings with but one finger; don't have a corner bare when you get through, as no good workman will do this through rubbing more on them than anywhere else.

Mix lead and a little lamp black together and add enough Japan to make it a mush; then thin with turpentine and add a teaspoonful of oil to half a pint of paint. Let this stand three days, and if you have plenty of time give a little more oil, but not too much. Mix the next coat the same way. This is generally enough for sleigh bodies.

To make rough-stuff, mix the filler with half rubbing varnish and half Japan; to a gallon of rough-stuff add two pounds of lead. Now if you have a mill, grind this, but it is not necessary to grind it fine like color or good lead. There is always coarse particles in all fillers; this you may notice at the bottom of a cup after using, and more or less gets on the body and does not make a firm, compact surface. The grinding reduces it all the same, and it works better also. Keep the rough-stuff in a pail or bucket, with turpentine on top ¾ inch deep; when you wish to use it turn the turpentine off in a cup, and set aside to place back when done. Now have a clean cup into which take the rough-stuff out of the pail and thin for use. I think a good flat 2-inch brush the best to put on rough-stuff with; it is better than an oval when it gets worn a little, and is not placed in water until it has been used some time.

I think there should not be less than four coats put on a body, unless it is a very cheap job, and these should be taken pains with, wiping around moldings, &c., squaring them all up nice. I prefer an inch badger or fitch for stick seats and some moldings, as a big bristle brush scrapes it all off. Sleighs should not be filled until after ironing, but we cannot always do this, although we should have all the coats on before ironing. After they are ironed, lead up the irons on the body, and as the gear is supposed to be primed, sand this off and give a coat of lead mixed to dry a little elastic.

Mix up lead with a little oil in, put it on to a piece of iron, sand off gear, and then you can tell how it will dry by the time you get ready for it. If it dries too flat, give a little more oil. Shade your lead according to what your color will be; don't put as much oil in for the irons on the body. Next day putty the irons, and when the irons do not fit good on the body crowd putty in, but don't leave it flush; it is easier to scrape off with the knife than to sand off. Now rub the body out of rough-stuff; don't rub against the irons with the stone very much, as they can generally be rubbed around; where they are bared it rusts the iron and will throw the paint off after awhile if it is not gotten well off. After rubbing look after these places, clean off and put lead on just where bare. Next day give the irons on the body another coat of lead. The rest of the body can be cleaned and the first coat of color put on.

The gear is now ready for another coat of lead. This mix so as to color next day, so there must be but little oil put in. Next day color the body, and as the gear only needs one coat of color, the whole job will come to the color varnish together.

If the color varnish is well rubbed on the body, of course there will be some spots to touch up, and another coat of color varnish, or with part of clear rubbing will cover these spots better than clear rubbing will. This coat, if put on smooth, will not need so very much rubbing. Unless this is to be an extra job this will do to finish over, but for good work it must have good varnish. The gear will do with one coat to finish over; it can be mossed off or rubbed with sponge and pumice-stone, or rubbed carefully with a rag. The job is now ready to stripe and finish.

C. E. V.

SCROLL FOR SLEIGH.

HOW TO PAINT SLEIGHS.

[THIS being our "Special Sleigh Number," we have thought it eminently proper to have a special article on how to paint sleighs, and Mr. F. B. Gardner has kindly prepared the following review of the subject.—ED.]

THE method employed in painting sleighs differs but little from that of carriages, the principal feature being a reduction of the labor and expense. In more northern latitudes, the sleigh is an almost constant necessity, and is therefore made with a view to durability, but the great majority of the sleighs built in New-York State and New-England must be classed as "cheap work." The shape or size of the sleigh does not alter the method, and a "Portland," an "Albany," or a "Pung," are all painted in about the same manner. The ornamental scrolling and profuse striping and plaiding, once popular, have been laid aside, and extreme *plainness* is characteristic of the most stylish sleighs now built in New-York. The fashions differ, however, in different localities, and moreover change so suddenly that plainness is at any time liable to take the outside track and let gold and splendor come in ahead. Nor should we regret such a change, for color display seems appropriate in connection with sleighs and four-in-hand coaches, and the new Canadian-pattern sleighs look most attractive when painted in bright colors.

The priming of a sleigh may be either white-lead or P. W. F., and the foundation coats may be as numerous as the painter desires; there is little to say on this subject that has not already been explained in connection with carriage work. I will say, however, that I prefer a priming of Wood Filling, two or three coats of roughstuff, P. W. F. over that, and then color and finish as usual.

The striping and ornamenting deserve more attention just now. The "Portland" is a style of sleigh that demands chaste and fine ornamental work and striping, while the "Albany" may be more showy in its embellishments. The colors used for the former are usually dark, as black, red, lake, carmine and dark green, relieved by a single fine line of gold. The Albany is generally gotten up with beautiful glazed colors, and filled with striping and scrolling. There is an opportunity for a good display of taste in the painting of the swell-side Albany, and we have prepared a few simple patterns for ornamental striping on such work, at the same time referring the painter to our serial on "Scrolling and Ornamental Painting" in previous numbers of *The Hub*, pages 15, 65, and 113.

How to paint sham Cane-work.—The arm-pieces of the sleigh may be plaided if desired, and this is done by striping and then glazing with transparent colors. Cane-work finish may also be used to advantage on these parts; but whatever ornamental work is done should be *well* done. "Sham-caning," as it is called, was at one time all the rage, and it may become popular again, so we will try to describe how it is done. The first appliance necessary for this work is a small bag made of sheep-skin or bladder, from the end or mouth of which there must be a tube made of tin, and having a very fine hole for the paint to run out of. Now, having filled the bag with cream-colored paint, mixed with japan principally, tie the bag and tube tightly together, and by a light pressure the paint may be made to exude from the end of the tube in the proper quantity to form the raised cane strings. The next thing necessary is the pattern. To prepare this, first take a piece of paper, and cut it to fit the exact size of the panel to be caned, including the swell, and lay it out with dividers and pencil, in lines as formed by the real cane. When this has been done, the lines must be pricked off in the same manner as in doing an ornament. Then lay the paper pattern on the panel, and keep it in place by a few tacks; pounce over it with a dust bag, and, on removing the pattern, we will find the entire panel laid out in white dots, and with a straight-edge we may draw the lines of paint, allowing one set of lines to get *dry* before the cross lines are drawn. Decalcomanie or transfer cane-work may be had of the dealers, and is very convenient. This comes in sheets, which are to be glued or otherwise stuck on, and it will be found inexpensive and durable.

gular shaped furnace, made of sheet iron and heavy wire, which holds a charcoal fire. The shape allows it to be held in corners, and it answers its purpose very well. A charcoal furnace, together with large irons, is also sometimes used, but this is a slow and clumsy way of doing it. An alcohol lamp may be used to advantage, and this is preferred by some. There are also several patented contrivances for burning off old paint, which do not require special mention here. Removing paint by alkalies and acids is not to be recommended (although it is practiced to some extent), as the wood in this case becomes saturated with the material, which is of course detrimental to coats of paint subsequently applied. The only difference in removing the paint from a heavy or a light job, that one occasions more labor than the other—the process is the same. In burning off paint from a job that was originally primed with P. W. F., the priming will be found in most cases as good as ever, and may be roughstuffed direct, but it is best to give another coat for safety.

While engaged as experimental painter with Messrs. Brewster & Co., of Broome-street, I was induced to test the qualities of a solution for "taking off the old varnish only," and leaving the foundation to build on again. It was much lauded by the inventor (?), and as nearly as I could analyze it, it consisted of 2 ounces creosote, 1 pint carbolic acid, and 1 pint turpentine. It took off the varnish after a time, but the paint came off with it in patches; and although the stuff would not harm a camel's-hair brush, it required about a gallon of strong potash water to remove it from the wood surface after it had eaten off the paint.

Having removed the paint by the burning process (we recommend no other), give the job a good cutting down with No. 3 sandpaper, and apply the priming; after which proceed in the same manner as with a new sleigh.   F. B. GARDNER.
New-York, July 23, 1877.

Designs for Corner Striping and Scrolls for Arm-pieces.—The accompanying designs may be picked and used direct for fine striping ornaments on "Portlands." They are intended for square corners. This kind of ornamenting requires a fine sable pencil—red sable is preferable—and the colors may be put in to suit the taste of the painter. The method of designing scrolls for the arm-pieces is fully described in the article "Scrolling and Ornamental Painting," already mentioned. Painters who can not readily do this work, may have recourse to decalcomanie or transfer designs. The manufacturers of these goods have studied the wants of sleigh painters, and some very fine patterns are to be found in their sample books.

Repainting Sleigh Work.—The first consideration when a sleigh comes in to be repainted is, how to remove the old paint; and this operation, to those who have no conveniences for the work, is sometimes a matter of considerable difficulty. Where gas is employed in lighting the shop, this may be employed for the purpose, and the work is easily done by simply attaching a piece of rubber tube to the pipe, with a burner at the end. An improved burner has recently been introduced for this purpose, which admits atmospheric air to the flame, thereby generating greater heat and avoiding smoke. This burner is the invention of Mr. S. G. Reed, of Boston, well known as the introducer of the gas tire-heater. The flame of the gas-jet being held close to the paint will cause it to soften or rise in blisters, when it may be cleanly scraped from the surface by means of a putty-knife or chisel. The next best plan, where gas is not available, is a trian-

THE CONSTRUCTION
OF SLEIGHS:

TRIMMING

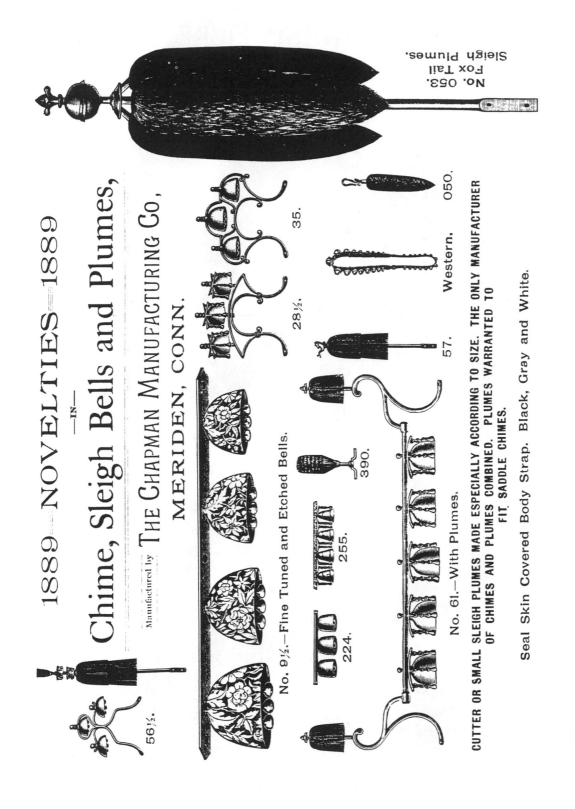

1889—NOVELTIES—1889

—IN—

Chime, Sleigh Bells and Plumes,

Manufactured by THE CHAPMAN MANUFACTURING CO,
MERIDEN, CONN.

No. 053.
Fox Tail
Sleigh Plumes.

050.

Western.

57.

No. 9½.—Fine Tuned and Etched Bells.

35.

28½.

390.

255.

224.

No. 61.—With Plumes.

CUTTER OR SMALL SLEIGH PLUMES MADE ESPECIALLY ACCORDING TO SIZE. THE ONLY MANUFACTURER
OF CHIMES AND PLUMES COMBINED. PLUMES WARRANTED TO
FIT. SADDLE CHIMES.

Seal Skin Covered Body Strap. Black, Gray and White.

56½.

EDWARD EICKE,

MANUFACTURER OF

Horse, Chime and Sleigh

Horse Hair and Worsted
PLUMES.

157 CANAL STREET, NEW YORK,

Carriage Monthly
November 1889

No. 51. Dash Plume with Star Collar.

No. 37.

CIRCULARS AND PRICES SENT ON APPLICATION.

The Hub
August 1886

SHAFT AND POLE CHIMES.

2578

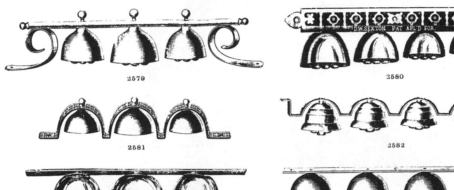

2579   2580

2581   2582

2583   2584

2585   2586   2587

2588   2589

2590   2591

2592   2593

2594   2595

C.M. Moseman & Brother

DESIGN FOR TRIMMING A TUB SLEIGH.

(See Illustration Accompanying.)

THE design illustrated herewith is intended for a sleigh with a full deep seat, such as that on tub bodies. It is novel in design and construction. The foundation of the squabs is made up perfectly plain, with a strong duck "rough-lining." The rolls are made up on leather backs. The piping on the squabs is made by stitching the outside to duck, leaving a little ful-

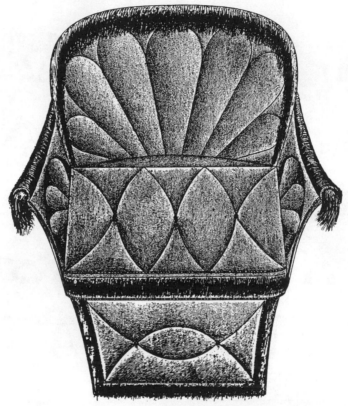

FIG. I.

ness, say ⅛ inch, to the centre pipe across its broadest point, and a proportionate amount to all others at their broadest part. Stuff with hair and draw taut over the foundation, and tack securely all around.

Make up the rolls upon leather cut to the required shape, cover with stout duck with sufficient fulness to give a heavy roll; then cover with bear or other long fur, and tack securely in place. Make the face of the cushion of fur of the same character as that used on the rolls.

The fall may be of plain fur, or with a fur roll all around. For all squab tops, cushions and falls, use seal brown plush or heavy cloth trimmed in this manner. The seat robe can be dispensed with.

TRIMMING SLEIGHS.

For sleighs, except those of the highest grade, the trimming should all be made so that it can be removed at will. Each squab and cushion should be made with an enamel cloth or leather back, and so fitted that by the use of a few knobs and straps they can be fixed securely in place, and easily removed when necessary.

For a plain Portland, a cushion fall and back squab are all that is necessary, as the sides are low and the seat robes furnish all the covering required. For four-passenger and deep quartered two-passenger sleighs quarter squabs are necessary, but in all cases the squabs and cushions should be quite flat. It is a good plan to carpet tops of rockers, etc., knobbing on the covering.

Warmth being a desirable requisite, cover the bottom with a well-fitted piece of linoleum, secured by knobs at each corner.

The advantages of loose trimmings are self-apparent, as they can be removed easily and hung up to dry.

The most popular material is plush, but heavy cloths are used by leading builders for their best vehicles. Leather is the least desirable of all materials, as it is cold and holds moisture. Springs and curled hair are preferable to all other materials for stuffing; next to these is Florida moss, while the poorest of all is rowen.

Strong but plain work is required, and if all pieces are well fitted, no more trouble will be experienced in the loose than in the fixed trimmings, while more comfort and greater durability will be secured.

The following tables furnish a general guide for the amount of material required to trim the respective sleighs:

MATERIAL FOR TRIMMING PORTLAND SLEIGH.

Width on seat, 30 inches.

2½ yards plush.	1 lb. moss.
1 yard enam. cloth.	3½ doz. buttons.
1 lb. harness leather.	1¼ " knobs.
2½ yards broad lace.	2 " nails.
8 " narrow lace.	3 papers tacks.
1 yard velvet carpet.	¼ lb. cord and twine.
2 yards buckram.	3 oz. thread.
1½ lbs. curled hair.	1 pint paste.
1 set cushion springs.	1 whip socket.

MATERIAL FOR TRIMMING SIX-SEAT SLEIGH.

Width on back seat, 3 feet 5 inches; spread of top, 5 feet 10 inches; 6 bows.

115 feet top leather.	2 papers nails.
4½ " jap. trimming.	3½ doz. knobs.
9 " soft russet for wings.	4 papers tacks.
9 " railing.	¼ lb. cord and twine.
8 " grain dash.	4 skeins thread.
4½ yards body cloth.	12½ feet molding.
6½ " head lining.	6 bows.
6 " cotton.	6 joints and props.
5 " burlaps.	10 rivets and nuts.
5 " cambric.	1 set slat irons.
1¾ " enam. cloth.	½ gallon paste.
1¾ " rubber.	8 buckles and billets.
11 " broad lace.	4 yards webbing.
39 " narrow lace.	16 pressed loops.
7 " velvet carpet.	2 back lights.
4½ " buckram.	2 side lights.
6 lbs. curled hair.	3 back curtain straps.
7 " moss.	4 pairs " "
12 doz. buttons.	1 pair safety straps.
	1 whip socket.

MATERIAL FOR TRIMMING FOUR-PASSENGER PONY SLEIGH.

Width on seat, 3 feet 2 inches.

7 feet dash leather.	3½ lbs. moss.
3¼ yards body cloth.	8 doz. buttons.
4 " cotton.	1½ doz. knobs.
2½ " enam. cloth.	3 papers nails.
5½ " broad lace.	4 " tacks.
29 " narrow lace.	¼ lb. cord and twine.
6½ " velvet carpet.	3 oz. thread.
3 " buckram.	1 quart paste.
3 lbs. curled hair.	2 cushion straps.
	1 whip socket.

Close Top for Portland Cutter.

ILION, N. Y., August 15, 1892.

EDITORS CARRIAGE MONTHLY: Can you kindly furnish me with a few pointers on building a close top on a Portland cutter? By doing so you will greatly oblige a subscriber. Yours truly,

CHAS. A. HALLIDAY, Ilion, N. Y.

We have prepared two illustrations for close tops on Portland cutters, the one showing the dimensions, while the other is to illustrate its appearance when finished. We have elected to make this top with a shifting rail, concluding that it is much better this way on account of its portability, and also because there is not much chance to fasten a top to the sides of a cutter, the panels being usually so thin there.

Of course, the seat must be ironed much the same way as in the case of a buggy seat, and we would suggest that in the back a sort of angle iron, with a hole to accommodate the rail, be used, it being remembered that we could not have the rail even with the top of the back, so this one angle iron would become necessary in the same way as when putting a shifting top on a park phaeton. The shifting rail for this kind of a job is made on the sides of half-oval iron, to which is fastened a block of wood, to enable the top to be fastened to it.

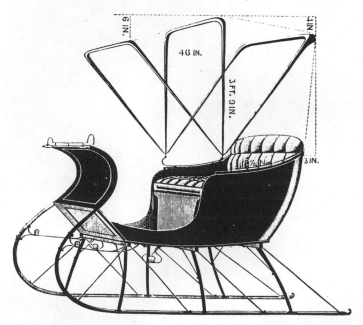

The illustration shows it as plainly as possible. It is rather difficult to give the exact measurements that would be appropriate for this job, but we give what we consider would make a good looking top.

We should always prefer to put on a three bow top. The dimensions are as follows: The goose neck is 19½ inches from the back corner of the shifting rail, the length of the top from front of first bow to back of rear bow is 47 inches; the height from the seat to inside of middle bow is 3 feet 10 inches; the front bow drops 6 inches from the

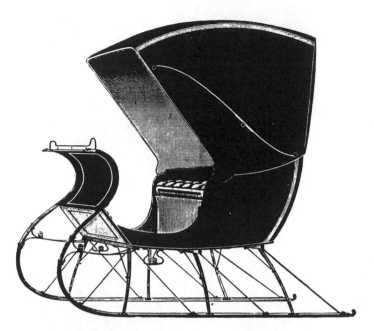

spirit level line, and back bow 4 inches; the back bow extends 3 inches over the rear of the body or shifting rail. There is not much to be said regarding the construction of this top, except that it is not advisable to use the " Brown " bend bow, as it is too short a bend to look well. The old fashioned bow, known as the wagon bow, is more appropriate. A regular cabriolet bow has most too much bend, unless the sleigh body is very round; in that case your own judgment will dictate which shape it is best to use.

It is best not to use a side light in the top. If it is desirable, however, we refer you to some of the back numbers of this journal, where you will find an exhaustive article upon the subject. You will please notice in the cut showing the job finished, that the usual cod piece is used; but if you use rubber it is necessary to line this cod piece, whereas if leather is used under no circumstances should it be lined, except with cloth.

We also call your attention to the finish on the bottom of the side quarter. It will be seen that the leather is left extending below the silver molding which finishes the tacks that are required to hold the leather in place. We would suggest the shape of joint seen in the illustration. The corners of this top should be just the same as on a landau, as the plain corners do not look as well as these.

panel is one inch thick, the roll should also be one inch thick in order to cover the edge.

It will be observed that, in order to keep the back in its place, the application of four small "pins" is resorted to, two of which are applied to the extreme bottom edge of the back, being let into the seat, thus securing the bottom part. These "pins" are about ¾ inch in diameter, and 1¼ in. long. The other two are utilized in the top of the back panel, and may be fastened either to the panel or to the wooden roll, fitting into a hole similar to the bottom edge. These "pins" are made very small, being but ½ in. long and not so heavy as the other two.

The whole, when completed as per directions, will give perfect satisfaction, because of its capacity to meet all the requirements of the office it is to perform, and being so readily taken out or put in.

The trimming design is very inexpensive so far as extra labor or material is concerned, yet certainly presents a pleasing appearance. The roll is 1¾ in. wide, the first row of buttons 1⅞ in., and the third row 4¼ in. from the first row. The second row will then form itself by drawing diagonal lines. These dimensions are furnished because they are neatly proportioned.

The plush is next cut out, it being presumed that plush is used on account of its appropriateness. The back is given one inch across, by ⅝ inch up and down in the diamonds, sufficient material being allowed on the edges. This kind of back may be stuffed with a stuffing-stick or by laying the hair; it is optional in this case, because plush will not show lumps so readily as most other materials.

It is not necessary to stuff the roll with hair, because the woodwork is already round, and four or five layers of cotton will answer much better in this instance than hair, when the finish is regarded.

The cushion is now made, the facings to be about 1⅞ in. wide. The top is made perfectly plain, and upon a frame of muslin, which will make a neater job, at the same time not being much more work; then again, the lining of the plush can be dispensed with if made up on a frame, whereas, if it were made any other way, it would necessitate lining the plush in order to apply cotton, which is such an essential feature in endeavoring to produce a smooth top.

The fall is made with raisers, because this finish is more pleasing to the eye than if it were totally plain. The foundation is the same as that employed in buggy work, it being duck canvas. The raisers are one inch wide, pasted ¾ inch from the edge; and the whole is then covered with the plush, and simply turned over the edges, and stitched and trimmed off.

The rugs are now finished with fringe, rather than with cloth or lace. A first-class sleigh should also have a mat, which can be procured of almost any color, that will harmonize with the painting.
HEAD LINING.

DIRECTIONS FOR TRIMMING A PORTABLE-BACK SLEIGH.

THE accompanying sketch, appropriate to our subject, represents a trimming design for a sleigh. It is not altogether new, but perhaps it may enlighten some as to a neat way to trim such work, as well as

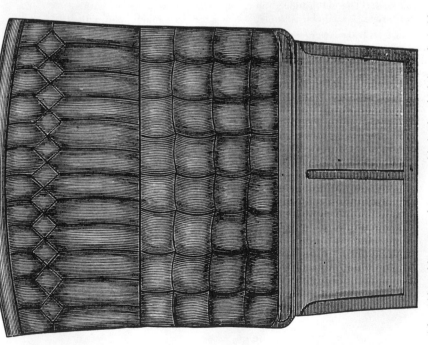

furnish an idea of how to make a portable back, which is so desirable, because of the limited amount of use to which the majority of sleighs are subjected, especially in our larger cities.

The initial proceeding, in trimming this sleigh, is to have the woodworker fit to the sleigh a wooden back, made out of poplar, having an additional piece of wood glued upon the back part of this back, for the purpose of forming a roll. It is about 1⅞ in. above the top edge of the sleigh, the bottom part to rest upon the top edge of back panel, being wide enough to completely cover this edge. That is, if the back

Trimming

INQUIRY ABOUT FUR TRIMMINGS FOR SLEIGHS.

AMESBURY, MASS., January 1, 1876.

TO THE EDITOR:

DEAR SIR : I see by The Hub, page 330, that you speak of *fur* trimming for sleighs, and recommend its use. I have a nice sleigh about ready for trimming, and should like some information in regard to it. Mr. C. E. Morrill was here yesterday. I spoke to him about it, and he thought I had best drop you a few lines. The length and breadth that I should want would be about 32 inches long and a foot wide for the back.

Cushion, 32 inches long and about 16 inches wide ; seat-fall, 32 inches long and 12 inches wide. This shows something near the dimensions. My sleigh is a light *black* sleigh. Now, can you tell me about what will be the expense, and the best color and kind, not to have it cost too much ?

I do not want to ask too much, but thought I could gain more information from you than elsewhere. C. W. L.

REPLY BY MR. A. H. WARD.

WE are indebted to Mr. A. H. Ward, fur dealer, of 52 Greene street, this city, for the following facts. Mr. Ward has spent considerable time abroad, has examined many French sleighs trimmed in this manner, and is fully posted on the details of quality, prices, and taste of finish. He says:

VARIETIES OF FUR, AND PRICES, MADE UP.

White fox, light color, price per square foot	$3 00
Wolf, " " "	1 25
Beaver, dark color, " "	3 00
Gray fox, light color, " "	3 00
Red fox, medium shade, " "	2 50
Coon, " " "	2 00
Black bear, dark color, " "	3 00
Brown bear, " " "	2 50
Black skunk, " " "	4 50
Gennet, " " "	1 50
Black Astrachan, dark color, price per square foot	2 00

STYLES OF TRIMMING.

To be most effective, the center trimming should be dark, bordered with light, or center dark, bordered with light, or any of the above for center, bordered with fox, wolf, or raccoon tails, or sides trimmed with tails and ends with half-raised heads. In other French sleighs, I have seen the cushions laid with dregget or rep cloth, and slightly lined with wadding, and edge of sleigh trimmed with row of tails above-named, with harness similarly trimmed. Any variety from the bushy-tailed animals may be used with advantage.

PRICES OF TAIL TRIMMINGS.

Tails, coon, per yard,	$0.75
" wolf, "	1.25
" fox, "	1.50

When finished as above, the cost of trimming an ordinary cutter would be from $10 to $30, according to the variety of fur employed.

I shall be happy to answer any further inquiries, addressed either to The Hub or to me personally. A. H. WARD.

52 GREENE STREET, NEW-YORK, January 8, 1876.

Sleigh Trimming.

There is manifestly a growing disposition to have sleighs trimmed in a more elaborate manner this season, than has been usual for several years back; the prevailing patterns last year were perfectly plain or the pipe-back pattern, but this season the diamond pattern promises to be the most prevalent; in consequence thereof we have prepared this article, not with the motive, however, that we are advancing anything new or original, but to sharpen our probably rusty minds upon the subject, thereby obviating any attempt which might perchance result unsatisfactorily.

In the accompanying design we have illustrated the back, squab, cushion and fall; the back and squabs are made separate, both having foundations of buckram of sufficient stiffness to permit making up; the job in question was trimmed with maroon plush; the back to be laid off as per design; the top row of tufts amounting to ten in number, the rest to correspond; the plush was given 1 inch fulness across by ¾ inch up and down; the tufts were plush, buttons to match.

The squabs were made similar to the back, the same fulness attending, but were put in their places before the back, thereby permitting the back to finish the mitre in the corners; the whole was finished with appropriate seaming and pasting lace.

The cushion, which was also of a diamond pattern, was made upon a frame; the front facing is 1¾ inches wide, which width is carried all the way around the cushion; all the facings are however stiff; the top, as before intimated, was made upon a frame and without plaits, being simply tufted as seen in the cut; the welts were of enameled leather, cut in 1½-inch strips; the cushion front has a 1-inch strip of kersey, but perfectly plain. The fall is made on duck canvass tacked to a board, and the dimensions of the fall marked thereon; a 1-inch strip of kersey is pasted ¼ inch from the edges, and covered over with the plush; when dry, a piece of leather is applied on the back part, 1½ inches wide, to allow the insertion of a fall stick which is such an efficient auxiliary to the durability of any fall; the edges of the fall are merely turned under and stitched; the fall should invariably be fastened to the cushion.

The rug was of a maroon color, matching the plush, and perfectly plain in pattern; it was bound with black fringe, about 2½ inches wide. The mode of binding a rug with fringe is simply "over" stitching the edges with thread to prevent the raveling out of the edges, and then sewing the fringe to the carpet by the aid of the sewing machine.

The whip-socket should be made extra long on sleighs; in this instance it was 12 inches long, and was made of skirting and dash leather pasted together, shaped in the form of a whip socket and bound on each end with binding leather.   BEN TACK.

INDEX OF SLEIGHMAKERS

Acker, Abram (Sing-Sing NY) 12, 13, 17, 27

American Carriage Co. (Kalamazoo MI) 67

Armstrong Mfg. Co., J.B. (Guelph, Ont., Canada) 60

Bailey, S.R. (Amesbury MA) 38, 45

Barber, J.M. (North Adams MA) 124

Beach Carriage Manufacturing Co. (Ypsilanti MI) 5

Bingham & Co., R.M. (Rome NY) 33, 149, 156 177

Brewster & Co. (New York NY) ii

Brigham, McRay & Co. (Ayer Junction MA) 122

Bryant, J.L. (Hillsdale MI) 87

Buffalo Carriage & Sleigh Woodwork Co. (Buffalo NY) 69

Carter, Chapman & Co. (Ludington MI) 132

Christie, A.E. & J.H. (Nyack NY) 14, 18, 32, 183

Cortland Wagon Co. (Cortland NY) 74, 76

Dixon's J., Carriage and Sleigh Works (Toronto, Ont., Canada) 140

Emond & Quinsler (Boston MA) 92

Fisher Mfg. Co. Ltd. (Homer NY) 98

Fuller Buggy Co. (Jackson MI) 61, 63

Gananoque Carriage Co. (Gananoque, Ont., Canada) 49

Goold & Co., James (Albany NY) ii, 4

Graves & Co. L.C. (Springboro PA) 62

Hallenbeck, E. (New Hartford NY) 22

Harper, J.D. (Christiana PA) 137

Healey & Co. (New York NY) 157

Hooker, Henry, & Co. (New Haven CT) 153

Isham, Brundage & Co. (Plattsburgh NY) 5

Jackson Sleigh Co. (Jackson MI) 64

Kemp, John (Detroit MI) 8, 20

Kimball, Peter (Hamlin's Gore, ME) i, 30

Kimball & Co., C.P. (Chicago IL) i, 70, 72

Kimball Bros. (Boston MA) 85

Kingman, Sturtevant & Larrabee (Binghamton NY) 71

Lariviere, P.A. (Montreal Canada) 136, 147

Marshall & Co., A.P. (Lancaster NH) 29, 89

McLaughlin Carriage Co. (Oshawa, Ont., Canada) 60

Muller, Adolphus (New York NY) 16, 24

Price & Shaw (St. John, N.B., Canada) 88, 151

Prouty & Glass Carriage Co. 78

Robinson & Vanderbelt (Albany NY) ii

Russell, Joseph (Portland ME) 26

Scott & Co., R.D. (Pontiac MI) 65

Shaw, P.H. (Albany NY) 11

Smith & Co., J.T. (Boston MA) 191

Spalding, S.W. (Binghamton NY) 2

Spencer & Co., J.L. (Oneida NY) 91

Stivers, R.M. (New York NY) 34

Sturtevant-Larrabee Co. (Binghamton NY) 67, 79

Sullivan Bros. (Rochester NY) 66

Wagner, G.W. (Philadelphia PA) 4

Willoughby (Rome NY) 119, 190

Worthen & Co., H.A. (Dover NH) 101